THE
WORK
REVOLUTION

THE
WORK
REVOLUTION

Gail Garfield Schwartz, Ph.D.
and
William Neikirk

RAWSON ASSOCIATES
NEW YORK

Library of Congress Cataloging in Publication Data

Schwartz, Gail Garfield.
The work revolution.

Bibliography: p.
Includes index.
1. Labor and laboring classes—United States—
1970–   . 2. Automation—Social aspects—United
States. I. Neikirk, William. II. Title.
HD8072.5.S38   1984   303.4′83   83-42623
ISBN 0-89256-251-X

Published simultaneously in Canada by McClelland and Stewart Ltd.

Packaged by Sandra Choron, Inc.

Composition by Folio Graphics Co., Inc.

Printed and bound by Fairfield Graphics, Fairfield, Pennsylvania

Designed by Stanley S. Drate

First Edition

To Ruth Ann
    —W.N.

To Lester
    —G.G.S.

"Oh, why don't you work like other men do?
How the hell can I work when there's no work
to do?"

—From "Hallelujah, I'm
a Bum, Anonymous

CONTENTS

ACKNOWLEDGMENTS

It is hard to select from among the many who have influenced us throughout our careers the names to be mentioned. Noted individuals such as Leon Keyserling, who set U.S. sights on full employment forty years ago and still has not given up the goal, and Wassily Leontief, the Nobel Prize winner who has both privately and publicly subscribed to the general thesis presented herein, are among them. But people who are far from famous were as important to the writing of this book as any well-known economist or policy maker. To all the ordinary men and women who told us they, too, sense the uncertainties of the future, both authors express their thanks.

More specifically, we would like to thank those who encouraged this work and helped make it happen. From Gail Garfield Schwartz, appreciation goes to the late Dean Harvey Perloff of UCLA, pioneer in the art of economic base analysis, and former Dean Paul Ylvisaker of Harvard University's School of Education. Thanks, too, to Katharine Lyall, Academic Vice-President of the University of Wisconsin, who made possible a research project at Johns Hopkins University which inspired this book. Anita Finkelstein researched vocational education. Kenneth Poole, research analyst at Garfield Schwartz Associates, did a conscientious job of tabulating statistics under a difficult time constraint, and Jennifer Miller typed the manuscript.

From William Neikirk, thanks go to R. C. Longworth and Charles Madigan, *Chicago Tribune* reporters who were partners in two series on working; the late William Jones, *Tribune* managing editor who encouraged this work; James D. Squires, *Tribune* editor, Douglas Kneeland, *Tribune* associate managing editor, and reporters James Coates and James O'Shea, all of whom provided encouragement. Thanks, too, to John Batty of General Electric, a fine devil's advocate; Carolyn Hardnett, librarian for the *Chicago Tribune's* Washington Bureau, who can find anything; and Raymond Coffey, *Tribune* Washington bureau chief, who understood.

THE
WORK
REVOLUTION

1

Introduction to the Future

This is a book about a quiet revolution that is changing our lives and threatening our livelihoods. It is taking place where we all work. It is a continuing revolution, still in its early stages. Yet it is very real and very powerful. Here are some of its sights and sounds, witnessed personally by the authors:

- It was a factory where they made airplane engine parts. Parts were piled high at various places in the cavernous building as computer-controlled machine tools did their work. One of the company vice-presidents conducting the tour stopped to show a work center where a middle-aged man was using a computer terminal to make sure each part was built according to specifications and was properly identified. Using the computer to handle this function was much more efficient than having it done manually, the company man said. The worker gave a demonstration of what he did, manipulating the machine to perfection, and then the factory tour moved on. A few yards away, the company man said, "Of course, this job is going to be eliminated, too, with further automation of the floor."

- In an insurance company's color-coded offices filled with functional furniture, several dozen women, each with a telephone headset, sat in front of computer terminals as they took calls from customers. There was little paper around. Each operator had access to the computer's memory bank of insurance files. Many aspects of the firm's business could be handled by a single person. "We were able to increase our office productivity dramatically," said one of the executives. In other words, the volume of business performed by each person had increased exponentially with installation of an electronic nerve center. Few new workers would ever be required.

- In an automobile factory on the East Coast, a union official cannot hide the fear in his eyes and in his voice about what will happen to jobs in the plant once robots are installed. The truth is worse than he suspected. Not long after our conversation, the plant is shut down. The company says it will reopen the plant only if the work force is reduced as labor-saving machines are put in and if the union accepts wage concessions.

- In a Japanese machine tool factory in Florence, Kentucky, just across the Ohio River from Cincinnati, the American sales manager explains how a fully automated flexible manufacturing system will run itself in the dark all night long without the assistance of a single human being. The company is getting many expressions of interest from U.S. industry because it is in the business of selling this automated system. The firm sees gains of up to 300 percent in productivity for those who buy its automated systems. American machine tool firms tell the same story.

- In Washington, D.C., an official of the International Association of Machinists says automation is the main issue of the 1980s. He notes that even the government is practicing it. For example, the air force has installed new metal-cutting machinery in its defense plants that also cuts back labor sharply.

- In a research laboratory in Pittsburgh, a bright young man describes how he is working diligently on a project that will enable a robot to see and sense an object clearly, so that it can distinguish one object from another. It is only a matter of time before this robot function is fully perfected, he explains.

• In a steel mill in Japan, the foreman tells a reporter he is extremely happy with his work and happy that his company provides subsidized housing and vacations—and especially happy that his company's steel is selling so well in the United States, where it is cheaper than American-made steel.

• In an appliance factory in the United States, the manufacturer is using automatic assembly techniques to insert a retaining pin into the spout cap of a tea kettle, instead of fastening it manually with a screw.

• In a shoe factory in Korea, the plant manager explains that he is able to sell his shoes for export much cheaper because the wages in his factory, located in a seamy section of Seoul, are low, compared with wages in the United States. Still, he says, jobs in his plant are highly desired by Korean people, as their standard and cost of living are much lower.

• In the headquarters of the Suez Canal, the supervisor explains how Japanese firms outbid American companies for millions of dollars in dredging work and new equipment. There could have been jobs for Americans in this, he says.

• Along the Saudi Arabian coast, where petrodollars that came from American and European pocketbooks are being employed to build vast new petrochemical complexes, a group of American newspaper executives is startled to see a team of South Korean workers busy at work on a construction crew. South Korean firms have landed many important contracts here, Saudi officials explain.

• At a convenience store in northern Virginia, a young Vietnamese cashier explains how he escaped from Saigon, made his way to the United States, and wound up in a job paying the minimum wage. A refugee from the turmoil in El Salvador sets up tables at a Washington, D.C., restaurant one and a half blocks from the White House. Though his job is low-paying, he is grateful for the work.

- In a neat air-conditioned office in Glasgow, the economic development official shakes his head slowly at the visitor who wants to learn how to stem the tide of unemployment in old, heavy-industry cities. Three generations of men here have lived on the dole, he laments, and all they can think about is getting back the shipbuilding industry. The shipbuilding industry will never come back, and Glasgow will be lucky if its 30 percent unemployment rate doesn't get worse.

- On a television talk show, a group of men and women debate whether women are capable of holding down jobs formerly held by men. The rhetorical heat rises when one of the men claims that he has found himself working harder because he has to do some of the heavier work his female co-worker allegedly can't do. The enraged women point out that soon he won't have to worry: None of the jobs in their shop will require any brawn, because robots will do all of them. Besides, they say, the man's claim is exaggerated.

The foregoing incidents may seem disconnected, but they are not. In one way or another they are all part of a revolution in work that is gathering force daily. Although the revolution is primarily driven by technology, it is affected by a wide variety of other economic and social factors that will forever change the way work is performed and the number of people who perform it.

The chapters that follow were inspired by these and similar incidents in the course of independent travel and research by an economist and a journalist who, in the course of their professional pursuits, discovered they were reaching the same conclusions about work in the future. These conclusions challenge the generally accepted wisdom that the American job market will settle down toward the end of the decade and that the unemployment problem will solve itself because of lower birth rates.

A visceral sense that there is something wrong with the way experts are looking at economic change has been bolstered by evidence that the more traditional beliefs about the growth of jobs in a growing economy were being perpetuated without a hard examination of what is happening in the real world. Complex equations applying to job creation and economic activity are painstakingly reiterated by mathematically oriented economists and used to project the number of jobs to be created for years into the future. Few, if any, users of these forecasts question the assumed sanctity of these equations, even though the mathematical relationships are not statements about actual cause and effect and were established in a different time. This is reason enough to challenge their applicability in a new world where both human physical labor and human intelligence are being supplanted by machines in many endeavors.

Our travels, interviews, and research have given us profound respect for the efficiencies, current and future, of the new technology that is being introduced into the nation's industries. But the work revolution is not just a technological revolution. It is a revolution involving world trade and migration patterns, greater expectations on the part of women and the elderly, and foreigners seeking to realize the American dream about work. It is a revolution that has exposed the nation's economic weaknesses as never before, right down to its educational system.

This book springs from our concern that economists, political leaders, and individuals are trying to apply outdated solutions to badly defined problems. The adage that for every problem there is a simple and wrong solution seems to fit the current situation very well. Both of us have witnessed the practical applications of the new technology in many plants and offices around the world. We have seen how political and social institutions at home and abroad mold and influence the world of work in different countries. Based as we are in Washington, D.C., we deal on a daily basis with the issues of national policy discussed in this book in various contexts. We are well aware that policy makers often operate in a reality vacuum. We have a healthy skepticism about the sanguine orthodoxy that dominates economic theory, but we are equally skeptical of superficial pronouncements of the economic mavericks. Neither of us is a Luddite.[1] The new technology of today cannot and should not be halted. On the contrary, its installation is essential.

But Americans should not labor under the illusion that the new technology is going to cure all ills. In fact, it is going to create as many problems as it solves and will force us all, individuals and policy makers, to cope with the high tech future that is coming so quickly. It will force millions of workers to

---

[1]Luddites were textile workers who attempted to block the introduction of new weaving technology in British mills in the early 1800s because they feared it would destroy jobs.

rethink their attitudes toward work and leisure and all of us to consider how to provide for those without jobs.

When President Reagan announced his economic program in 1981, he said that it would lead to creation of thirteen million jobs over a five-year period if the economy grew as expected. The new tax changes he propounded, including the fastest tax writeoff of new equipment and machinery in the nation's history, were going to be an especial boon to job creation. These promises were based on the administration's convoluted economic theory and on econometric models that spat out the potential job opportunities as if they were certainties. The recession, high interest rates, and massive budget deficits soon tempered this original optimism about how much economic growth could be achieved, but the government never backed away from its original belief that the anticipated jobs would have materialized had the economy performed in line with forecasts.

This book will challenge such assumptions. It will also challenge assumptions about the alleged improving quality of work. Those who labored in the dirty factories of smokestack America might have found the jobs difficult and not especially rewarding, but the high wages they received over the years prompted many to yearn for those old jobs when they were laid off. Our visits to so-called high tech factories, making everything from semiconductors to television sets to black boxes for F-5 jet fighters, revealed that many of the vaunted high technology jobs are low-skilled and low-paying. For example, assembly jobs involving putting circuit boards in television sets or checking circuit boards for flaws can be handled by almost anyone who walks in off the street. We saw these same types of jobs being performed just as skillfully in so-called high tech factories in Mexico and Asia. This means that such jobs are highly vulnerable to foreign competition. It also means that new is not necessarily better when it comes to jobs.

Interestingly enough, the television factories in the United States are owned by the Japanese and run by Japanese nationals. At Sony's San Diego plant, a Texan wearing a ten-gallon hat works on the assembly line while the Japanese engineers, who have high-paying jobs, relax in a company cafeteria eating hamburger with chopsticks. It is perhaps an ultimate example of how foreign competition and products that are superior from a technological standpoint have destroyed the higher-paying jobs for Americans and supplanted them with lower-paying jobs. But this is better than nothing. In some industries, like bicycle manufacturing, just about all jobs have been wiped out by foreign competition. It is no surprise that America became more protectionist in the 1970s and early 1980s. Nearly every industry—including many high tech ones—has become sensitive to the foreign challenge, which comes from every quarter. To cite but one instance, no sooner had America entered into an economic relationship with mainland China than an economic battle broke out over textile imports and Coca-Cola exports.

In contrast to the confident attitude of many economists and politicians, we have found many ordinary Americans deeply worried about the availability of jobs in the future. The economic equations cannot measure these fears, just as they cannot measure the future job picture adequately. These fears do not arise from some abstract boogeyman speaking to workers in their nightmares; they arise from daily contact with work and the difficulty in making ends meet. The changes have already led to the effective displacement of millions.

This book looks into the causes of these fears and assesses the powerful economic forces impinging upon American workers. While the message may be frightening, it is not intended to frighten, but to inform. As far as it is within our ability to do so, we have tried to provide some informed advice on how workers in the future should proceed with their education and their job search. Our real purpose is to give a glimpse of the immediate future as we see it in the hope that the worst does not come to pass. The way to ensure that the work revolution has a less devastating effect is to plan for it, both at the personal and at the institutional level. Revolutions have a way of sweeping up innocent people and quickly making them victims. Our hope is that the number of innocent victims will be kept to a minimum.

2

The Work Revolution

On a warm, rainy day in spring 1982, a hundred or so unemployed electronics workers—mostly white Americans—invaded the strawberry fields of southern California. Their mission: to steal the pickers' jobs from the migrant farm workers—mostly Mexican. A few miles away, tools lay idle on the computer assembly line in plants from which the electronics workers had been laid off. The ostensible reason: a deep recession. The real reasons: more and more semiconductors were being made elsewhere, outside the United States (and even in Mexico), and electronics were increasingly replacing people in many of the tasks needed to build computers.

In California, the news of "Anglos" trying to survive stoop labor was akin to "man bites dog." The Spanish-language radio and newspapers crowed proudly when, after four hours, the invaders gave up their attempt, admitting that the work was too hard. Presumably, the workers gave up to look for jobs more suited to their experience.

The unemployment rate in California, land of both the past and the future, was .2 points higher than the outrageously high national average of 9.7 percent in 1982. So the strawberry scene brought an ominous message, not only to California, but to the rest of the nation as well. The message was that American workers face a double paradox. They are losing the jobs they once thought secure, but they don't have the skills to capture the jobs that will be available. Compounding the problem is this dismal reality: Even though population projections suggest a steep drop in the U.S.-born work force within a few years, there will nevertheless be a long-term jobs shortage.

The first paradox is acted out in a thousand daily dramas. The most common, perhaps, is this: A fresh-faced high school grad rushes to the newspaper each morning to search the help wanted ads. Though he possesses untapped native talent that could be useful to a business, he has never developed it. He has no plans for college because his test scores fall just a mite short of the requirements. The classified ad section is thick, brimming with hope and with jobs. But once again he finds the exercise fruitless. Page after page calls for computer specialists, for engineers, for education, for experience, for qualification. In no more than a couple of minutes, he drops the section in frustration. Nowhere have the ads described him.

The second paradox is not so apparent, but it is just as real, and its dramas are almost as common. A middle-aged automobile worker is on a nine-month layoff and putters away his time waiting for the recall that has always come in similar periods previously. He's doomed to disappointment. He will never get his assembly line job back. If Japanese imports haven't wiped it out, a working army of industrial robots will. A black man getting along in years is pounding the pavement looking for another short order cook's job, but they are all taken by funny-looking people whose language he doesn't understand. A young Puerto Rican woman, the first in her family to finish school on the mainland, can't find the hoped-for job as file clerk in a big company with big fringe benefits because computers are doing the filing, not people.

For millions of Americans, job opportunities are being destroyed by a fierce combination of forces, the most threatening of which is technology. The time has come to worry about automation again. After 1990, when current technology has gone through more than half its expected development, it will take perhaps only 75 percent of the work force to do 100 percent of the work. The nation is only at the beginning of a technological revolution in electronics and communications. This revolution promises to increase factory and office worker productivity as dramatically as mechanized farm machinery has increased the output of an acre of land—so much so that 3 percent of the work force now produces all the food we can eat and more.

Americans do not fully perceive the threat as yet, because the revolution is so young. Many think that electronic offices, for example, will make work easier, not faster. But technology is now being used inefficiently and in a trial-and-error fashion. Once the revolution ages, America's managers will treat their sophisticated new machinery less as a status symbol and more as a workhorse. Then jobs will be displaced.

The coming age of electronics is only one reason a job crisis is in the making. America's workers are more vulnerable to foreign imports; our market is wide open and foreign goods are cheap and of high quality. Illegal immigration is out of control. At the same time, the steady march of American women into the work force will further increase the number of job seekers. Because of medical advances and harsher economic times, the elderly will remain at work longer, additionally restricting job opportunities down the line.

If the lower birthrates of the late 1960s and 1970s had been the only factor to consider, the nation would not have to worry about a job crisis. Indeed, looking at demographic factors alone, 1985 would have marked the year when the trickle of youngsters into the work force would be so thin that the pipeline of job applicants would finally be unclogged. But the birthrate is but one of many factors. In their obsession with lower birthrates, technocrats have diverted the nation's attention away from other dangers lurking in the future.

The coming job crisis will shatter the uneasy tranquility of American workers. Setting worker against worker, it will ignite bitter wars between the old and the young, between men and women, between white and nonwhite, between native-born and new arrival. Every group will have its favorite scapegoat. Some will insist that we would have no "real" unemployment problem if only those women who bring home a second paycheck would stay in the kitchen. Others will blame the elderly for hogging jobs. Some will fault the "ethnics." Everyone will blame someone.

Politicians who ignored the problem when it was developing will fan the flames of conflict when it suits their reelection campaigns and, once they are elected, try to placate the "losers" in the job struggle with palliative programs.

And what about those inevitable losers? Who will they be and what will they do?

THE THREAT OF A NEW INEQUALITY

The United States stands at the edge of a new inequality. In the face of shrinking work opportunities and diminished skill requirements, the organized and educated elite may well strengthen its grip on the available good jobs in the private economy, throwing scraps of social programs to the jobless. An alternate possibility is that elected officials, management, and workers themselves will find ways to redistribute work opportunities so that everyone has a chance. However, possibility two will occur only if people understand the emerging problems, take their heads out of the sand, and consider the realistic choices that can be made.

The Work Force Explosion

Some say it was the pill. Others say it was a mass shared concern that the planet was on a collision course with disaster because of threats of a nuclear war, the population explosion, and environmental degradation. At any rate, it happened and it happened unexpectedly. Beginning in the 1960s, America's birthrate slowed down. It slowed down so much that births even fell below the replacement rate—the rate at which the number of children born would offset the number of people dying, so that the total population would remain the same. The actual fact of zero population growth would not occur until late in the twentieth century because of the number of fertile women in the population, but if the low birthrate were sustained, America could look forward to a jubilant day when its population bomb had been defused.

Job experts were delighted. Because of the postwar "baby boom," they had forecast a long-range job shortage. Now the apparent solution was here. They saw a measurable, definable demographic certainty: fewer youngsters moving up the ranks and into the world of work. The people pipeline would no longer be clogged. The arithmetic was clear, impressive, and precise, with equally clear, impressive implications: By 1985, the drastically lowered birthrate would make its mark on the labor force, and unemployment would no longer be a threat. To most labor market experts, the numbers suggested there would be nothing to worry about once the "baby boom" population matured. Not only would competition for jobs gradually diminish, but the United States would enter an era of labor shortage. At that point, we would have to import workers rather than limiting foreign immigration as we do now. Or, it was suggested, if the United States did not have to look abroad for new workers, certainly the end of long-term unemployment would be at hand. This new era of plentiful work would bring jobs for new workers and security for older workers fearful of a younger generation snapping at their heels. Parents could rest easy about the employment prospects for their children and their children's children. The numbers promised security, happiness, and fulfillment of the American dream.

Technology Destroys Jobs

The native-born American labor force will indeed increase at a much smaller rate; the numbers are undeniable. But to rely on a smaller-growing U.S. population to solve the nation's unemployment problem is to ignore the job-disrupting, job-eliminating potential of computer chips made into clever, tireless robots cheerfully performing monotonous tasks for seven years on end without a coffee break. It ignores the talented, obedient word processor that enables one highly skilled operator to produce 105 words of perfect text per minute, entitling her (or him) to a salary of $22,000. It ignores the ability of computer technology (in all its forms) to revolutionize the services that now dominate the economy, making almost all processes more efficient and permitting more work to be done with fewer people.

Americans have always placed supreme faith in technology, and for good reason. Inventions have reduced the toil and drudgery of work; at the same time, they have brought about great strides in efficiency. By opening new vistas, technological advances have also provided new jobs. During the industrial revolution, electrical-mechanical technology created initial fears about widespread job losses, but these fears were soon overcome by an explosion of new work opportunities. Canal workers initially felt threatened by the new railroads, but the country soon came to realize that this new form of transportation would carry it into an era of unparalleled economic development. Canal workers didn't always like losing their water-transport jobs, but railroads gave them new jobs right away. So it went through the years as America developed the world's most advanced and productive economy. People tolerated the job-displacement effect of a new piece of machinery because it was demonstrated over and over again in the industrial economy that the new technology created new markets and new jobs.

This past happy relationship with technology has prompted most of the nation's economists to glow with optimism about any new development. In their sanguine view, *any* new technology will create more jobs than it abolishes. But this viewpoint is rooted in tradition and in the outdated industrial model of development. It does not adequately take into account the new realities of the world economy or the quantum leap in the efficiency of production of goods and services made possible by electronics.

The truth is, the new economic model for America will be patterned after the agricultural revolution, not the industrial-mechanical revolution. The number of people required to produce food in the United States declined steadily as mechanization of agriculture developed in the nineteenth and twentieth centuries. When chemical fertilizers were added to farmers' investments, productivity per worker grew even faster. In 1940, it took 35.2 man-hours per acre to produce 26 bushels of corn. By 1966, it took only 6.2 man-hours per acre to produce 68 bushels of corn. In other words, by 1960 one-sixth of the work could produce more than twice as much corn. Now only 3 percent of American job holders feed the entire country and much of the rest of the world as well. This extreme productivity has created economic hardship. In good crop years, American farmers produce huge surpluses and therefore must be protected by price supports and subsidies to keep low prices from driving them out of business. The agricultural revolution in the United States has created the ultimate absurdity: To provide enough income for those left in the production process, we pay them not to grow food or pay them not to sell the harvested food. Plenty creates scarcity.

The same process is promised by the electronic revolution. Like the agricultural revolution, it promises to raise output higher and higher with fewer and fewer people.

In testimony before Congress, Nobel Prize–winning economist Wassily Leontief shared a glimpse of the future. "While in many operations even dirt-cheap labor could not compete effectively with very powerful or very sophisticated machines," he said, "a drastic general wage cut could temporarily arrest the adoption of labor-saving technology." But he continued, in the long run the process is uncontrollable unless it is forbidden or otherwise deliberately slowed down by public policy.

DIMENSIONS OF THE NEW UNEMPLOYMENT

High unemployment rates in the range of 25 percent usually conjure up visions of a depression. During the 1930s, the jobless rate actually reached 30 percent, and millions lived in poverty. Our economy is bound to have its ups and downs in the future, but it need not plunge into the abyss of poverty. Like agriculture, the economy will go on generating income. Our society will be growing richer in the aggregate. But how do we distribute the largesse, so to speak?

Charles Wilson, a former engineer who worked his way up through the ranks to run the General Dynamics plant in Fort Worth, Texas, is a man who understands and appreciates flow charts and the industrial process and the way technology works to make a highly sophisticated piece of machinery such as the F-16 jet fighter. As he whips his gasoline-powered cart up and down the aisles of the cavernous assembly plant, he smiles with pride. The new machines that help make the F-16 fighter jet whiz and whir as they trim a fighter wing to precise tolerances with the aid of computers. In another section of this mile-long complex, said to be one of the world's largest fighter assembly plants, newly installed robots handle yet another aspect of the assembly process. Yet in the vastness of this building, something seems out of balance, even eerie. Considering all the machines at work in these thousands of square feet, there are not many people. The machines are now more tended than they are operated. Wilson, like any good manager, boasts of the productivity and cost-saving aspects of these marvels. When asked how many workers they have replaced, he responds with an engineer's economy of words: "Quite a few."

"Quite a few" is the way many engineers and businessmen respond when they ponder the labor-saving capabilities of the emerging technology. They have not yet assessed its full impact, especially in the context of an economy that has changed fundamentally since the industrial revolution flowered. But the impact will be enormous. "Every time the cost of labor goes up one dollar an hour, a thousand more robots become economical," says Roger B. Smith, chairman of General Motors. Smith is a man challenged by foreign competition. His aim is to boost productivity and lower the cost of his automobiles.

Productivity means what you can produce with the tools and materials and time and labor at hand. It is the output per unit of input, to use the economic definition. When people work harder or when the machines they use enable them to produce more per hour worked, they are rewarded for this increased efficiency with higher pay, more leisure, or more fringe benefits. This is especially true if productivity increases gradually every year.

But suppose there are quantum leaps in the speed and accuracy with which machines can perform tasks? It is then that jobs are threatened. This threat exists now. It is unlike any that has preceded it. For one thing, change is moving much faster. For another, it is attacking all parts of the economy at the same time—factory, office, store, warehouse, even home. And for a third thing, workers are much more vulnerable than ever before and therefore less able to defend the standard of living gained in the past. "Your job or your paycheck!" may well be the choice many workers face.

There will be a big problem in deciding who works and who does not. Should we have early retirement and heavier social security burdens? Should we have compulsory higher education and delay the time of entry into the work force? Should we have a law that says only one person per household may work, or a law that confiscates the second worker's income through taxation? Or should we have a new national wages and hours law, putting a twenty-hour limit on the work week and forbidding overtime?

These are some of the far-out options that will be promoted when the competition for work heats up. The biggest danger is that there will be no planning for the future, so that some people get all the opportunities and some get none. Then the already existing underclass of some six or so million people who have never held a permanent job at a living wage rate would swell to double its present size. The involuntary idle would reach a quarter of the work force—a potential powder keg.

Such a high degree of individual idleness is a sure prescription for social upheaval. Not only will a larger proportion of the population live in poverty, but also a growing gap will emerge between the rich and poor. Not only will there arise a confrontation between those who work and those who don't, but crime will soar. Riots could be common occurrences. If violence does not in fact occur, there will surely be a shattering of democratic principles. The sense of elitism felt by those who work and the sense of rejection felt by those who don't will destroy all pretenses of an egalitarian, humanitarian society.

But we don't have to permit increased joblessness to defeat us so handily. The United States could go either way—more unemployment or more leisure. More leisure for all is preferable because it would salve the tensions, prevent the confrontations, and preserve the nation's democratic principles. In order to avoid the job crisis, the United States must rethink traditional work patterns and how the available jobs will be distributed and shared. An unemployed class of 25 percent of the work force seems out of the question. But such a large pool of unemployed is not out of the question if nothing is done.

The United States has had its automation scares before, the latest occurring in the late 1950s and early 1960s. These scares were accompanied by dire predictions of widespread unemployment caused by automatic machines that displaced humans. But these eventualities failed to materialize. Some displacement did take place. But as workers left manufacturing, they found jobs in other sectors, especially in the fast-growing services area. That gave hope, picked up the slack. The typical services—secretary, bank teller, insurance clerk—weren't that automated then. The whole services area expanded with people, not machines.

Within factories, the machines of the 1950s and 1960s and 1970s did not cause the massive layoffs some anticipated. Machines were limited in what they could do, so they did not cause fantastic leaps in efficiency. Their installation actually enabled workers to bargain for better working conditions, shorter hours, and a higher standard of living. This was the American way—passing productivity gains on to workers. The fact that industrial workers were highly organized also minimized the automation scare and enabled them to share in the benefits of new profits earned through the efficiency of the new machines.

There were other reasons why job abolition was postponed. Fat and happy American industry did not feel the heat of competition from abroad. Emerging from the ruins of World War II in an unparalleled number one position, industry in the United States found no reason to move aggressively and rapidly into investment in labor-saving machinery. Japan was exporting what Americans perceived to be low-quality goods; it was only an infant industrial giant. The temptation for American firms was to let the old technology run its course, and rake in the profits. Many workers' jobs were spared through this lack of foresight—but only temporarily.

By the early 1970s, the failure to innovate and invest in an aggressive fashion had left its mark. Americans were better employed than they otherwise might have been, but their basic industries were under threat because of a shortsighted reinvestment policy. By their inattention to longer-term issues, like developing new markets and products, American industrial managers had invited worthy competition from Japan, Europe, and a host of fast-emerging developing nations.

U.S. industry in the 1980s must plunge forward into the newest technology in order to survive. This time the new machines are more formidable from a worker's point of view. Robot technology, or robotics, is only in its first generation, yet it threatens to eliminate thousands of jobs in the automobile industry alone. That much is evident in the tour of a factory or two. Walter K. Weisel, vice-president of Prab Robots, Inc., of Kalamazoo, Michigan, says robots have the potential to improve every manufacturing process dramatically. "Envision the results if we were to properly apply thousands of robots in our existing processes, each adding up to fifteen to twenty percent increases in production."

Robots that can build robots are being built. The new robots and computer-aided machines on factory floors achieve their work with a speed and, more importantly, a precision that were never possible before. Precision is the key to cost control, because it ensures quality control in mass production. Even on the engineering side of factories, the revolution is apparent. Gradually replacing the drafting table is the CAMCAD, the computer terminal where engineers design supersophisticated machines with the same gusto of a teenager playing a video game in an arcade.

Yet the technology is still in its infancy. Robots have yet to achieve the intelligence of those pictured in *Star Wars*. Most consist of nothing more than mechanical arms and a computer memory, enabling them to do simple garden-variety assembly line jobs. Every minute, though, robots are being equipped with more "intelligence." They are being groomed to handle infinitely more complex tasks in the future. Computers are the pets of hundreds of engineers and technicians whose goal is to replicate or duplicate human intelligence. Herbert A. Simon, Nobel laureate in economics and professor of psychology and computer science at the Carnegie-Mellon Institute, sees no limit to the intelligence that computers can attain. Earl C. Joseph, futurist at Sperry Corporation's Univac Division, predicts that "expert systems" no bigger than a calculator will be available by 1990. They would serve as a professional "mind amplifier," like a magic encyclopedia.

The power of computer tools, as all who use them will say enthusiastically, is that they "talk" with the user—and they never say anything irrelevant. Interactive computers with nearly infinite memories are almost here. William G. Howard, Jr., vice-president of technology and planning at Motorola Inc.'s Semiconductor Group, forecasts that by 1990 a single thumbnail-size computer chip will hold one million bits of data, more than fifteen times the amount of stored data now possible. His prognosis: Computers will be about the size of a basketball and do more sophisticated work than today's mainframes.

Historically, at least fifty years are required for any innovation to be taken through all its major possible ramifications. We have lived through only 20 percent of this time lapse in connection with the electronics revolution.

A big leap in robot use is at hand. General Motors plans to spend more than $1 billion by 1990 to install more than fourteen thousand new robots, pushing many more workers out of the automobile industry. Almost every major American manufacturer is rushing into the robotics revolution. In Kentucky, a robotized factory to produce robotized factories is under development. By the turn of the century, the totally automated factory will be commonplace. Just about all of the operations in those factories will be performed by robots—even management functions. Automatic inventory and tool management and automatic machining, assembly, finishing, and inspection will be routine.

Even as the cost to industry of these technological marvels is coming down, the amount of work they can do is obviously increasing. They do not complain about working conditions or organize themselves into unions. Their "wage" is the cost of maintenance and depreciation, and this compares very favorably with wages and fringe benefits paid to people. Semiskilled as well as skilled industrial workers will find their jobs threatened as robotics becomes more widespread during even the next decade.

The expected surge in efficiency and the almost total displacement of workers in the goods-producing industrial sector weaken the argument that robots will somehow create jobs in the industries where they are installed. A new market for goods produced by robots may well be created because of lower costs, but more jobs won't necessarily follow.

Even before the new automated technology came on the scene, it was apparent that the factory worker was a fading phenomenon in America. The U.S. economy has undergone a basic transformation within the past twenty years, with a remarkable shift from manufacturing to services. People are not aware of this personality change, because the goods are still being produced. But more than three-fourths of all jobs are now related to services, not goods production. America is now well into a "post-industrial" world, where knowledge is the product and communications are paramount.

At the same time that robot technology is dampening job opportunities in manufacturing, the computer will be creating a job crisis in the services area. Office work has long been noted for its low productivity. The office system was built around paper and memos and big, bulky files. Job opportunities were created because business bureaucracies lived in the dark ages of inefficiency. An office was aptly called a paperwork jungle. People, not machines, were needed to make them function, however badly. Computers are the new machetes that will tear down these jungles—in banking and finance, in retail trade, in communications, in every service industry. The revolution is already taking place. It will pick up speed.

The secretary who had to take dictation with a pencil, type at the rate of sixty words a minute, and file yards of paper in phalanxes of cabinets will be replaced by a word-processing technician who types from voice tapes, files by computer, and by satellite transmits printed or electronic (video) output anywhere in the world instantaneously. In the electronic office, one person will do the work of at least three previous employees.

But this is only part of the story in the services sector. In supermarkets, the people who once marked the prices on items are no longer needed, thanks to new "scanners" being introduced. Soon radio band communication will update such information instantly. In banks, thousands of check-processing and record-keeping jobs are being eliminated. In warehousing, neither human brain nor brawn is required to do the job anymore. An automatic forklift handles most of the heavy lifting. Automatic inventory control performed by computers handles the paperwork problem.

Little companies as well as big corporations in every field are finding ways to improve productivity and cut cost with relatively cheap computers. A mere $7000 allows one person to automate financial statements, ledgers, inventory control, and a host of other business records. Computers make wonderful little bureaucrats; as they get smarter with the introduction of even more advanced technology, they will be able to streamline the office bureaucracy even more.

In short, America's service-type firms are finding that they can do lots more with lots less. Computer technology is increasing exponentially their ability to expand business volume without hiring new people. Communicating with customers, processing sales and claims, and filing reports and information can be more efficiently handled by these new marvels. Banks, insurance companies, and stock brokers can offer a vast amount of new services to the public without a correspondingly large increase in their work force.

To be sure, opportunities are being changed by this new technology. The nation has long counted on growing industries to provide future jobs as declining industries lose their dynamism. Repair and service jobs and programmers' and designers' jobs are being created by computer technology, but there will not be enough of them to meet all the needs of would-be workers. The new automated machines have created a squeeze effect on workers such as they have never experienced before. In the past, after workers had lost a job in a factory, they searched for jobs wherever they could find them, usually in another factory. Or their wives found jobs. Relatively unskilled jobs in the services sector were the old standby. Typically, the pay was low, but it was a job, even if it was in a supermarket or department store. In the future, factory workers will be pushed out of the manufacturing sector in increasing numbers as companies rush to automate, and when these workers go looking for a service job, they will find the search frustrating.

THE TOUGH WORLD ECONOMIC GAME

If the threat to jobs were limited to technology, it would be more manageable. Unfortunately it isn't. What makes the technology problem so menacing is that it is piled on top of another big threat to jobs—foreign competition. In the somewhat innocent generation after World War II, the United States enjoyed a position as an industrial power second to none. But the 1970s jolted the American people back to reality and made them realize they are not insulated from the winds of international competition.

America's economic innocence was built on some fortunate foundations. Capital and energy were plentiful and relatively cheap between 1946 and 1972. Japan and Europe, devastated by the war, were still rebuilding and were no threat economically. The United States was at the center of the international financial system. The dollar was the strongest currency, and the United States provided it freely to help rebuild the war-torn economies.

The United States also had a special commitment to free international trade. It renounced restrictions on trade and money flows in order to help other economies recover and to open up markets for U.S. goods and services. By selling exports to the United States, other countries earned the dollars needed for investment at home. In most cases, foreign goods sold in the United States were no real threat to the powerful corporations that had emerged from World War II in a strong position.

And then others began to catch up. Japan and Western Europe found the openness of the U.S. market an invitation to sell new goods produced with the help of U.S. money, technology, and expertise. Exporting to the U.S. market would keep their employment levels high. Japan's export-minded policies turned it into an industrial giant at the expense of hundreds of thousands of jobs in the United States. The bicycle, radio, television, and sewing machine industries in the United States were virtually wiped out in less than a decade.

U.S. companies began protective tactics. Among other strategies, they increasingly went multinational, building factories around the world to take advantage of lower wages. Suddenly the American worker found himself vulnerable to forces that he did not really understand. Low-priced imports were great until they threatened his job. His average pay was higher than in almost any other country in the world, but he was losing his paycheck because those imports meant that he was competing not with his equally well-paid neighbor, but with Japanese, Taiwanese, and Korean workers.

Optimists argue that America's technology is still much more advanced than that of any other nation and that this leadership will save us no matter what. They assume we will always have that edge. But there are two big problems with this view. In the first place, in some key industries we are losing our technological edge. The Japanese, using a more strategic plan of industrial development, are rapidly jumping ahead of the United States in several areas of high technology. They are aiming to take the world lead in development of the most advanced computers. Already they are rushing ahead with the development and manufacture of robots. Many industries in the United States already use numerous Japanese automated machines.

America's old competitive edge was based on its superior research laboratories. But no idea is any good unless it is put into practice. American industry, still suffering from the hangover of short-term thinking that characterized its management in an earlier generation, is slow to put new technology into practice, compared with other countries. For example, America developed miniaturization in electronics, but Japan first understood how miniaturization could be applied and marketed around the world.

Even more important, U.S. multinationals (which, after all, are at the leading edge of technological change) are not exclusively limiting their use of the new techniques of their plants in the United States. On the contrary, they are spreading new technology around the world. Foreign factories are equally likely to have licensed American-invented equipment making goods at low cost to be shipped for sale to U.S. consumers, whose higher wages permit an extensive market. The new technology is highly portable. National borders cannot restrict its usage, no matter if it is originally spawned in some American laboratory. To see thousands of Mexicans busy at work assembling integrated circuit boards or electric irons just south of the border is to understand the future.

Yet another factor makes the U.S. worker vulnerable to foreign competetion—the unwillingness of other nations to open their markets to foreign goods as freely as the United States. Although the United States is not entirely pure on this point, Japan and some European countries have used exports to create jobs and raise their standard of living while enforcing "buy our own" policies at the same time. U.S. workers understand that free trade is unfair if it is a one-way street. They are demanding either that other countries' goods be kept out of the United States or that other countries open their markets fairly to our exports. Political leaders hear and heed; trade policies will be more carefully scrutinized in the future.

WORKERS DISUNITED

Tension will also develop between the United States and foreign workers on the home front. When the optimistic job analysts tell us that the unemployment problem will be virtually solved by lower birthrates, they overlook one of the fastest-growing segments of the work force—illegal immigrants. They ignore the alarming increase of illegal immigration and the hordes of desperate, impoverished Caribbean, Latin American, and Asian people for whom death is a small risk compared with the hope of gaining a foothold in America. The thousands of illegal Mexican immigrants who pour across U.S. borders each year will be supplemented by another group—the new refugees fleeing impoverishment, repression, and war in Central America.

No one really knows how many new illegal immigrants pour into the United States each year. The White House has estimated that perhaps 500,000 net new illegal immigrants come in each year. This estimate is based on the belief that 1.5 million cross the borders, but 1 million are caught and sent back. The figure may be low—as low as one-third of the real number. If it is, and there is good reason to believe that it is, all the optimistic predictions of a slower-growing work force in the late 1980s are wrong. By the end of the decade, the improvement in employment that America was expecting because of lower birthrates would be wiped out by illegal immigration alone. And this does not even consider all the effects of technology, foreign competition, and other forces adversely affecting the job market.

Where illegal immigrants are already clustered, they are branching out beyond the farm and restaurant work previously considered their only hope. They, too, are picking up skills, taking jobs once held by American workers.

Tension between many worker groups is already apparent in some areas of the nation. Blacks rage against Koreans taking over neighborhood shops. Unskilled Puerto Ricans resent the Dominicans and Mexicans who get the low-level jobs they would have had. American garment workers in urban factories fear the Chinese women who will tolerate sweatshop conditions. Illegal immigration is a ticking time bomb—one that will produce intense and bitter political debate about whether the United States should begin to limit its historic role as safety net for the world.

The optimistic view about the job market also ignores the rising expectations of more than half the population: women. The number of women who decided to abandon housework for a paying job rose dramatically in the 1960s and 1970s, stunning labor analysts. Now there's a tendency to believe that this dramatic surge of women into the work force will slow down.

But women's participation in the work force continues to build. Youthful women who are just getting out of high school or college are seeking work at a much higher rate than middle-aged or older women. As these career-minded, work-oriented, nontraditionalist women age, they will replace those middle-aged and older women. As a result, the participation rate of women in the work force will continue to rise. Look at the figures. In 1979, 58 percent of women aged fifty-five to sixty-four chose not to look for work, compared with 27 percent for men. But only 42 percent of women aged forty-five to fifty-four were not working or seeking work, compared with only 9 percent for men of the same age. The participation rate of women who are just getting out of college or high school is well over 60 percent. Women hold 42 percent of the country's jobs now.

Women still have a long way to go before they approach the degree to which men participate in the work force. But the numbers indicate that the traditional woman who chooses to stay home or raise a family is being replaced by the woman who finds work either an economic necessity or a deep satisfaction, or both.

What is the saturation point of women in the work force? Some would answer that question with value judgments about the "proper" role of women in work. But there is no such proper role, and the saturation point is the same as it is for men—no more, no less. Some analysts have argued that there would be no unemployment problem in the United States if female employment could somehow be discounted. The implication of this remark is that women, who in the past were generally not much involved in the great basic industries that paid top dollar, like making cars or steel, are "extra" workers. It is now ever so ironic that men are increasingly being pushed out of these jobs, too. The basic industries of the future won't need the same skills as those of the past. Women might be better equipped than men right now to take the new jobs.

If women are being overlooked by the optimists, so are the aged. Advances in medicine have increased life expectancy; the elderly in the United States are able to work longer than in the past. When a worker leaves the work force permanently, he or she leaves a slot to be filled by someone else. This frees up jobs all the way down the job ladder, even for the beginning worker. It used to be that for every worker who retired, a new job was created for a new entrant into the labor force. In the future this won't be the case, because so many retirees will already be redundant. If those who might have retired cling to their jobs, the squeeze will be on younger workers.

Those who look at the job statistics with rose-colored glasses counter that a trend toward early retirement is well established and will continue. But this ignores several key factors. First, the susceptibility of the U.S. capitalist system to cycles of inflation and recession has made many elderly workers realize the need to stay on the job longer. A strong social movement is already well advanced among the elderly—they want to work longer for a "psychic income." They enjoy working. Congress lifted the mandatory retirement age from sixty-five to seventy a few years ago. Now the administration is proposing to abolish it. Earnings restrictions now in the social security system are being phased out so that the elderly can work without seeing a decline in their social security paychecks.

Not yet foreseen is the degree to which automation will enable the elderly to stay on the job longer. One reason many people retire early is that they are literally worn out by the drudgery of their employment. But what is so physically demanding about pushing buttons to make an automated machine work—either in the factory or in the office? The optimists believe that the nation will need more elderly people at work to make up for a presumed labor shortage in future years. It is more likely that the opposite will happen. Fierce intergenerational competition will result.

As the implications of all these forces become more evident to the worker on the street—or in front of the TV or in the bar, because he/she has nothing better to do—panic may replace complacency. The last thing to hope for is an epidemic of robot phobia. Already the symptoms are beginning to appear in the dying autotowns of the Midwest, from where a new migration to the Sunbelt is a trickle that could become a flood. As a vocational education expert in Milwaukee told a conference convened by former Congressman Henry Reuss, "Everybody's talking about the demand for machinists going unfilled, and I can't place half our graduates. I'm beginning to suspect it's a great big red herring, like lulling us to sleep while they sneak in the robots."

Panic can be avoided by taking realistic steps toward achievable goals. One approach to the coming job crisis is to let things take their course—workers who are smart and worthy will train themselves for the new jobs, and welfare will take care of the rest. A better approach is to try to figure out what changes will mean for skills needed, places they are needed in, and the time they will be needed.

A moderate dose of foresight and strategic planning should reveal that Americans are far from helpless in face of the work revolution. For one thing, the work revolution will also bring about a revolution in leisure. We may have seen the last time card punched in some industries, while their new prosperity will allow them to support, through wages and taxes, a better life-style. Many jobs that now go undone can get done, and many people can be retrained or newly trained to handle them. Instead of welders, we'll need robot maintenance people. Instead of file clerks, we'll need "techniteachers" to help children learn the *abc*'s with interactive computers they can carry around with them.

Ringing the job crisis alarm also signals new opportunities. A high tech society can use its technology to prepare both its youth and its experienced workers for a future that is approaching faster than ever before. After all, for the first time in history, a society has the knowledge, the technology, and the means to meet the future head on.

3

The New
Technological Revolution

In 1983, the Reagan administration offered farmers a unique program: Don't plant your fields this year, and the government will give you surplus grain already in government warehouses, which you may sell on the open market. You pay nothing for the grain you receive, and you keep what you earn. The program was called PIK, for payment in kind.

Naturally, farmers facing plummeting prices could not pass up such a deal, and political leaders were eager to embrace a farm-support program that did not add to the already swelled silos. It seemed the perfect solution to the crisis of agricultural overproduction. Only 3 percent of the total American work force was feeding America and other countries as well and still building up vast stockpiles of surplus commodities.

And the program worked. At least it seemed to work—until adverse side effects started to materialize. By the early summer, reports of unanticipated consequences were trickling back to Capitol Hill: You may have helped the farmers, but you plowed under those who live off the farmers. Farm machinery and fertilizer sales were poor. Seasonal workers who depended on farm work had to look elsewhere for employment. Pilots who dusted crops were idled. The income normally brought in by the economic activity associated with plowing, planting, growing, and harvesting was never generated. Wherever the land was idle, many pockets were emptier. Many farmers had planted enough in one season to last for two seasons, and parts of agricultural America came face-to-face with the paradoxical poverty of plenty.

This bit of recent history is more than a metaphor for what is to come in the rest of the economy; it is a promise. The U.S. economy is passing through the final stages of the mechanical–industrial revolution and into a technological revolution brought about chiefly by two successor technologies: electronics and optics. Together, the scientists and engineers and technicians in these fields have opened up a vast new world of information management and communications. They are the force behind the new "knowledge-based economy." Their discoveries complement one another and will reduce by enormous quantities the amount of labor needed to produce a given amount of product or service or data.

Like previous technological revolutions, this technological revolution will play itself out in many areas of endeavor over many years of development. During previous technological eras—the electro-mechanical era, the age of steam, the age of the human- and animal-drawn wheel, and the hand tool age—innovations were constantly multiplying the yield of human labor by substituting energy in a physical form. The fifth technological revolution differs from all others in that it is substituting energy in a mental form. To be sure, this energy may be harnessed to a physical contraption. When it is, the physical performance is enhanced many times over by what drives it, and what drives it may no longer be a worker, but a string of binary numbers. This revolution replaces moving parts with integrated circuits. It replaces telephone cables with spun glass that transmits sound by converting it into light and transmits it many times faster than does copper wire. It replaces scalpels with lasers—which is light amplification by stimulated radiation. It also replaces people with chips, robots, keyboards, light pens, and other miraculous electronic tools.

This revolution will rapidly spread in factories, offices, banks, stores, and warehouses, not to mention schools and homes. It will drastically alter the way we work in every area of activity and in almost every walk of life. The effects of the fifth technological revolution will echo the agricultural revolution that ended in the pitiful irony of PIK. We will be able to produce more and more with fewer and fewer workers, and there may come a time when we can cheaply produce far more than we can sell at prices we need to support the high standard of living we are used to.

This revolution goes far beyond simple automation. That is why the history of the assembly line and of the computer-based automation of the 1960s and 1970s is irrelevant.

Industrialization in the era of mechanization might have replaced the Luddite weavers and their like, but it did create more jobs than it destroyed. Similarly, in the last two decades, the big mainframe computers also created more jobs than they replaced. There were three reasons for this. First, the computers were used primarily for organizing and keeping track of information—for data handling. To use them, it was necessary to convert all the hand-kept records they processed into machine-readable form, and this was a very labor-intensive activity. A second reason the first generation of computers did not destroy jobs was that firms used them to add more products or services in a growing economy. So even as production became more efficient, sales and employment rose. The third reason for employment stability was that the computers were very expensive; they took up a lot of space and were not very mobile. Only well-capitalized firms could afford them.

All of that has changed. The magical chip has changed it. Silicon chips no bigger than a fingernail can store 128,000 bits of information. They have vastly reduced the price of electronic hardware and enabled the miniaturization of equipment so that electronic technology can be applied in every work setting. Soon, a 256,000-bit chip will be widely marketed, making possible computerized linkages that only electronic engineers can now imagine. Supercomputers, or Very Large Integrated Systems, will process limitless amounts of information in a twinkling.

But the microchip is just the workhorse of the electronic era. It is how it is put to use that will determine what the work world looks like in the 1990s.

THE FIFTH TECHNOLOGICAL REVOLUTION IN THE FACTORY

In Erie, Pennsylvania, an old industrial town by Lake Erie, General Electric's newly automated facilities for producing electrical locomotives give a glimpse of the industrial model's swan song. Inside a huge old warehouse of a building where a beehive of men in grimy work clothing once toiled amid noise and grease, one man in a computer-control room guides the production of engine frames while automated machine tools do all the rest of the work as the big parts roll down the assembly line. Two other men are on the factory floor to tend the machines and handle any maintenance, but there appears to be little of either. In fact, according to a GE official, little maintenance is required, because the machinery itself has been built to finer specifications than ever before, thanks to computer technology. Because of this so-called flexible machining center, GE has been able to cut its time for production and assembly of a complete engine block from sixteen days to sixteen hours.

Even more remarkable is the capacity of this automated facility to engage in flexible manufacturing. The automatic machine tools can be programmed to shape one part a certain way as it rolls down the line and then adjust automatically to cut and shape a completely different part right behind the first without the line having to shut down to change the tools. "The ultimate batch is one," says a proud GE official. Such a revolution in manufacturing is only of recent vintage, as computer technology has been incorporated into production. The old assembly line could make one part model *ad infinitum,* but the line had to be stopped and retooled every time a new model was to be made. This not only consumed time, but it required many more people to do the work.

These computer-programmed inventions are quickly bringing the agricultural model of production into the industrial realm. Cutting the cycle time of production from sixteen days to sixteen hours is a dramatic achievement that compares favorably with the reduction in cycle time in agriculture when the tractor replaced the horse.

What is already taking place in industry insofar as automation is concerned is light-years ahead of what was done only a decade ago. But this is actually only the first big wave of integration of computer technology into the manufacturing process. The level of sophistication, as marvelous as it is, still has a long way to go before maturity. In addition, the technology now available has not yet been fully incorporated into the manufacturing process. General Electric, one of the nation's largest and best capitalized firms, still has not fully modernized its operations with available technology. At its Erie plant, for instance, it will be 1986 before all the robots, computerized machine tools, programmable controls, and other automated systems are in place. GE estimates that these improvements will bring a 25 percent cut in direct labor costs, but a 33 percent boost in the capacity to produce. Although the company has said it is optimistic that the pickup in business caused by a more efficient plant will result in little more unemployment, union leaders at the plant are justifiably skeptical.

THE FAST AND THE CHEAP

The speed at which the new technology will be installed is critical. Companies are realizing that failure to invest in it will put them far behind competitors who do. They see that it is in their own self-interest to plunge ahead. In addition, the cost of the new technology—including the cost of robots—continues to fall. Thus, the speed of installation is going to be much faster than widely believed.

Even the smallest firms are getting involved. Take the example of a machine shop in California that employs ten to fourteen people to make precision parts for spacecraft. The spotlessly clean plant floor has several computer-controlled tool-and-die-making and milling machines turning out the same amount of work as noncomputerized shops with twenty-five employees or more, according to the firm's youthful president. But, as he observes, the new technology has raised productivity, and without it, small companies would go under. We have conducted dozens of interviews with similar small manufacturers who tell the same story.

A 1977 study by Donald N. Smith and Lary Evans showed that computerized numerically controlled (CNC) machines cut machining time in half and cut costs by one-fourth. It is probable that with today's equipment cost savings are even greater.[1] All the automobile manufacturers are now using robots on their assembly lines. That industry, threatened by Japanese competition, is spending billions in the midst of difficult times to modernize its plants with new technology. General Motors

---

[1]"Management Standards for Computer and Numerical Control," Ann Arbor, University of Michigan, cited in Bureau of Labor Statistics, *"Technology in Four Industries,"* Bulletin 2104, Washington, D.C.: U. S. Government Printing Office, 1982.

plans to have at least fourteen thousand robots in its facilities by 1990, compared with only three hundred in 1980. In 1983, there were an estimated five to six thousand robots in the entire United States, each one of which can work for half the hourly cost of labor. The survival instinct—which in business is roughly equivalent to the profit instinct—is at the heart of the question of how fast the new technology will be incorporated in U.S. industry.

But what's being installed now is only a precursor of the sophistication to come. If the race among U.S. firms to modernize their operations seems fierce, consider the battle between the United States and Japan to see who will be first to develop a new generation of "superchip" technology that some say could make possible a much more intelligent computer than is now available. Many engineers believe that by 1990 the technology will be available to produce a semiconductor chip that will hold one million bits of information, with potential applications that could supplant many human endeavors in the workplace. Aware of the implications of this race, the U.S. government has encouraged cooperation among high technology firms to develop that technology before the Japanese do, and a consortium of U.S. firms has chosen a Texas location to develop a supercomputer.

The survival instinct among countries is also a major factor in how quickly the new technology will be developed and installed. Considering how quickly the technology is developing, it is not too futuristic to predict that a robot that responds to voice commands is only several years away. The Japanese are talking of developing a computer that will be able to duplicate some aspects of human intelligence, such as reacting to changed circumstances in performing a task. This is in connection with Japan's drive to create the next generation of computers.

ELIMINATING HUMAN HANDS

The totally automated factory is closer than most people realize. James Albus, director of the industrial systems division at the National Bureau of Standards, supports the view that total factory automation is only fifteen or so years away. In such factories, robots will perform most, if not all, of the operations that now require human skills. There will be totally automatic inventory and tool management and automatic machining, assembly, finishing, and inspection systems. Automatic factories will even be able to reproduce themselves. That is, automatic factories will make the components for other automatic factories. (The ancestor of such factories already exists in the Nissan plant in Smyrna, Tennessee, where a robot greets a visitor at the door and leads tours of a plant floor where robots are producing equipment for robots.)

> Once [automated factory construction] occurs, productivity improvements will propagate from generation to generation. Each generation of machines will produce machines less expensive and more sophisticated than themselves. This will bring about an exponential decline in the cost of robots and automatic factories which may equal the cost/performance record of the computer industry. For the past thirty years, computing costs have spiraled downward by 20 percent a year. This is at least in part due to the fact that computers are used to design, construct, and test other computers. Once automatic factories begin to manufacture the components for automatic factories, the cost of manufacturing equipment will also fall exponentially. This, obviously, will reduce the cost of goods produced in the automatic factories. Eventually, products produced in automatic factories may cost only slightly more than the raw materials and energy from which they are made.[2]

Many firms have already linked computer-assisted design and engineering with manufacturing. From the conception to the delivery of the goods, computers are reducing the human work involved in making things. GE's Erie plant, like most large manufacturing operations, is already equipped with an automated warehouse. "We envision a paperless factory," says one of the local GE executives. In fact, the aim is to link all the manufacturing operations together via computer, so that every aspect of business, from the financial department to the assembly line, can be seen and assessed at any time.

That the job-destroying capabilities of the new technology outweigh the job-creating capabilities has been demonstrated mathematically by Wassily Leontief, the Nobel Prize–winning economist. Leontief's input-output analysis, a technique for showing how labor and capital move through a given economic system, was applied to the Austrian economy. The results: If

---

[2] James A. Albus, "Industrial Robot Technology and Productivity Improvement," *Proceedings of the Workshop on the Social Impacts of Robotics*, Office of Technology Assessment, Washington, D.C., July 1981.

technology were fully applied, white-collar jobs would be reduced by 50 percent. In blue-collar jobs, the percentages were higher, reaching 77 percent in machinery. Austria found that with full mechanization and no reduction in the work week, unemployment would climb to more than 10 percent, unheard of in that country. No comparable study has been done for the U.S. economy.

Leontief emphasizes the important point that the cost of capital relative to labor is escalating rapidly. A new job that would have required $50,000 of equipment and plant a generation ago now requires twice that, he says. And he predicts that in another generation it will require five times as much. However, employers and companies will be willing to make the investment in equipment because, once in place, it goes on producing without costing fringe benefits and without getting sick or being late.

No one has financed an input-output analysis of the impact on American technology because Americans pride themselves on not planning ahead. Americans are optimists who prefer, for whatever reasons, to believe that all will be as it was before. American economic thinking is still dominated by the thought processes of the industrial age: We expect to create new jobs faster than we destroy old jobs.

Many cite this comforting rationalization as they go about destroying work opportunities and using government subsidies to do so. When Congress approved the generous Accelerated Cost Recovery Act of 1981, which reduced business taxes through faster tax depreciation of new plant and equipment, it bought the argument that new investment would create millions of new jobs, despite evidence of declining manufacturing employment associated with new technology. This act, known as 10-5-3 (each number refers to years in which a particular investment could be depreciated), was, in the words of one observer, "the most important manpower legislation in the history of Congress." He was referring to the impact of jobs that would be destroyed across a wide range of business because of accelerated investment in automated machinery as result of the legislation. The fiction that this law would be a gigantic job creator was reinforced by economic analyses by many private econometric firms using the formulas of the outdated industrial model to project trends. These formulas build on past relationships between investment, job creation, and output. Besides being admittedly incorrect in their macroeconomic projections of gross national product, inflation, and unemployment, these economists' toys do not even speculate on the job displacement capabilities of the new technology.

We are not arguing against capital formation, by any means. We are merely pointing out that government encouraged capital formation is being sold as something it is not. It may well increase wages and should boost profits, but it will not necessarily reduce unemployment. And those corporate leaders who argue for capital investment subsidies and against larger unemployment insurance taxes are arguing for the right to disemploy people with impunity. Fortunately, there is a growing cadre of enlightened business leaders who see the need for security for workers as well as a need for the most advanced technology.

In a later chapter, we will provide some job scenarios that do take into account the job displacement effects of technology. These scenarios, developed by Dr. Schwartz, are considerably more pessimistic than those projected in a recent book on robotics, by Robert Ayres and Steven Miller. According to them, 4 million workers could be displaced from manufacturing by the end of the decade, and that would exceed the total employment increases for manufacturing for that period by 1 million workers. They maintain that the impact will not be great, given a total work force of more than 100 million people, especially considering that joblessness will be concentrated in a few metalworking industries.[3] But, 1 million more jobless workers would push the total number of unemployed up to 13 million, and from the workers' perspective, this is a significant number.

What is exciting about the new technology is the pace of innovation going on in laboratories and workshops around the nation. This innovation will lead to new applications that will in one way or another reduce employment. Once a new technology such as this is launched, it challenges the human mind so that all the possibilities for application come to be tested and tried until the technology reaches a mature stage.

The mature stage is not yet here. You can see that when you visit laboratories such as those at Carnegie-Mellon University's Robot Institute of America in Pittsburgh. Here researchers are

---

[3]Robert U. Ayres and Steven M. Miller, *Robotics Applications and Social Implications*, Cambridge, Mass.: Ballinger Publishing Co., 1983, p. 212.

seeking ways to broaden a robot's abilities, such as enabling it to identify a specific object, pick it up and put it somewhere else, and then ascertain that it has done this job correctly. That may sound like a simple task, but it requires an enormous amount of complicated circuitry to do it. This is just one example of how robotics is in its infancy and how efforts are under way daily to make improvements. If this kind of task can be mastered, the capacity of robots to work on assembly lines would be greatly expanded.

Most robots are incapable of small-parts assembly. They are still used primarily for difficult, routine tasks such as welding, painting, handling of materials, cutting, drilling, die-casting, and forging. Consequently, many assembly line workers thus far have escaped the effect of automation. On an automobile assembly line, for example, much of the hand work involved in assembly after the major components have been put into a car still has to be handled by human labor. But strides have been made in increasing the complexity of robots, and it seems only a matter of a few years before more complex robots will be put into operation, and many more assembly line jobs will be put in jeopardy.

The job-displacing impact of robots has already created a proposal by the International Association of Machinists for a "robot bill of rights" that attempts to put controls on their installation and to impose a "robot tax" on all machinery and production systems that displace workers and cause unemployment. This proposal has caused deep concern in the machine tool industry, where little, if any, retraining has taken place.

IT'S NOT JUST ROBOTS

But while everyone talks about robots, that's not the extent of automation in manufacturing. Consider the commonplace job of sewing. Automation of sewing is not far away, and this will have an enormous job impact among textile workers in the United States and elsewhere. Three researchers at the University of Illinois' Chicago Circle Center for Urban Development found a Chicago embroidery firm planning to cut its labor force in half because computer-run sewing machines were to be installed. Computers will "digitize" sewing patterns and then guide the actual sewing work. "Company officials state that they expect to cut labor costs and produce a better quality product with the new machines."[4]

What is striking about this is the pervasiveness of the application of the technology. Studies of the job impact of technology tend to focus on certain jobs in certain industries, but if there is one sure thing about the new technology, it is its ubiquitous nature. This magnifies the job of estimating its impact.

Those who are optimistic about the effect of technology on jobs say that brand-new jobs will be created that will partially offset the impact of automation. The argument goes something like this: Workers may be displaced, but there will be new demands for computer programmers, robot-maintenance workers, and other new skilled positions. This is true, but the number of new jobs created is far outdistanced by the number of those destroyed.

Maintenance of robots will obviously be a growth area in the job market, but many who cling to the hope that the job numbers will be vast should reassess. What's impressive about the new technology is the fundamental improvement in quality of both the product being made and the robots doing the work. For instance, GE officials report that their new programmable machine tools require little maintenance. There are simply fewer breakdowns. This is because the technological revolution begins with the very design of a product. You can see this dramatically at General Electric's computer-assisted engineering facilities in Cincinnati, Ohio: CAE International Inc. and SDRC Inc. Here the job of the engineer has been incorporated into sophisticated computer software. In designing a part or a product, all the stresses and strains can be simulated right in the computer—and much more accurately and to finer tolerances than can be done by hand. One of the results of this work was a lightweight, plastic axle designed for the Volkswagen Rabbit, which, GE says, passed all the tests and created a radical new design for an axle.

According to the software experts, the chief advantage of computer-assisted engineering is the leap in quality, simply because the computer permits better testing and finer tolerances. This is a big advantage to companies making a large

---

[4]Robert Mier, Art Strobeck, Jr., and David Ranney, "Technological Change and Chicago Industry: A Preliminary Study," Chicago: University of Illinois at Chicago Circle Center for Urban Economic Development, January 1983.

number of products, because it sharply cuts the number of prototypes they have to build. When this technology is fully incorporated into industry, say the experts at CAE International, it will result in products that last longer. Such technology will lead to higher-quality products as industrial firms compete to satisfy the demands of consumers for better quality. Companies that try to retreat back into their old routines of cutting corners will find their competitors making the sales. Besides, quality can now be achieved in many products at a lower cost than previously. And, the new capability for quality will affect not just consumer goods, but industrial equipment and machinery as well. In other words, fewer maintenance and repair workers will be required.

Building longer-lasting products, especially such expensive machines as automobiles, could further reduce the need for workers to build them by reducing total demand—unless, of course, cars become so inexpensive that everyone can afford one or more. For the moment, it looks as if the retirement age for autos is on the rise, although that could be a recession-induced situation. Still, unless we move to a strong protectionist position and keep out foreign cars in a large way, the pressure will be on to prevent obsolescence and offer a better, competitive product. Because quality is now technically more feasible, it is a more essential marketing strategy. Added quality may help employment in a firm that is making higher profits by responding to the demand for quality. Over time, though, as consumers keep their goods longer, demand will slacken.

Office Automation

Now that the United States has been thrust into the information age, many analysts feel that millions of new jobs will spring up in the offices of America. White-collar jobs in banks, finance and insurance companies, the administrative offices of manufacturing corporations, and in other office-based services are counted on to take up the job slack caused by the loss of jobs in manufacturing. But this is a false hope. Automation of the office is proceeding as quickly as in manufacturing, perhaps more quickly, because it is in the office that electronic technology and optics technology come together to completely change the amount of human labor needed to produce information. As far back as 1953, the sociologist C. Wright Mills warned that office automation would change the nature of work in offices faster than automation would change factory production lines.

To fully appreciate what the new technological revolution can do in an office, one must keep in mind what is done in offices: Information is gathered, processed, stored, analyzed, altered, and transmitted to people who need it. Different people use the same data in different ways. Different combinations of information are sent to different audiences and in different "packages," ranging from a simple table of numbers to a slick annual report. Thus the office is the one place in which there is an almost insatiable demand for labor saving equipment that can be applied to office workers' functions.

The office worker's main labor saving device in the mechanical-industrial era was the typewriter, invented in 1900. For decades, the typewriter was the chief contributor to office productivity, and its significance is underscored by the fact that it was not until 1983 that Smith-Corona stopped making a nonelectric typewriter. The first electric typewriter was introduced around 1950, and it increased office workers' productivity, too, primarily by allowing typists to work faster. In the 1950s and 1960s, the gigantic electronic computers hit the back offices—the places where records are kept, cases are counted, inventories are controlled. To transfer all of the material that had formerly been typed, proofread, and calculated on a mechanical adding machine to the computers, armies of keypunch operators were hired to type data onto cards and later onto magnetic tape that the computers could read.

All of this made office work more efficient without destroying more jobs than it created. But the microchip is another story, because it reduced the size and the cost of electronic data handling enormously. In the 1970s, microprocessing was born, and the front office began going electronic. The front office is where the managers work and make decisions, write letters, plan and compose reports. The first equipment to appear in the front office was designed for the typing pool: It was the electronic word processor, which stored data on small disks that could be edited and altered without touching the parts to be retained. This saved hours of retyping time and hours more of proofreading time. A typist who could type 90 words on an electric typewriter or on an electronic typewriter with a small "memory" could type 130 words a minute on a word processor. But the major efficiency improvement was the time saved in controlling quality.

Meanwhile, another set of miraculous machines was invading the office: the communications systems. This is what makes possible the production of more than one copy of a document so that many people can view it at the same time or save it to view at different times. Since the first photostat in 1910, through the invention of microfilm in 1920 and photocopying in the 1950s, communications have grown so fast that we are at the brink of the paperless office. Magnetically coated and photosensitive recording materials will almost eliminate photocopying—and thus the need for files and file clerks. Computers and word processors can communicate with one another, bypassing paper all together, as evidenced by the fact that the authors of this book edited each others' words without first printing them on paper. Multiple copies can be made now at the rate of 140 characters per second; the speed could double in a few years. Thanks to fiber optics, as many copies as are wanted can be automatically copied, collated, and stored. The magic of fiber optics, which consist of very slender strands of glass that conduct digitally coded information in the form of pulses of light, is just beginning to be explored. "Intelligent" copiers can handle twenty pages a minute and can merge materials from different sources, all with a few keyboard instructions. In the future, spoken mail can replace telephone communication and hardcopy communication. A person will speak into a computer, which will store the message and forward it later to its destination, where it can be read on a screen or filed on a disk or printed on paper.

These innovations will affect far more than the back office workers or the front office support staff. They will greatly alter the professional and managerial jobs done in offices, too. With a simple microcomputer at their sides, staff members can compose reports, send them to superiors and subordinates, receive comments, and alter the reports—all without paper. Software enables them to do complex math, including graphs, and to try out different combinations of numbers. The software available now is easy to use for anyone determined to learn it; in a few more years, or perhaps months, it will be so simple that even people who have computer phobia will be able to use it.

But the first effects will be felt by the clerical staff, because saving their labor costs is more important to management than saving professional and managerial labor costs. Already the signs are there. According to Working Women, the national association of office workers, computers have encouraged enormous expansion in the volume of office-based transactions, with little or no growth in employment. The organization has studied this phenomenon in banking, one of the first industries to adopt computer technology. From 1960 to 1973, banking transactions increased by 8.3 percent a year and employment by 4.5 percent a year. But from 1973 to 1976, as computer technology became more pervasive in banking, banking transactions still continued this sharp growth while employment growth slowed to 3.2 percent a year. The government projects that the growth rate in banking employment will fall to 1.8 percent by 1990, but financial transactions are expected to continue their rapid growth.

Although no reliable estimate for office automation has been made in the United States, studies in Europe reported by Working Women suggest it will be substantial. A 1978 report by Simon Nora for the French Ministry of Industry predicted that 30 percent of clerical workers in the banking and insurance businesses could lose their jobs by 1990.[5] In England, two researchers estimated that office automation could lead to a permanent 20 percent office worker displacement.[6]

Eileen Applebaum, a distinguished economics professor at Temple University, noted these estimates in a paper for the Office of Technology Assessment of Congress. "These guesses (and I emphasize that they are only guesses) suggest an increase in labor productivity in the office of about 25 percent. Even if these guesses are too high by a factor of 2 or 3, they suggest the severity of the technology unemployment problem that may emerge if programmable automation spreads through both manufacturing and nonmanufacturing sectors."

With so few clerical workers belonging to unions, they are ultimately going to have trouble reaping the benefits of higher productivity. Right now, this is not a serious problem, because there is a relative shortage of personnel with experience on the equipment, and the shortage will last for another three years at least. Word processors command high salaries and have a wide choice in choosing a company to work for. But toward the end of the present decade, the picture could well change, and the choice for office-support labor then will be either to organize to keep wages up or to accept lower pay to keep their jobs. But either way, according to Applebaum, "The rapid growth that has characterized clerical employment in the last decade is

[5]Simon Nora, "The Next French Revolution," *New Scientist*, June 1978.
[6]"The Future with Microelectronics," *New Scientist*, April 1979.

likely to slow, further compounding the problem of providing jobs for new labor entrants."

Whether or not office automation will reduce the demand for professional, managerial, and administrative labor is a more difficult question, because there will be many new products and services to develop, and sales and marketing will become increasingly important to companies in a competitive economy. It is true that automation will make such workers much more productive. Insurance adjusters can handle more cases; analysts can examine more alternatives; actuaries can assess risk more often as new data come in. Salespersons can spend less time writing up sales reports and more on the road. Certainly automation will reduce drudgery and make the job more rewarding. But there is a drawback for thousands of middle management executives throughout the United States. The ability of the computer to keep better track of the business through sophisticated communications networks internally has caused many firms to reduce the size of their executive force, which has been growing too large since the post-war period.[7]

Again, only a few scientific studies dare to support this anecdotal information, and they are, notably, not American work. Richard Stursberg of the Ottawa Ministry of State for Social Development noted in 1982 that most researchers continue the tradition of "relentless optimism" begun by sociologist Daniel Bell in his classic 1977 book, *The Post Industrial Society*.[8]

The Automated Shopping Spree

Billed as the world's first robot-salesperson, it looks more like a box than a person. It certainly is one of the more unusual features of Woodward and Lothrop, the Washington, D.C., department store. It's in the "domestics" department, where sheets and towels are sold. A customer can punch in the type, size, and color of the item wanted after viewing real fabric samples on the console. The computer calculates the cost, the customer pays, and the goods are delivered by mail. According to the store, the robot also automatically records the change in inventory for the information of the warehouse and the store's buyer.

[7]"A New Era for Management," *Business Week*, April 25, 1983.

[8]Richard Stursberg, "Productivity and Employment: A Review of the Debate on the Implications of Information Technology," paper prepared for the American Political Science Association annual meeting in June 1982, p. 9.

Robot sales forces may not proliferate too rapidly, because not all items are as standardized as sheets and towels; standardization makes it easy to routinize the sales processes. But the technological revolution has already made many inroads into retailing and can make many more. The black and gray bars printed on grocery shelf items are scanned by a laser, transmitted digitally, and stored in computers that remember price and track inventory. In Columbus, Ohio, subscribers to the experimental Warner Communications QUBE cable system can do their shopping by video. Citibank is preparing HomeBase, which will allow bank customers to do all of their financial transactions from their home, including paying the bills. Some banks already have systems that provide for automatic payments to creditors.

Automation in both the retail end of shopping and the wholesale end has advanced further than most people realize. Warehouses are manned by computer-controlled automatic forklifts, which can roll down an aisle, pick out and stack a quantity of given items, roll on to deliver the items to a truck or train, and keep records of what has been moved, where it is going, and how much it costs. All the necessary basic instructions are preprogrammed into the forklift, and miles of warehouse shelves can be "manned" by a single person.

The machine now used by the (human) sales clerk in a shop or department store records every necessary bit of information about the goods sold: the department number, inventory code, sales clerk, customer's identification, price. Once the information is punched in, necessary changes in information about needed inventory are also made automatically and routed automatically to those people who need it. All these changes mean the customer waits longer while the transaction is being completed, but they also mean that no clerks in back office cubby holes are needed to record and copy data onto different work sheets or punch it into computer cards.

WHERE WILL THE WORKERS GO?

Relentless optimism about the economy's ability to absorb workers displaced by automation derives from the comforting assumption that the economic pie will grow fast enough so that increased business activity will create enough demand for new jobs to keep a growing percentage of the population in gainful employment. When certain sectors of the economy got too productive, as did agriculture, it was assumed that the gains in productivity would be reflected in lower prices. Lower prices for those goods would mean that people had more money to spend on more of these or other goods. The portion of the savings spent on other goods would generate more demand and would lead to new job formation in other industries. So, for example, if the price of food or television sets should fall, more money would be spent on cars or vacations. Jobs in the car industry or the travel industry would increase faster than they would have had the food-producing sector or television industry not become more efficient.

Unfortunately, this theory works only under ideal circumstances that economists like to postulate but that seldom occur in a pure form. Look at what has actually happened in agriculture. It is beset with a complex system of price supports and government help that add billions to the tax bills and food bills of ordinary Americans. The productivity gains in agriculture that theoretically would have lowered the price of food have been offset by government mechanisms that keep food prices high. The reason is that the remaining farmers found that they could not live on the low prices that increased productivity had brought. They created so much plenty that the government had to take steps to convert plenty to scarcity. Farmers have been unable to make up in volume what they lost in unit prices, because they are in competition with other countries and because U.S. policy has limited sales to Communist nations. Giving away the food to poor nations in great quantities has never been seriously considered, although some believe that would be a cheaper way of disposing of surpluses than the current price support system. So theory did not work out in practice.

There are many reasons why theory may not work out in practice during the work revolution in manufacturing and services, either. The theory will be the same: reduced labor costs in the auto and steel and clothing and other basic industries should reduce the costs of those goods enough so that people will have more money to spend on other goods, like home computers, audio cameras, recreational vehicles, and opera tickets. The money spent for new goods and services would in turn create more jobs—enough to offset those lost in the automating industries. At the same time, the workers remaining in the automating industries would earn more as a result of wage gains associated with rising productivity.

That is the theory, but in a society where automation is taking place across the board and a huge pool of labor is available, many firms would be in the driver's seat in paying their employees. Their motivation for passing along the benefits from productivity increases would not be high. So wages might not go up as much as expected.

In addition, any new money freed up for spending for new goods and services would not necessarily create new jobs. It could be spent on services that were also being automated, on goods that were being imported, or on goods being made in automated plants. Unless the freed-up spending is concentrated by choice or by law on labor-intensive industries, theory will not hold up as it did, for the most part, during the industrial era. Earlier technology did not have the same widespread application that current technology has. The new electronic and fiber optics technology is leapfrogging ahead to transform every aspect of the economy at the same time. This is a vast, sometimes unappreciated work revolution.

The mechanical revolution on the farm released workers to man the mechanical revolution in the factories and helped America become the industrial giant of the world. But the transition was not all smooth then, either. When farm workers moved into Detroit and Chicago and the great industrial cities of the Midwest, they were moving to plants that were expanding output, but not all of them found jobs, and not all the jobs were very well paid. In fact, full employment was not reached in the United States until after the Depression *and a world war.* And even without war, conditions during the 1920s to 1950s were very different than they are now. Farm workers were moving to assembly line jobs that were easy to learn and that needed almost no education to perform. The difference now is that the new technology is invading every sector, and its biggest impact will be to eliminate precisely those kinds of low-skilled jobs.

FROM UNDERUSE TO REVOLUTION

The great migration off the farm and into smokestack America took about thirty years, or one generation of workers, to complete. During this time, technology inside the factories did not change very much—not because new equipment wasn't available, but because companies were making enough profit milking the old equipment to its last productive drop. For example, continuous casters have been available for steel manufacturing for twenty-five years or so, but barely one-fifth of American steel is made by this cost-effective system, as compared to almost 100 percent of overseas production. When everyone began to notice that the Japanese were taking over our markets for cars, televisions, bicycles, cameras, and steel itself, the cruel joke was told: Japan really won World War II, because all its obsolete plants were bombed out and new ones had to be built from scratch.

There's an element of truth in this gallows humor. After the war and conversion of factories back to peacetime use, U.S. firms in many industries were slow to replace facilities and introduce new technology. There were several reasons for this. For one thing, the United States was the strongest economy in the world by far, and it had no concern about international competition until the 1970s. Second, Americans did not save a high percentage of their money—savings that could be tapped by industry to plow into investment. They were not encouraged to save as, for example, Europeans were by high equity requirements for home ownership. In fact, many laws passed during the 1940s and 1950s actually discouraged savings by subsidizing consumption in various ways. Third, tax laws and inflation discouraged new investment domestically, and overseas investment opportunities became relatively more attractive, especially since the labor cost of overseas production was so much lower than the labor cost of domestic production. Finally, there was the human tendency to continue running old equipment for as long as possible to squeeze the last penny of profit out of it and to avoid the expense of new machines.

Many who have tracked these habits of American industry believe the delayed investment strategy was perfectly logical. But in truth it was foolhardy and tragic. It was failure to invest earlier that led to the compulsion to invest later, once the true noncompetitiveness of American firms became clear. But when the need to invest was finally clear, the sales demand to justify investment was not there. In 1982 the United States found itself with the highest unemployment rate, the lowest utilization of existing (however obsolete) capacity, and the lowest rate of new capital investment since the Great Depression.

This is what is causing the great dilemma today. No one wants to look at the fast track of technological proliferation and rejoice that increasing productivity will push the unemployment rate up. Yet it is clear that American firms, for survival's sake, must install state-of-the-art equipment if they are to compete. It is also clear that progress never stands still and is moving ahead at an ever-increasing rate. Some say more discoveries have been made in our lifetime than in the previous 500 years. It seems logical and simple to advocate the most rapid possible diffusion and application of these new discoveries, and the United States is beginning to do so as a matter of policy. There are a variety of government responses, from new laws encouraging investment in research and development with tax incentives to new energy in high risk, venture capital markets.

But with this accent on the need for the new, few people have paid attention to the need for understanding what this new technology will do to the workplace and the workers. Finding a balance between being the best technologically and the best in human terms is the tall challenge that faces us all as technology revolutionizes work.

4

The International
Job Crisis

Inside the union hall in Anderson, Indiana, the signs betray the
workers' main concern: "Buy GM—Buy America" and "Hun-
gry? Eat a Toyota." A woman worker in her twenties, divorced
and with a small son, explains what it is like to be laid off from
her job at the Delco plant, hard hit by recession and imports.
She feels the stress, tries to cope with headaches, and generally
feels useless. She was offered a job in another state, but the
father of her son objected and, besides, she had to worry about
who would take care of her son in another location. She found a
part-time job as a computer operator, just for the training, and
explains she wants to go to school for further training with the
federal "trade adjustment assistance" money she's expecting.
"If I could ever find a job in the computer field . . . " she says
wistfully.

Pain. Change. Fear of the unknown. Adjustment. This is the
common story of American workers caught up in a new economic arena, one that stretches beyond the comfortable borders
of the past. International trade may not be one of those intri-
guing topics that is on everyone's lips, but it has become a major
influence on the lives of average Americans in the past decade as
imports have devastated industry after industry. The pace of
this change has been breathtaking, disrupting the lives of hundreds of thousands of workers and their families.

And therein lies a message. Those now trying to plan their futures should be aware of the forces now gripping international commerce and threatening their job opportunities. Americans need to sit down and think through the implications of the trade and technology challenge as never before. Trade will play an increasing role in whether the country is healthy economically and in who will get the jobs in the future. Those who do not take the trade outlook of an industry into account when they plan their future fail to do so at their own peril.

Thinking about trade does not mean becoming obsessed with the esoterica of exchange rates, tariffs, and quotas. The real fundamentals that make international trade so important to everyone are: Who has the best technology and the best trained and educated work force? Who is the best organized from an industrial standpoint? Who has the highest wages? Who has the resources? Who has the highest unemployment rate?

The trade story too often emphasizes international politics, when in reality it is about how workers worldwide are trying to survive and cope by using the resources and technology at hand. In a visceral sense, trade is social Darwinism; the fittest survive as they adjust and specialize. Protectionism is attempted survival by the unfittest.

The new story to be told about trade will not have a neat, tidy ending, producing a safe system for passing out the buy and sell opportunities. It's going to become much more of a people story and potentially much more tragic. Trade is going to be the action-forcer that will make countries recognize the need to move rapidly into newer technologies and revamp their economies in fundamental ways—ways that may hurt many individuals.

TRADE CONTROL OR DAMAGE CONTROL?

For Americans, as far as jobs are concerned, the trade story is one of damage control. Workers should not be tempted to cast their lot in with an industry merely because it seems to be doing well selling goods overseas. As a matter of fact, in the large-volume, high-growth sectors of U.S. manufactured exports in the 1970s, total employment grew very little—and shrank in some industries. In aerospace, the total number of jobs rose by less than 2 percent from 1978 to 1983 despite the fact that exports went up by 50 percent. The job outlook for the next several years in that industry is poor, and aerospace is typical of a number of industries. In the construction machinery industry, one of our hottest overseas performers, there was a sharp jump in exports of more than 60 percent from 1977 to 1981, yet total employment actually dropped.

In addition, workers should not be lulled into the belief that the destruction of jobs caused by foreign imports in the 1970s is over. The destruction will continue in the same industries as in the 1970s and in others as well. The key for workers is to know where to look and what to avoid and to understand the new world of international trade.

What to avoid will be made clearer as one's understanding of future trade forces increases. Where to look is probably in the high technology area, but workers have to look behind that easy answer. There are many different kinds of jobs in high technology industries that might actually be susceptible to trade competition. Where to look is closely related to one's education, skills, innovative abilities, and the international situation in the job sought. High technology firms in the United States are beginning to feel the pinch of imports, too.

But the most important reason to become more aware of the internationalization of trade (and work) markets is the need to make necessary changes at home. The new international scene will require well thought-out and concerted national policies for survival. Collective awareness of the challenge must precede action.

THE TIES OF TRADE

From 1960 to 1981, the value of U.S. exports doubled as a percent of total national economic output, to 8 percent. The value of imports in that same period tripled, to nearly 9 percent of output. This means that more of our jobs and national income are dependent on foreign trade; it also means that other countries are more dependent on our economy for their jobs and national income.

You do not have to tell automobile workers in Detroit, steelworkers in Pittsburgh, or machinery workers in Peoria of the devastation caused by imports. A few numbers document the terrifying story. In the automobile industry, employment fell by over one-third between 1979 and the middle of 1982; at the same time imports went up 9 percent. In the steel industry, jobs declined by nearly one-third and imports rose by over one-fourth during the same period. Several other industries felt the same pressures. When these trends occur, everyone wants to blame the other guy. And the worse international conditions become, the harder it is to take an objective view of cause and effect. As William Brock, the U.S. special trade representative, told President Reagan in a confidential memorandum on November 3, 1982, "Other countries who do not share our well-founded reluctance to intervene in the economy are increasingly taking actions that protect their narrow national interest—to our disadvantage." But it is not only other nations' protectionism that is causing the shifts we've seen.

THE FLOOD/TIDE OF TECHNOLOGY DISPERSION

The job crisis brewing in the United States is part of an international job crisis. The same economic forces requiring enormously less human labor for an even higher economic output are present in every industrial country. It is a future from which they cannot escape. The developing countries cannot escape either, despite the fact that they have made impressive economic strides using cheap labor. The trade and technology challenge looming before the world economy is one of the most dangerous in history, and no one can predict its outcome. But it is especially dangerous for the United States, where the economic, political, and military leadership of the Western industrial world is at stake.

From an economic perspective, the new era will be every bit as dangerous as the inflationary 1970s—and we suspect more so. The reality of widespread technological unemployment in America, Europe, and Asia will strain old alliances as each region tries to meet the political challenge posed by it. Technology is going to speed up the process by which the world economic system becomes more efficient. If you think about it, you can see why. Computers, robots, and machines with the power to replace human labor and intelligence in the workplace are going to be employed by industry on a worldwide basis to improve the efficiency of economic output.

No industrial country that aims to stay in the competitive game is going to let another get too far ahead, if it can help it. A race for the economic survival of nations, driven by the quiet efficiencies of the tiny silicon chip, is already under way. The newly industrializing Third World nations, those noted for building up their economies with cheap labor, are catching on. Taiwan is hoping to become the Silicon Valley of the Far East, moving away from the types of low wage, high employment industries that helped wipe out jobs in the American bicycle, toy, shoe, and apparel industries. The long-run choice appears to be between more unemployment or *much* more unemployment.

THE LIMITS OF PROTECTIONISM

Nations have tried and will try even harder to prop up their employment with overt and covert measures to make exports cheap and imports dear. The measures range from quotas on imported items to low-cost financing for exports, and they include a number of ingenious ways of defeating the free-trade purpose of international agreements. But there is a limit to how far any nation can go in beggaring its neighbors by keeping out foreign goods and services. The reason is that if A keeps away B's major exports, B will block A's exports to it—or to another trading partner, C, who will then lack the means to purchase A's exports.

It is the interdependence of nations that is the final police force in maintaining negotiated trade agreements. The question is, will that interdependence survive the pressures that the great technological diffusion is going to bring to bear on the international trade system? Countries with a long history of protectionism are not only those with relatively high wages, but those with higher wages will be the most threatened by the diffusion of production opportunities around the globe. The political pressures in these countries to save jobs will be great, but if they go too far down the protectionist route, retaliation by other nations could cause more harm than protectionism causes good. Each country will have to deal with the economic costs of protectionism in its own way, but international trade tensions are sure to rise as the installation of labor saving devices becomes more widespread.

Some international truths are now becoming very clear. The higher a country's wage structure, the more susceptible to automation it will be. Indeed, to stay ahead in the international game of trade, countries will be forced to automate. Mass production of standardized items will continue to move to low-wage nations, unless they can be almost wholly produced by automated equipment in the advanced industrial nations. A corps of the working elite, highly educated in technical and scientific skills and expert in applications of new technology, will dominate in each country. Income distribution within countries will become much more of a political issue worldwide. These trends are international extensions of the same phenomena already noted on the domestic scene.

Currently, the wealthiest economies are beset with a number of imbalances—call them sicknesses if you will—that make them especially vulnerable. These are, more or less, the imbalances that result from a maturing of the industrial revolution. Many factories are aging and in need of modernization. Wage scales, the result of gains that came because of the economic uplift resulting from the industrial march forward, are now as much a factor in the international competitive situation as are the goods themselves. Wage scales are now vulnerable. Many industries are still officially protected and highly inefficient. They must modernize and shrink employment or die. They will probably have to give up markets as well.

It is already happening. In fact, it has happened more in the past decade than Americans realize. But there is still a reluctance to believe that these forces will become so strong as to threaten employment worldwide. One reason is that faith in the old industrial model is still strong because so much has been invested it it. Orthodoxies are like dead vines. They have a tendency to cling on long after reality has destroyed their vitality. Orthodox economists have not yet come to grips with the full implications of the new artificial intelligence that will dominate the production and delivery of goods and services. They have yet to assess what impact such a breakthrough as flexible manufacturing will have on world trade and jobs.

COMPETITION FROM FOREIGN "SWEATSHOPS"

In a company-owned dormitory in Seoul, Korea, young women sleep ten and fifteen in a room, waiting for the next shift in a large textile mill. They earn only a few dollars a day tending the clattering machines or testing the material destined for export around the world. The dormitory is right next door to the mill, convenient for the young women workers and for the company. The plant manager explains that the young women come here to work and save money before they get married sometime in their early twenties. And there's never a labor shortage. There is always a replacement for the worker who leaves. This plant has modern machinery purchased from Japan, as efficient as any textile mill has in the United States. The combination of low wages and high efficiency keeps the price of the goods down. Outside, on the loading dock, the plant manager explains where much of the material will wind up: in clothing purchased by Americans in their largest retail stores.

This scene is repeated in many other places, in different degrees, and with different products—in Taiwan, in Mexico just across the U.S. border, in Singapore, Hong Kong, and other places. The products include not just textiles, and sneakers and cheap plastic toys, but microchips, sophisticated electronic consumer goods, machine tools, and even automobile motors. These modern sweatshops are not like those of the industrial era's family-owned companies. The big difference between Seoul in 1980 and Lowell, Massachusetts, in 1890 is that in Seoul, American multinational corporations played a big role in establishing the foreign competition. The developing nations were as eager to advance into the modern era as the corporations were to expand production in areas where labor is cheap.

The unique combination of the new and the old—cheap foreign wages and modern machinery—became the new international model of mass production in the 1960s and 1970s. Henry Ford's boldness in paying workers the unheard of wage of $5 a day in 1914 (roughly double the national wage) had long since faded into history and out of the memory of modern American managers. Ford did not have to worry much about imports from Japan, so he came to the conclusion that paying his workers more money than other industrial workers would stimulate the American economy and establish a higher demand for goods and services. The new international era changed that. Horace Greeley's "go west" advice was supplanted by "go east," and that usually meant Asia.

The developing nations meanwhile showed considerable entrepreneurship of their own. They developed—or, more correctly, borrowed—the techniques of modern industrial management and discovered that they could mass produce goods of equal, and sometimes better, quality than those produced in the United States—and at a cheaper price. And while working conditions in foreign factories do not provide the same amenities and wages that American workers receive, they do provide desperately needed income for workers with considerably lower expectations and consuming habits than Americans.

Nevertheless, jobs that were in the United States only fifteen years ago have since been exported to far-flung factories. Here workers use essentially the same machinery U.S. workers use. Sometimes it's better technology, because companies put the latest machines in new foreign plants when they decided to expand overseas.

Analysts such as Martin Feldstein, the chief economic adviser to President Reagan, are fond of saying that the modern foreign sweatshops sprang into existence only because American workers had priced themselves out of world markets. While this assertion has the strong ring of truth, on closer examination one finds it does not represent a comprehensive understanding of the dynamics that brought American workers to their current state. To claim that they priced themselves out of the market is to suggest that only American labor was arrogant and short-sighted—so much so workers blindly sacrificed their own long-term best interests. It might just as rationally be asserted that American management bought labor peace (no strikes, please) at a temporary high price until foreign countries provided new opportunities for plant expansions out of the reach of high-priced American labor. American workers were merely trying to enjoy the fruits of the American dream, pressing ahead to increase their standard of living at the prompting of politicians and economists. The doctrine of spiraling and continuing economic growth was espoused by all in the 1960s and early 1970s.

The concept of fair compensation also played an important role. Workers were thought to be entitled to wage increases equal to the rate of inflation plus increases in efficiency, or productivity, in their industries. This pay pattern dominated American industry in general—and still does to this day. But in much of American manufacturing, it soon became inconsistent with the new world economy. The mistake many workers made was to assume that standardized, mass production on U.S. assembly lines was superior, when in fact it was no longer unique. The industrial model of endless production of one item with the same design and specifications was actually rather old, the stuff of Henry Ford and the Model T. The Japanese and others found it easy to duplicate this system, adding efficiencies American managers found hard to achieve.

HIGHER AND HIGHER TECH

If there is a strategy to counter the export of jobs, it is the strategy of specialization. Should Americans try to beat themselves over the head competing against the newly industrializing nations and their masses of low-paid people equipped with modern technology? Probably not. Let the foreigners industrialize. Let us take our economy out of college into graduate school, so to speak, and move into more and more sophisticated forms of technology. Our new industries are already incubating in the laboratories and workshops of the nation, waiting to be born. The United States can increase its national income if it stays on top of the technological ladder, creating goods and services (especially services) that are not now in existence.

The biotechnology and computer software industries are prime examples. We have manufactured interferon—a life substance that promises to cure a dozen diseases. Americans are the world leaders in the gene splicing techniques that made interferon possible. Our firms have created hundreds of computer programs that monitor nuclear plants, defuse bombs, control aircraft flights, and do many other tasks that improve the quality of life. When we develop a new good or service that people find desirable, we create new markets heretofore unperceived. Sooner or later, new ideas blossom into industries with new employees. Because the resultant new goods or services have behind them an array of talent and sophistication that can't be matched elsewhere, the producer can afford to charge dearly for them, increasing its total income. This pattern enabled the United States to increase its wealth and its employment in the halcyon years immediately after World War II.

Climbing the ladder of higher and higher technology is America's destiny and the key to economic survival. But it should not make us sanguine about future jobs. There is no eternal relationship between the creation of one high tech job and support jobs.

Some economists have insisted that every new high tech professional job will create as many as 3.4 jobs in support industries such as accounting, trade, banking, and custodial and other services. However, this academic faith in the "economic multiplier" ought to be approached with caution. It is based on past relationships; it does not take new technology into account either in the basic high tech jobs or in the support industries. Any observed past relationship between one job and its spin-off jobs was noted at a time when high technology was just aborning. Inefficiency and its newness made for new job slots. For instance, during the 1960s and 1970s, rapid growth in banking jobs occurred to support newly computerized "back office" record keeping. But now computers themselves perform many of the clerical tasks people performed for computers a decade ago. The story is the same in almost every service industry and in many manufacturing industries, too. It is rumored that soon robots will make the wire harnesses, or central nervous systems, of computers. We do not believe that the payoff in new jobs in high technology support industries will be nearly as big as some have indicated.

THE BIG IF: CONTROLLING TECHNOLOGICAL DIFFUSION

Neglected in the debate about climbing the high technology ladder is the degree to which our new sophisticated inventions find their way to other nations, either via industrial espionage or through outright sales by industries to other nations. Industrial espionage is no small problem, as the Hitachi case in 1982 indicated. The allegations of technological theft in the Hitachi case were described by many experts as only the tip of the iceberg, although no actual figures are available on how much has been stolen.

Theft and sale are not the only ways technology gets around. There is a big danger that arrogance about America's supposed technological superiority will get us into even deeper trouble. Science and technology are not easily locked up. There is no national monopoly on intelligence or inventiveness. Many nations besides Japan, including Sweden, Finland, and the Netherlands, are right on the heels of the United States in technological development and are actually ahead in some areas. The Japanese often set the pace, though. They have already moved much faster into robotics than the United States. They have targeted the computer industry as one in which large financial and scientific resources should be devoted for the forseeable future. The Japanese have proved to be very inventive people and especially adaptable to the new high tech world. Japan was able to move light-years up in technological development after World War II because U.S. firms found a ready market there for the new inventions developed in their laboratories. The technology was sold for a fraction of its development cost and literally put the Japanese on the map economically. One analyst has called it "one of the greatest fire sales in the history of the world."

Out of this developed one of the great delusions of modern economics—that the Japanese are great imitators and terrible innovators. This phrase has been repeated so often that the Japanese have a national inferiority complex about it and have redoubled efforts to prove they are as good at inventing as they are at applying. Tobioka Ken, director of Japan's Human Science Institute, wrote recently in *Japan Echo* that "science itself has little value unless it contains far more creative potential than the technology derived from it. And in this regard, Japan has far to go." But Japan is nevertheless growing faster than the smug American innovators ever thought possible. The Japanese have moved far beyond imitation and miniaturization to innovation. In so doing they have given the lie to the cliché that they can only imitate, not invent.

Besides, imitation is the highest form of flattery. When will we begin to imitate the Japanese?

BEAT 'EM OR JOIN 'EM?

Japan has proved that government and industry cooperation on a grand scale can produce even grander results. Its most extraordinary effort is to create a machine with artificial intelligence. Increasingly complex computer chips are the secret here, and eight of Japan's largest electronics companies have combined resources with the Ministry of International Trade and Industry (MITI) to form the Institute for New Generation Computer Technology (ICOT). The institute's aim is to create a computer that will respond to vocal commands, program itself, make inferences, interpret visual images, translate foreign languages, and even learn from its own experience. One computer expert, Yoneji Masuda, recently said that Japan's national strategy, which had been to match IBM, has now changed. "Instead of equaling IBM, we want to develop new technologies," he told *Popular Science.*

American business executives do not need to be told of the Japanese challenge. In a survey of 142 business leaders—conducted by Yankelovich, Skelly and White, Inc., for Motorola—the executives said they feared that Japan would score major successes in industries such as computers and telecommunications. To the extent that Japan can grab away markets from U.S.

competitors with its own technological developments, it can create jobs at the expense of U.S. workers. But the plain truth is that there is no way to beat the competition in today's international situation. Because we can't beat 'em, we try to join 'em.

When video game manufacturer Atari announced it was firing a quarter of its work force and moving production overseas, many analysts took the news calmly. They even argued that moving production to low-wage areas would only cut the cost of Atari goods and permit Atari to maintain its U.S. market share. This, in turn, would enable Atari to create new jobs in the United States. Moving up the technology ladder means, in other words, that jobs constantly have to be exported overseas whenever a newly developed product enters mass production and threatens to reflect the relatively high U.S. costs in its price.

Does this mean that to stay ahead in climbing the technology ladder, the American job market must constantly be in a state of turmoil? Probably yes, with jobs being created and destroyed much faster than ever. This is no doubt the game we will have to play far into the future—exporting jobs to other countries to save our own economy, giving up something so that we can have something. It sounds so contradictory, but it is in the finest tradition of comparative advantage or survival of the economically fittest.

If U.S. high technology companies are even to stay abreast of this competition, they will constantly have to evaluate and question the need for jobs involving production in this country. James Baker, a senior General Electric executive, says the United States has only three choices in the future: "Automate, emigrate, or evaporate." This is a sound analysis. But other nations are automating, too, realizing that the cold, harsh fact of the new international market in almost all goods and services makes that choice necessary. Thus the process of automation is feeding upon itself, speeding along as nations realize that others will do it if they don't.

FLEXIBLE MANUFACTURING: OUR SALVATION?

Our first encounter with flexible manufacturing was in Florence, Kentucky, just across the Ohio River from Cincinnati, one of the nation's largest machine tool centers. In one of those industrial parks that all seem to look alike, U.S. executives of Mazak Corporation, one of Japan's big machine tool firms, demonstrated how their newly automated machine tool center would work. Mazak's flexible machine tools, totally computer operated, have a huge carousel filled with various tools. It looks vaguely like a massive Gatling gun. Little robot cars carry the parts to be machined to these steel automatons; human labor is required only to load the parts onto the robot cars.

Compared with the way machine tools worked just a few years ago, these new machines are amazing. They do not have to be stopped when they go from making one part to another part. The machine is told by the computer to keep going when a new part comes up for shaping. The carousel whirs around automatically, and the tool required for cutting, drilling, or grinding goes to work. There's no down time to speak of. A part is made quickly and without interruption. Furthermore, large companies are using flexible manufacturing in conjunction with computer-assisted engineering and design. From start to finish in the manufacturing of a part, most of the real work is done by computer. These new "numerically controlled" machine tools even have the capacity to judge how much their own cutting edges have worn and to adjust themselves automatically for that fact.

The number of workers required in Mazak's flexible manufacturing center is minimal. Once the loading is done, the machines can pretty well operate on their own. In fact, the third shift runs all by itself. Flexible manufacturing will increase the productivity, or efficiency, of a machine tool plant by more than 300 percent in some instances, Mazak executives told us.

Many U.S. firms are now making and installing flexible manufacturing systems. They will be particularly beneficial to the automobile industry, which has always been cursed with huge retooling costs. Flexible manufacturing systems have a big advantage in "small batch" manufacturing—they make the manufacture of small volumes of a product much more economical, according to numerous experts.

Why is this so important in the international picture? Because whatever country has the most of these manufacturing systems will be best able to produce many different, highly specialized varieties of a particular product. The United States, now at a disadvantage in competing with low-wage countries in the manufacture of standardized, mass-produced goods, could find itself able to maintain a manufacturing base by specializing in goods of which the consumer requires many different varieties. To dream a little, the U.S. automobile industry could regain some of its momentum by creating a design-it-yourself car. It would take only a few hundred orders of a prototype to make its production economical.

THE NEW PROTECTIONISM: KNOWLEDGE

In a knowledge-based economy, information is the most valuable commodity. Those who work in some aspect of the fast-growing telecommunications industry are keenly aware that the free international flow of data is necessary to their companies' profits and to their jobs. As the U.S. economy moves higher and higher up the technological ladder, the expert information developed by the new technical class of workers will account for a higher percentage of the country's potential income. The success of manufactured products also will depend on how this expertise is incorporated into the design of goods. The flow of information is crucial to every industry.

In the days when information had less value than it does now, few restrictions were placed on its flow across national borders. But that has changed in recent years. Information is becoming a victim of protectionism in the same way that textiles, automobiles, and steel were in the 1970s. West Germany requires telecommunications data to be processed locally before being transferred out of the country. Canada requires banks to keep and process all data relating to customers within its borders. Many nations have restricted their citizens from using computer facilities in other countries. Some countries require that foreign firms use local engineering, law, and advertising services and fail to give adequate protection to trademarks, copyrights, and technology. They often impose discriminatory licensing or buying requirements and establish other discriminatory standards. At times, West Germany, France, and Scandinavia have excluded U.S. airlines from their seat reservation systems. Brazil, which built up its economy on the leverage of American bank loans, requires foreign companies to buy Brazilian equipment and use Brazilian labor when building data bases. It also requires use of Brazilian software in computers if that is similar to other software that might be employed.

There is a trade war of sorts in information. The restrictions have become so pervasive that the number of executives who attend regular State Department briefings on the problems of the information war has increased dramatically. The Commerce Department's National Telecommunications and Information Administration has issued a report warning that the restrictions on information could be catastrophic to U.S. firms over the long run. At the same time that other nations are restricting the flow of information, the United States is deregulating its telecommunications industry.

It is difficult to quantify the effects of these restrictions on U. S. jobs and income growth. The most ominous aspect is what they portend: As information and services become more and more important, the danger of further restriction looms. Communications has become so sophisticated, especially with the development of satellites, that information can travel instantly around the globe. How do we ensure its unfettered flow? Only an international trade agreement will do that, but it is a task that will take years. Until then, there's little the United States can do—restricting information here would only result in further retaliation. The painful lesson: Whatever nation gains the upper hand in the business of the future should expect that others will try to protect themselves. No area of working life is exempt from protectionism and its ill-understood limitations on the expansion of world income. Moving up the ladder of high technology is not always an easy trip.

CAN EXPORTS SAVE US?

The 1981–82 recession was hard on American exporters. The dollar stayed sky high because of high U.S. interest rates, so that everything they tried to sell to foreign countries was at an immediate price disadvantage. High unemployment rates worldwide stirred up protectionist sentiment everywhere against all imports. And Third World nations such as Mexico, Brazil, and Argentina nearly buckled under the weight of heavy debt.

Since one in six American jobs depends in part on exports, it was a bad time. Cities like Cedar Rapids, Iowa, with heavy-machinery plants that produce for export, felt the pinch. Business was so slow that many townspeople weren't sure the jobs would ever come back.

Despite these difficulties, many leaders believe that the United States can increase its exports sharply over time and that this will go a long way toward solving its unemployment problem. The optimism, though, seems misplaced. The dynamics suggest otherwise. Here's why: High unemployment worldwide is going to linger for several years. That will keep protectionism strong, limiting markets for U.S. goods. The debt problems will linger, too, limiting markets especially in Latin America. And even though the dollar isn't likely to remain as high as it did during 1981 and 1982, the U.S. economy is still regarded as a safe haven for funds from around the world, a factor that tends to keep the dollar's value higher than it would otherwise be.

All in all, the dream of an export drive that would rescue the United States from a dismal world trade picture and provide vast amounts of new jobs is not realistic. Government officials will latch on to some schemes anyway, such as the new law that makes it easier to set up export trading companies, if for no other reason than a faith in artificially created export drives, which has always been part of our economic mythology. It may provide some profits, but not enough employment to make a difference.

THE WORLDWIDE WORK REVOLUTION

The work revolution will have a massive impact on trade, and trade will have a massive impact on the work revolution. New technology will spread quickly throughout the world, causing widespread job displacement. This will affect trade patterns and provoke protectionist tendencies. Trade itself will not necessarily result in increased job opportunities.

Workers should take steps to protect themselves from the uncertainties of the new international market in goods and services. They should avoid jobs in smokestack industries where little or no modernization has taken place—these industries will continue to be vulnerable to imports. So will most assembly line jobs where a standardized product is involved.

The process of international trade will speed up the work revolution. Those who fall behind in installing new technology will suffer greater unemployment than those who do not. The United States has far to go in guaranteeing that the free flow of information continues unabated. Many jobs and income depend on it.

Whatever the case, the job crisis is international and will severely test the industrial democracies. Many Third World nations will be more severely affected, especially if the new technology displaces the jobs of workers who have learned to depend on export-related manufacturing.

The winners will be those who recognize that preserving national income is the key to maintaining the highest level of employment. The choice is between high unemployment and even higher unemployment.

5

Smart Jobs
and Dumb Jobs

The draftsman who used to make a thousand versions of an engine design for the new automobile at Ford, General Motors, or Chrysler isn't doing that anymore. The designs are created and recreated by a program that can instantly alter every factor and create facsimile models of scores of different engine designs in a matter of minutes. The journeyman machinist who used to build prototypes to stress test gold-tipped fasteners that will fly to outer space isn't doing that anymore. A computer program analyzes the characteristics of a set of specifications, and the stress is tested automatically before ever a bolt is even made.

The master of business administration who once was the only person in the real estate developer's office who could figure out the rate of return on a proposed investment is no longer alone. A computer program allows anyone, even someone with a degree in archeology or Sanskrit, to key in the numbers that allow the computer to calculate that fraction. The attorney who was the only one in the office who could remember how to search the law library for esoteric cases is no longer the guru he used to be. With a computerized search, newcomers just out of law school can handle the search as efficiently as the old hand.

The new technology, with its expansive facility for speedy calculation and ability to outperform humans in key areas, is transforming the way work is done and the place in which it is done. In the process, it is destroying a hierarchy of skills that has prevailed for generations, actually taking the need for specialized skills out of many jobs. In the past, a person could start at the bottom of the career ladder and work up to a more responsible position as experience and knowledge were gained and absorbed. Now, increasingly, we will have positions that demand a great deal of basic skills from the beginning and other positions that require almost no skills, either at the beginning or at the end of the career path.

In other words, the jobs of the future are going to be either "smart" jobs or "dumb" jobs. (We use the term *dumb jobs* not to cast aspersions on those who are physically mute, but as an expression to refer to the amount of intelligence and skills required for positions in the future.) Most of us see this happening in various ways in the workplace as we watch how computers transform jobs. The anecdotal evidence is overwhelming. The splintering of the work force into two distinct camps is an enormous change in our history, one that will take years of adjustment and lead to a far-reaching reassessment of our society.

To understand what is happening, consider the push button. It's a simple enough metaphor. The amalgamation of human knowledge and intelligence that goes into research, development, and production of a complex piece of machinery that can be run by a simple push button is enormous. Yet, the person operating the push button need not have much knowledge of the system his finger activates nor the towering intelligence required to understand how it operates. He just pushes the button, and the gigantic press starts up and operates automatically or the cash register figures the total and the change or the automated assembly line swings into action. All the worker has to know is when to push the button and under what circumstances. Within the complex wiring and organization of the machinery are represented many human skills that have made ingenious contributions to the system; at the user's end are the button pushers. They perform a simple operation regulated by computer chips, wires, and automated machinery of all types.

The current pace of technological change increasingly suggests a split of the work force between smart jobs and dumb jobs. The last automation scare, in the 1950s, had the effect of reducing the skill levels required on many jobs. In 1958, James Bright, a professor at Harvard Business School, looked into the skill requirements of manufacturing companies and discovered that automation had made unnecessary much of the long experience and training previously required in many machine-related jobs. But automation in the 1950s never had the productivity potential that the computer/electronic revolution has.

Computers themselves were difficult to operate initially, but improved technology has changed that. Now computer programming itself is divided into two categories: the highly creative, skilled tasks performed by systems analysts and the more routine jobs performed by computer programmers and coders.[1]

There will be several big groups of smart jobs. The largest group, which will require college and post-college professional training, will involve analysis and decision making. This group will include scientific researchers, lawyers, accountants, business managers, investment managers, public relations and marketing experts, engineers, social scientists, economists, journalists, systems analysts, teachers, real estate developers, government managers, and administrators in every type of organization. Without exception, practitioners in these fields will depend upon the new technology, and the sooner they learn to apply it in their area of expertise, the better equipped they will be to qualify for the smart jobs.

Another group will involve practitioners of medicine and related personal-help professions: physicians, surgeons, psychologists, social workers, nurses, dentists, physical and speech therapists, and medical and dental technicians. Such careers will probably not be affected negatively by technology. On the contrary, the same number of people will be able to do more work successfully, thanks to the technology—especially if you believe with some psychiatrists that computers are compassionate, as some pioneers in the field do. In fact, one may hope that there will be more practitioners per capita in this group than there now are.

A third group will be the support group: people who operate certain types of equipment but are not expected to analyze information. Rather, they will organize it or monitor it. Some of these jobs will require a two-year training program, but others will require college. They include office managers, tenders of power plants, travel agents, airline sales agents.

Another group of smart jobs will be in sales and marketing. This group will be very important in the future because, as more products proliferate on the market, selling will be more important. Already we have seen the home computer war, in which sales are more dependent on the advertising campaigns than on the quality of the product itself. As the applications of the new technologies multiply and as firms try to expand in new markets at home and abroad, sales will be one of the most important smart jobs available.

And finally, there will be the entertainment jobs—those that involve creative arts and for which talent is (or should be) the main criterion of success. These, too, will not be much affected by technology, other than in the ways the product can be distributed to the audience.

That makes five groups of smart jobs, each demanding some type of specialized education and training. And the other jobs? The rest, unfortunately, will be just plain jobs. They won't be very interesting. They won't change much over time. They won't demand much of the people who do them, except following instructions exactly. They may be much more boring than working on an assembly line. These dumb jobs will range from janitor to fast-food service person, from pushing the button on the machine that chooses a combination of paint colors for a car and then sprays the car, to the job of starting the computer that records the results of a laboratory test.

Needless to say, there will be many of the same kinds of unskilled jobs in the economy of the future as there are now—fruit pickers, delivery persons, etc., will still be needed. But even these will be in competition with the new technology. Robot fruit pickers are now being experimented with, and they work, on some fruits under some conditions. Fast-food shops could be much more automated than they are now—in fact, our hamburger shops are less automated than the grandfather of the fast foods, the Horn and Hardart Automat in New York City, where you put your money in the wall and opened a trap door to get your food. Robots are being trained to clean factories, and it is now possible, if you own an IBM personal computer, to attach a robot arm to it that can do such helpful things as hand you your coffee.

JOBS THAT WILL BE DE-SKILLED

Here are just a few of the jobs in which the "de-skilling" of existing work is almost certain. In most of these occupations, a reduction in the number of workers needed to produce the present volume is also very likely.

Blue-Collar Jobs

PRINTING AND PUBLISHING. Automatic scanning and plate making reduces the need for scanners and plate makers. Electronic typesetting further reduces the need for typesetters. Web-offset printing, a photographic process on a continuous roll of paper, increases efficiencies and eliminates feeders of sheet paper. This process is already used in about 40 percent of American printing plants, according to the Bureau of Labor Statistics. Lower prices make absorption into other plants likely: 80 percent of all plants are likely to use advanced technology. A major impact will be on operatives who formerly stacked and fed paper and on crafts workers who formerly managed the sequence of printing tasks.

STEEL. Continuous casters, used in about one-fifth of all large integrated mills, will be added in more mills, virtually eliminating the need for manpower during the process of forming a slab of steel. Miniplants using electric furnaces or oxygen furnaces will proliferate, eliminating the need for blast furnace tenders. Reduction in operatives and craftsmen needed on the job will be by at least one-fourth; it could be much higher.

PULP AND PAPER. Already capital intensive, this industry features football-field size rooms tended by one person. Continued expansion in use of Fourdrineri paper machines and diffusion of computer process controls for making paper and for controlling pollution can be expected. Operatives' jobs will continue to be eliminated.

APPAREL. Automatic contour seamers, profile stitching machines, and numerically controlled sewing machines will guide material automatically through sewing operations, so one worker will be able to tend more than one machine. Operatives will require a lower level of skills. Laser cutting and numerically controlled computer cutting devices will be less expensive and be more widely used, eliminating the need for skilled cutters.

MOTOR VEHICLES. Robots; computerized work flow management; automated assembly lines; computerized and numerically controlled cutting, welding, and painting machines; and improvements in transfer lines will further reduce needs for both craftsmen and operatives. Job descriptions will no longer match the traditional work tasks. In addition, cost cutting will reduce administrative and managerial positions. Even engineers and designers will be less in demand relative to the number of models, because of computer-assisted design and model-building.

FABRICATED STRUCTURAL METALS. Motor-powered conveyers, automatic welding machines, computerized numercially controlled shape-cutting equipment, optical tracers for creating templates where CNC machining centers are not available, and cold-cutting saws, all available now, will be more widely diffused, reducing the need for grinders, helpers, machine operators, welders, template makers, burners, and feeders. The skill levels for machine operators will be reduced. Some new skills will be needed, such as in programming, but fewer of these will be needed than the number of skills being eliminated.

TELEPHONE COMMUNICATION. Electric switching equipment, fiber optic cables, and digital transmission will reduce the demand for installers and maintenance and repair personnel. Widespread use of modular user-installed telephone equipment will further reduce the need for installers.

White-Collar Jobs

TELEPHONE COMMUNICATIONS. Increased use of computerized switching and call forwarding, credit card verification, and intercept calls will reduce the need for telephone operators and back-up white-collar personnel. Computerized record keeping and billing will reduce the need for back office personnel. Restructuring of the Bell System may have a hastening effect on attrition of personnel. Service demand growth will probably be handled with existing or smaller work force.

RETAIL SALES. Computerized credit transfers and credit checking and computerized billing and sales announcements will reduce the need for back office workers and mailroom and delivery workers. Computerized inventory via vendor-source-marked ticketing will reduce the need for sales personnel and stockroom clerks and will reduce overall post-sales operations. Shopping by video and microfilm could increase, further reducing the sales force without increasing the stock-delivery force. Price marking manually will be eliminated by automated central retail distribution systems. Dependence on the universal product code and optical scanning systems in supermarkets will eliminate pricing and reduce the need for stock clerks while increasing the speed of cashiers, thereby reducing the number of cashiers needed per shift. All of this technology is already in use and will spread further.

INSURANCE. System-wide hookups of minicomputers with central mainframe computers will handle electronic data processing for all tasks, eliminating the need for file clerks, keypunch operators, typists, and other clerical workers. Photoelectric optical character recognition will further eliminate workers, as will sensor writers that create machine-readable data by tracing printed copy. Portable computer terminals will allow insurance agents to process insurance applications in computer-compatible format, further depressing the need for clerical staff and reducing the number of agents and brokers needed per unit of insurance sold. The extent of diffusion depends only on the cost and rate at which user-friendly software is created for salespersons.

As discussed in other sections of the chapter, the potential for job reduction in the support staff of large offices and even in the need for lower echelon administrators and managers is also quite strong. However, it is more likely that the lower-skilled jobs will be eliminated first and that the higher-skilled jobs will be de-skilled, rather than replaced.

All of these changes, most of which are now taking place, can be expected to accelerate as long as the nation's firms are making a strong effort to compete and as long as there are greater incentives offered by the government to replace labor with capital than to retain workers. That is one reason why some labor unions have called for a tax on machines, or a payroll tax on robots. Although that sounds attractive to those who want to preserve jobs, it will not help our companies keep their prices lower than those of foreign competitors. Moreover, such action could just drive production overseas. There is little to stop word processing from being exported to the Bahamas if someone starts taxing the equipment too heavily to make its utilization in the United States cost effective.

IS UNCLE SAM RIGHT?

With technology destroying and de-skilling many of the traditional jobs in the American workplace, it is harder to know where the smart jobs will be. Figuring this out requires a leap of imagination, because what was true in the past is not going to be true in the future. Indeed, that is the main point about the work revolution: It represents a watershed in American economic history. There is no way to draw a straight line from the events of the past into the probabilities of the future. Yet, that is precisely what many analysts of the job picture in the future attempt to do, despite the fact that extrapolations of past events have proven wrong.

For example, the U.S. Bureau of Labor Statistics (BLS) indicates its expectations by occupation. In 1980, it estimated that 2 million new jobs would be created annually during the 1980s. In fact, during the first three years of the decade, one million jobs were lost. (Total jobs, according to data derived from employers by the U.S. Bureau of Labor Statistics, cited in the BLS *Occupational Outlook Handbook*, were, in 1980, 90.4 million; in 1981, 91.105 million; in 1982, 89.984 million; and estimated for 1983, 89.1 million.) The bureau predicted that jobs in the goods-producing sectors—agriculture, mining, forestry, construction, and manufacturing—would rise 13 percent to provide 3.8 million new jobs by the end of the decade. One-third of the way into the decade, these sectors provided 2.7 million *fewer* jobs than they did in 1980. Goods-related employment in 1980, according to the establishment data from the bureau, was 25.6 million. According to the preliminary data in April 1983, goods-producing employment, again based on establishment data, was 22.9 million.

That initial job projections proved to be in error is no accident. These forecasts are derived on the basis of assumptions that are debatable at best. Some of these assumptions are politicially motivated. Some are determined on the basis of extrapolations. Some are mere guesses. Some are based on questionable methodology.

The job forecasts were based on the following economic assumptions for the 1980s: Inflation would reach an average annual rate of 5.2 percent throughout the decade. No major institutional changes would occur. No major technological or social upheavals would occur. The labor force participation rate would not increase substantially. And labor productivity—the amount of work produced per hour of labor—would not rise.

Reaching the decade-long 5.2 percent inflation rate will be difficult, even with major productivity increases provided by new technology. As recovery sets in, there will be upward pressures on wages. If the federal budget deficit is not brought under control, there will be upward pressures on interest rates, which help drive up costs. Even the pickup in demand for credit as the economy recovers drives up prices. The handmaiden of recovery will be inflationary pressure.

On the other hand, improvements in productivity will far exceed the Bureau of Labor Statistic's forecasts. Until 1973, the annual rate of increase in productivity was about 1.7 percent. After 1973, productivity increases dropped to zero in all sectors except manufacturing, and even in manufacturing, productivity gains were only one-fourth as great as in previous years.[1] As a result, the productivity picture is like a dammed-up lake: There is a huge backlog of investment to be made, and when it is made, the new technologies will sprout up everywhere. This has to happen if American firms are to produce goods and services that can match and surpass those of competitors in domestic and world markets.

The largest productivity gains will be achieved in manufacturing industries initially, continuing historical trends. But for the first time in many decades, large gains in services will also be possible. There are many services in the United States that are more labor intensive than is necessary. That includes private services, such as fast-food dispensing, and public services, too. According to the director of finance of the city of Boston, it is possible to increase the number of transactions each public service worker handles by one-fourth, while reducing the work force by 30 percent. And this is only the beginning, according to Lowell Richards. All this is possible because microprocessors to keep records, to dispatch police, firefighters, and ambulances, and to track traffic violators are so efficient.

Perhaps the greatest oddity about the government's job forecasting is the way it treats the unemployment rate. That rate is an input, not an output; it is not the result of *all* the calculations, as it should be. To make this clear, consider how it's computed. The bureau looks into its crystal ball and makes economic projections, including an unemployment rate for 1990. Suppose that projection is 4.5 percent. Then, it looks at the projected size of the labor force and calculates how many jobs will be needed to yield that specified unemployment rate, which can also be stated as an employment rate of 95.5 percent of the work force. After that, it distributes the total number of jobs predicted to various occupations, based on past relationships of the proportion of all jobs represented by each occupation and the past growth rates within occupations.

This is a strange way to determine where the jobs will be or

[1]Bureau of Labor Statistics, USDL 83-153, April 6, 1983.

how many there will be. But if the method is odd, consider some of the other assumptions behind the bureau's data. Although revising its forecasts for 1990 to reflect greater pessimism about recovery from the recession of the early 1980s, it still forecasts its job picture on the basis of a postulated unemployment rate in the 6 percent range. Although it revised its assumptions about job growth in the auto and steel industries, it still asserts that many industries will grow as a result of heavy military spending, even though that is a questionable outcome in view of widespread protests against the heavy military buildup. Even if the buildup is approved, it will take a couple of years before the effects start rippling through the economy.

Alternative scenarios developed by Dr. Schwartz develop job pictures that build from the bottom up rather than from the top down. Instead of beginning with a wish list that reflects where an administration in power hopes the economy will be in seven more years, she began with "likely" or "possible" occurrences within each major occupation group. This approach assumes that past job growth rates in a given group are no more likely to continue in the future than they are unlikely to continue—that there is no built-in growth curve for jobs. In some cases, the growth of job prospects in a particular occupation are just the same as those used by the government. But in other cases, they are different.

The net result of this exercise, as shown in the chart on pages 98–99, is that in 1990 there could be 12.7 million fewer jobs than the Bureau of Labor Statistics has forecast. If the most pessimistic assumptions about internal growth in each occupation are used, the total number of jobs could be no more than we have today. Again, these scenarios are not certain. However, they are more likely than the ones sketched by those who think that things will be as they have always been.

WHERE WILL THE SMART JOBS BE?

In order to see where the smart jobs are likely to be, given some realistic premises about demand in particular industries and the degree of automation that will be put into effect, refer to the job chart. In doing so, the rule used by the Bureau of Labor Statistics will have to be kept in mind. The bureau's estimated growth rates, based on past growth rates, are:

Fast—50 percent
Average—15–27.8 percent
Slow—6–14.9 percent

The bureau says "no change" can mean anything from a decline of as much as 6 percent to an increase of the same magnitude. When the bureau says that the jobs will grow at about an average rate, it is only saying that they will grow at this rate because they grew at the average rate in an earlier period. It is merely a projection of the past into the future.

Another important point to bear in mind about percentage projections is that if there is a small number of jobs in any given job category, a big percentage change will not add that many opportunities to the total. By the same token, if there are many jobs in a given category, a small percentage change will add a substantial number of jobs to the total. So the job hunter should not only look at the percentages, but also at the base or number of existing jobs.

A third consideration is that a strong projected growth rate by itself does not mean that the work prospects in a particular occupation are excellent or reasonably good. There also may be many people available to fill those jobs. The bureau tries to take this "elasticity factor" into account when preparing its job outlook forecasts. But if the supply of labor in any one occupation increases suddenly—as it now promises to do with computer courses oversubscribed at just about every major college in the country—then the predicted supply and demand can change very suddenly.

The bureau uses a cluster approach to job forecasts. The clusters do not mix all occupations in a given field or industry together. Instead, they mix together all occupations that demand a certain combination of skills or training and offer a certain level of advancement. So health technicians are not classified with doctors or dentists, but with service workers. You might guess that only occupations that demand high levels of education—the professional, technical, and managerial occupations—will offer smart jobs in the future, but that is not the case. There will be smart jobs at all levels of training, but they will be harder to find and to keep. In fact, one of the consequences of the work revolution will be to so alter the skills that are associated with any occupation as to put the traditional clusters out of synchronization with the real job market. But in order to see what happens when we make different assumptions about the job market, we have to rely on the bureau's established clusters of jobs.

These are the clusters defined by the bureau:

Administrative and managerial
Engineers, surveyors, and architects
Natural scientists and mathematicians
Social scientists, social workers,
    religious workers, and lawyers
Teachers, librarians, counselors
Health diagnosis and treatment practitioners
Registered nurses, pharmacists, dietitians,
    therapists, and physician's attendants
Health technologists and technicians
Technologists and technicians outside of the health field
Writers, artists, and entertainers
Marketing and sales
Clerical
Service
Agriculture and forestry
Mechanics
Construction and mining
Production workers
Transportation and material moving
Helpers, maintenance, laborers
Military

Taking each one of the occupations, one can go through the *Occupational Outlook Handbook* and question the assumptions behind the forecast.

To consider which types of jobs offer the best smart-job opportunities for the future, we can collapse the twenty BLS job clusters into nine groups. These are the white-collar jobs: professional and technical workers; managers and administrators; sales and clerical workers. These are the blue-collar jobs: craftsworkers; operatives; farmers; laborers; private household workers; and service workers.

It is definitely in the blue-collar groups where the most jobs will disappear. Operatives will be the most vulnerable. Among craftsworkers, the least vulnerable to automation are construction workers, who can expect to be called back to work in increasing numbers as the economy comes out of its cyclical trough. Still, even the construction worker isn't immune from technology. Housing production is moving gradually into the prebuilt mode, and the rate of increase in on-site construction workers per dollar of housing construction will probably be much lower than historically was the case. Jobs in farms and forests will not likely pick up much either, as these are relatively capital intensive, not labor intensive. Other than "amusement farming," the long-term trend away from family farms, which are somewhat more labor intensive, does not seem reversible.

The rate of attrition will be the fastest in heavy industry as many assembly line operatives and a substantial number of craftsworkers are replaced by computerized machinery and robots. All in all, the total number of blue-collar jobs in 1990 is likely to be smaller than it is today, even though more goods are being produced. There are about twelve million industrial craftsworkers and almost an equal number of semiskilled production workers in the present labor force. One-fourth of these workers could be redundant by the end of the decade, which would mean 600,000 fewer jobs in these occupations than in 1983.

Growth in the white-collar occupations will not offset declines in blue-collar growth rates, as it has in the past. Although white-collar jobs will increase, it is doubtful that they will increase as fast as they did in the last decade, because fewer workers, assisted by computers and electronic communications, will be able to do many more tasks. If the output of the business service sector were to remain the same in 1990 as in 1980, it could likely be created with three-fourths to two-thirds of today's work force. If output increases by 2 percent per year, or 20 percent over the decade, it is likely that output could be produced by the same number of workers as now labor in this sector.

If blue-collar jobs shrink and white-collar jobs do not grow, there is still one category of jobs that could grow under certain circumstances: the pink-collar jobs. These are in the caring-for services—the licensed practical nurses, dietitians, beauticians, barbers, most of whom require less than two years of education. These jobs have traditionally not been considered smart jobs. They are relatively low-paying, and they offer virtually no career ladder. Yet they do demand some strong skills if they are to be done well. Many workers in these jobs do not have the skills that would make their performance highly valuable to the client for their services. Although interpersonal relations are a key element of work in the pink-collar jobs, there is no screening for talent in interpersonal skills. Yet it is virtually certain that need for these jobs will increase at a faster pace than demand for most other workers.

The greatest job growth in the decade of the seventies occurred in the white-collar and pink-collar job categories. By no means was all of this growth in smart jobs—that is, jobs that required judgments and decision-making. White-collar jobs increased by more than one-third, from about 38 million to nearly 51 million. All told, in 1980 there were 30.8 million blue-collar workers and 50.8 million white-collar workers—a ratio of 1.6 to one.

The greatest percentage increase occurred in professional and technical jobs, which climbed 40 percent. However, the total number of such jobs at the end of the decade was only 15.6 million—far fewer than the 18 million clerical workers. Other "smart" white-collar jobs are found in the managerial and administrative occupations, which grew by almost 32 percent, but which at the end of the decade provided only 11 million jobs. By contrast, there were nearly 14 million operatives in 1980, nearly 13 million private-sector blue-collar service workers, and 12.5 million craftsmen.

Look, too, at the distribution of occupations. In 1970, 35 percent of employment was in blue-collar occupations, while by 1980 this share had fallen to 31.6 percent. White-collar workers, who had held 48.3 percent of all jobs in 1970, held 52.2 percent in 1980. The major growth areas in the blue-collar occupations were in the health and food service categories, not in professional or business services. The question for the future, therefore, is whether the high growth rates in the smart-jobs categories will continue and, even if they do continue, whether they will provide enough jobs to substitute for those that will assuredly be lost in the blue-collar occupations. We believe they will not.

THE FUTURE LABOR FORCE

The economists who believe that the nation's jobs problem will be solved in the future tend to focus on the growth in jobs, rather than on the imbalance between the number of people who want to work and the number of jobs available. But the good-news seekers are likely to be disappointed in the future, because the rapid upward trend in the creation of jobs is over. From here on in, the trend at best will be modestly upward and, at worst, negative. Because the labor force will keep on growing, unemployment will keep on growing, too.

To see why this is the case, let us first take a look at the projected labor force and see how it compares with the present labor force. At the beginning of 1983, there were approximately 112 million people in the labor force. (This was about half a million fewer than had been in the labor force in June of 1982.) By 1990, according to the Bureau of Labor Statistics' moderately high projections, there will be about 128 million people in the labor force—an increae of about 16 million workers. The assumption that only 400,000 immigrants per year will be added to the labor force, which is part of this projection, is probably false. The real labor force is likely to be much larger. Nevertheless, for argument's sake, we will accept the assumption. Expecting that 2 million workers will remain in the military, the civilian labor force in 1990 will be 14.5 percent larger than it is today and will include 126 million people.

If the 126 million people are to be employed, there would have to be 6 million more jobs than the 90 million that were counted in 1983. If the same proportion of the labor force that involuntarily worked part time in 1980 were to work full time in 1990, only about 2 million of the total of 126 million jobs would be part-time jobs.

This many new jobs would mean adding about 85 percent more jobs than were added during the seventies, when the number of employees, full- and part-time, rose by 19.5 million. Even if we were to accept a 6 percent unemployment rate as normal, there would have to be 118 million or so full-time jobs—28 million more than are now available.

Then, remember that of the jobs added during the seventies, only 16 million were created in the private sector. Therefore, if we are to retain the public sector at roughly its present level of about 16 million workers, achieve 6 percent unemployment, and employ everyone else in 1990, private industry would have to provide 100 million jobs. This is an increase over seven years averaging 3.7 million jobs per year.

It is fair to say that this is at least 50 percent higher job generation than is likely. As shown in the accompanying chart, our pessimistic forecast is that only 115 million jobs will be created *in the private and public sectors together*. The rate of increase this scenario projects is roughly half the rate of job increase projected by the Bureau of Labor Statistics in its most optimistic forecasts.

JOB OUTLOOK FOR THE 1980s

Occupational Cluster	Employment in 1980	1980–1990 Growth in Percent		1990 Projections		BLS Projection Less Alternate Projection
		BLS* Optimistic	Alternate† Pessimistic	BLS	Alternate	
Administrative and managerial occupations	3,314,700	26	21	4,188,042	4,019,965	168,077
Engineers, surveyors, and architects	1,359,700	37	37	1,865,022	1,861,500	3,522
Natural scientists and mathematicians	539,900	45	60	785,261	861,944	−76,683
Social scientists, social workers, and religious workers	1,406,800	26	14	1,768,023	1,600,397	167,626
Teachers, librarians, and counselors	4,268,000	4	4	4,442,008	4,442,008	0
Health technologists and technicians	1,233,900	42	39	1,750,125	1,708,942	41,183
Health diagnosing and treating practitioners	759,500	34	29	1,018,025	980,746	37,279
Registered nurses, pharmacists, dietitians, therapists, and physician assistants	1,439,200	45	40	2,083,715	2,014,880	68,835
Mechanics, repairers, and installers	3,937,600	31	21	5,144,812	4,771,124	373,688

98

Writers, artists, and entertainers	995,400	23	10	1,228,389	1,090,964	137,425
Technologists and technicians	1,746,200	36	37	2,381,648	2,392,294	−10,646
Marketing and sales	17,570,800	26	10	22,079,051	19,327,880	2,751,171
Administrative support occupations, including clerical	17,230,700	26	8	21,747,511	18,654,734	3,092,777
Service occupations	15,547,000	30	18	20,227,425	18,330,008	1,897,417
Agricultural and forestry	3,023,000	−8	−17	2,785,109	2,520,458	264,651
Construction and extractive occupations	3,750,900	28	24	4,814,656	4,656,949	157,707
Production occupations	12,662,500	24	5	15,746,478	13,233,411	2,513,067
Transportation and material moving	4,345,900	25	11	5,433,048	4,840,945	592,103
Helpers, handlers, equipment cleaners, and laborers	6,975,600	21	13	8,465,570	7,899,367	566,203
Total	102,107,300	25.3	12.8	127,953,918	115,208,516	12,745,402

*Rounded off from an aggregation of the Bureau of Labor Statistics' highest projected increase by occupation.
†Projected by Gail Garfield Schwartz on the basis of a low-growth scenario for all jobs that are technology-sensitive and medium-growth projections for interpersonal jobs, knowledge-based jobs.

CREATING NEW SMART JOBS

One way to end some of the pessimism over the slow growth in smart jobs is to value some jobs more highly as the nation changes in many dramatic ways. This is an option that hasn't received much attention. It goes to the question of what the nation is willing to pay for. Each person could construct his or her own list of what is needed—everything from construction workers to rebuild the nation's decaying public facilities to public health care specialists.

As the population ages, there will be a greater need for health care for the elderly. People will have a harder time finding and maintaining a career; thus we could use more well-trained and empathetic career counselors than we have now. The children of America need a far better education than they're getting now, so the teacher work force could be increased. The job of pollution inspector could be increased tenfold, and there still would not be enough inspectors to detect all the violations of air, water, and toxic waste control laws.

Many of these jobs aren't currently being performed to the degree needed because many of them are in the public sector. The current trend to turn these duties over to the private sector has resulted in a shrinkage of the number of people performing them. As a result, the streets are dirtier, the trees less cared for, the schools unpainted, the potholes unfilled, and the air and the water less healthy.

There are many jobs that would enhance the quality of life in America, but which are now understaffed. We do not have enough well-qualified attendants in mental hospitals. We do not have enough well-qualified guards in prisons. We do not have enough occupational therapists or teachers' aides or nursing school teachers. Why not? Because we do not want to pay for their services. One way out of our job dilemma is to increase the demand for these services.

SPLITTING THE WORK WORLD

The tendency of the new technology to split work up between smart jobs and dumb jobs is well documented, both historically and anecdotally. In terms of sheer numbers, the quantity of smart jobs anticipated to be created in the future looks small in relation to the number of people seeking them. The competition for these jobs obviously will be keen. Not all of America's bright minds will find a job that they consider satisfactory, both in terms of the quality of the work and the wages it will pay.

This splintering of the work force poses many challenges and dangers for the nation's economy, not the least of which is the continued erosion of middle-class jobs by the new technology. The hierarchy of jobs that has dominated the American economy for so long has undergirded the nation's social structure, with its great, gray middle class. The emergence of the middle class has given the nation an extremely stable political system and staved off radicalism of the left and right. As middle-class economic security erodes over time with the installation of the new technology, the political security of the nation will face new threats as well.

6

Who Works?
The War over Jobs

The war over jobs is millions of quiet little skirmishes, like these four:

- It was one of those late-night radio talk shows. The host was trying to fill air time by picking a controversial subject in hopes of seeing the switchboard, and his ratings, light up. His choice, immigration, obtained the desired results. He had to end the program with a number of people still hanging on the line waiting to be heard. What was remarkable about the show was the intense, bitter anger of so many callers who insisted that immigrants—legal and illegal—were the main reason why they or their relatives were out of work. One black caller complained that his teen-age children could not land a job in convenience stores simply because Vietnamese refugees had taken them all over.

- In Akron, Ohio, a fifteen-year veteran of a tire plant, worried sick over a potential layoff, said he would be more than willing to accept concessions in pay and fringe benefits, if necessary to preserve his job. The seniority he thought would protect him turned out to be no safety net at all.

103

- In Philadelphia, the young woman had just completed her schooling as a computer programmer and went looking for a job. Surprisingly, in company after company, all the openings had been filled. "Everybody wants to be a programmer," she was told. Finally, out of desperation, she took a job with an insurance company keeping the computer printers in operation—which simply meant tearing off the paper regularly. Despite an apparent glut of programmers on the market in her area, she said she still aspired to be a programmer one day.

- The white mechanic worked for a defense contractor, and his (white) wife worked in a high tech factory before they decided to take early retirement—only to discover a few years later that the pension money they thought would be sufficient turned out to be meager. The mechanic took a low-paying job as a part-time school custodian to bolster the family income; he deprived a young black man of a job he had hoped for. The mechanic and his wife cursed their decision to retire so soon. In fact, many people their age had decided upon the opposite course, to continue working past sixty-five because of what they regarded as inadequate income.

These skirmishes may seem trivial enough until they are related to the real war—a war over jobs that is squeezing opportunity throughout the work force. This war has been brought on by a convergence of forces that will affect the job market for many years. It comes at a time when professional job analysts naively project the job future with optimism because the low birthrates of the 1960s and 1970s suggested a dramatic slowing of the work force growth rate in the 1980s and 1990s. But the diminishing stream of youth will be offset by a growing number of immigrants and older women in the work force, and the older male workers will stay in the work force longer. In the face of technological job displacement and increased foreign competition, inadequate pension and retirement systems, and increased life expectancy, a frightened work force will scramble to get and hold onto any job, even if it means accepting pay concessions.

A time of great turmoil is ahead. Even as technology destroys many jobs and transforms others, it creates new work opportunities as well. But the number of new jobs to be created will be insufficient for the army of unemployed people, swelled as it is by dislocated workers, women, older workers, and legal and illegal immigrants. The nation could easily become a battleground in the fierce competition over who will work and who will not. America has already seen some of this competition erupt in strife between various groups; this threat will grow worse as time passes.

The Bureau of Labor Statistics forecasts a labor force of 124 million in 1990, of which 122 million will be the civilian labor force. This assumption is too low, primarily because the estimate of immigrants is too low. The 1980–1990 increase in the labor force of 16 million persons, projected by the Bureau of Labor Statistics, is a 14.3 percent increase, an average of 1.47 percent per year. The expected 1990 civilian labor force participation rate is 67.9 percent, as compared to 63.6 percent in 1980.

CLOGGING THE JOB PIPELINE

This huge labor force will be literally fighting over jobs—smart jobs *and* dumb jobs. So, the normal process of freeing up job opportunities—through new job creation, retirements, advancements, and resignations—will be disturbed. Since the job growth rate will not keep up with the labor force growth rate, those with jobs will become extremely anxious about keeping them and will become more conservative—and rightly so—about taking chances and moving to another company or community. Job availability and mobility will thus be even further restricted by the ancient human instinct to play it safe.

Supporting this prognosis are Census Bureau figures showing that the percentage of the population moving from one area to another each year has declined from 20 percent to below 18 percent. Several factors caused this decline. One is the fact that in many households both husband and wife work, so that changing one job means sacrificing a second income at least temporarily. Another is that if job mobility requires uprooting a household and finding new housing, the process of moving itself can wipe out a year or more of income gains. And income gains are not always in the prospect, anyway—the grass is not always greener in another city, especially for many blue-collar workers. The 1982 and 1983 newspapers were filled with reports of laid-off workers making fruitless treks across the country to find good jobs. The soup line or at best a minimum-wage job was often the only reward. The deep-seated suspicion lurking in the mind of many workers that it is better to stay put and hang onto what you have has a strong base in reality.

Bolstering their lack of risk-taking with jobs is the fact that many people are not pushing their adult children out of the nest. Another Census Bureau survey showed that nearly twenty million adult children were living with their parents in 1981, up by two million in one year. Many of these children are still at home because the recession so severely limited job opportunities. Others could not afford a home of their own even though they had a job. Many social scientists who have noted this basically economic phenomenon believe that the present generation is also having a hard time with the psychological dependency that results. The even older tradition of an extended family relationship that reflected the constraints of limited economic opportunity may have its positive aspects, too, of course, but the fact remains that the restriction of job opportunities is in turn restricting the economic and social independence of millions of young people.

YOUTH: AT THE END OF THE PIPELINE

The fact that many young people are moving back in with their parents is the job opportunity problem in a nutshell. Young workers seeking an entry-level position will be the big losers in the clogged-up job pipeline. From an employer's point of view, they are less experienced and less reliable, therefore less employable. Employers will no longer have to go to young people exclusively for jobs that were once classified as entry level. The glut in the labor market will make even dumb jobs increasingly desirable to more experienced workers, including many who have one or more years of college.

Those with college credentials naturally have a leg up on those without a degree. The lack of job opportunities is creating ferocious competition among young people for available entry-level jobs. The Bureau of Labor Statistics reports that the pool of college graduates who are either unemployed or in jobs for which a college degree is unnecessary has been growing at the rate of 200,000 annually. The pool at the end of 1982 totaled between two and three million people. The 1983 "Endicott Study of College Placement" published by Northwestern University showed 50 percent fewer offers being made to college graduates than in 1982. Especially those graduates who have majored in a liberal arts curriculum to the exclusion of anything else are finding jobs hard to come by, and their average starting salaries dropped 7 percent in 1983, according to the National College Placement Council. Even those with special skills are finding starting salaries 5 to 10 percent lower than a year ago.

Young people who have credentials in a highly desired discipline or in two or more disciplines are landing the few positions available. Employers can pick the cream of the academic crop, leaving those who have eked their way through college in dire straits—and those without college education in deep trouble. College graduates who are unable to find entry-level smart jobs are competing with high school graduates for the dumb jobs. In the virtually certain continued competition, the high school graduates will be at a disadvantage, and high school dropouts will be lucky to land even a dumb job.

Who gets the work depends on who gets the credentials. Who gets the credentials depends to a growing extent on who has the income to pay for a college education. The competition for jobs among young people is more than a matter of individual merit; it's a matter of the current distribution of income in the nation. Those who have the highest income are able to finance credentials for their children much more easily than the lower-paid workers, putting their children at the head of the queue for jobs at the beginning of the pipeline. Because of their relatively unfavorable economic position at the onset of this job crisis, many American families will discover that their children are frozen out of opportunities in a way that they had not experienced.

A college education may not always fetch the high income it once did, but it could mean the difference between an income and no income at all. At the end of 1981, 42.1 percent of the unemployed were just high school graduates; 40.7 percent of the jobless had not even finished high school; 11.5 percent had attended but not completed college; and only 5.5 percent had a college degree. Clearly, college credentials are a factor in obtaining and keeping a job—and the more education, the better.

The fact that college graduates are not obtaining the kinds of jobs they want has led many analysts to conclude that the American work force is overeducated. This is based on statistical evidence showing that between 1962 and 1969, 90 percent of the four million graduates found jobs in relatively high-paying positions, while between 1969 and 1976, 64 percent of the eight million graduates found relatively high-paying jobs. One of the amazing things about this statistic is that the number of college graduates doubled within a seven-year period. But *overeducation* is a highly pejorative term. Rather than being overeducated, it is more plausible to say that many of the young people were *wrongly educated* for the kinds of skills required in the work revolution.

Youth Without Hope

Young people without skills will still be the dregs of the job market. Most of these will, as now, be blacks. The future of black young men is particularly bleak, since their dropout rate from high school is higher than black girls' or white boys' or girls'. And it's Catch-22 in the job market: Without experience a person can't get a job, but only the cream of the crop gets experience. While many teenagers work part-time—some eighteen million according to a *Washington Post* article—most of the jobs go to white youths. Teenagers without job experience will be far at the end of the hiring line. That is one reason why conflict between blacks and other minorities is heating up in communities around the country.

Many analysts see the United States as a country with a permanent black underclass imprisoned in large cities and living on the edge of mainstream America. The grandchildren of black men who never held steady work will see no reason to try to improve themselves. The underclass will grow bigger each generation, unless it explodes into violence.

While those blacks, both men and women, who secure jobs are as likely as whites to keep working for a long time, the real problem is getting employed in the first place. A study by Robert E. Hall of the National Bureau of Economic Research showed that 26 percent of blacks could expect to work twenty years or more, compared to 29 percent of whites. Still, only 49 percent of all blacks were working in 1983, as compared to 64 percent of all whites, and only 60 percent of black men, as compared to 72 percent of white men, were working.

Blacks also are much more likely than whites to be relegated unwillingly to part-time work or to work that does not pay a living wage. A government study of underemployed people showed that in 1974, 43 percent of black men were underemployed for five years or longer, whereas only 30 percent of white men were underemployed that long. *Underemployed* in this study meant having earnings only 25 percent higher than the official poverty level in 1974. This study went so far as to categorize the workers earning such wages as members of a "surplus population" suffering not temporary, recession-induced work shortages, but permanent, irreversible underemployment. The study showed that an underemployed youth is more likely to be permanently underemployed than an underemployed adult.

As an aside, it is interesting that underemployed workers of both races and all ages tend to move around more than fully employed workers, with about one-third of the underemployed moving out of a given place within five years. Only one-fifth of the fully employed move that frequently.

THE AGED: SECURITY ABOVE ALL

America's elderly population has discovered after years of economic crises that their private pension plans and social security do not provide the economic security they had counted on. If ever they had counted on them before, as a general rule they no longer do, because of the enormous public attention generated in 1982 and 1983 when the social security system teetered on the edge of bankruptcy. (Social security was never actually designed to be a retirement program that would permit an elderly person to maintain the same standard of living after leaving his or her job, although millions perceived it that way for years.) Private pensions also have proven inadequate. In the first place, only 45 percent of the civilian workers have private pension coverage of some type. In the second place, most private pension plans are not indexed to reflect the annual increase in inflation.

The realization that the nation's system of income security is insufficient will change the elderly's attitudes about remaining in the work force, reversing a trend toward early retirement that had been continuing for years. Attitudes of the entire work force about working after age sixty-five are changing. According to a poll commissioned by the National Commission on Social Security, only 31 percent of those surveyed said that they would prefer to retire at the normal age of retirement if their income was adequate. And that is a big if.

The number of elderly people looking for jobs declined steadily from 1960 to 1981, according to the Census Bureau. In 1960, for instance, 36.6 percent of the male population sixty-five and over who were living with their wives were in the work force. That had dropped to 20 percent by 1981—an astonishing decline. But early retirement was encouraged during much of that time; both the social security system and private pension plans provided for retirement income at age sixty-two. In addition, the social security earnings test, which reduced benefits dollar for dollar for all who earned above $5500 annually, served as a powerful disincentive for the elderly to seek jobs. With the new social security legislation approved in 1983, that limitation will be phased out, and since $5500 is close to poverty level, many more elderly will try to work at least part time.

Earnings are not the only reason older people will want to stay in the work force longer. There will be fewer physical reasons forcing them to reduce their activity. Work itself in many fields will require little physical exertion. People will be healthier, even though older. Life expectancy is also rising, even more dramatically than previously projected. For many years, life expectancy for men and women rose only slightly, remaining at around age seventy for men and seventy-eight for women. But now scientists have reported that greater breakthroughs in medicine, particularly in treating heart disease, have pushed the average life expectancy up dramatically. By the year 2000, they say, it will be seventy-four for men and eighty-six for women—startling changes in longevity. Add to this a new ethic about exercise and better nutritional habits, and the prospect of the elderly working longer takes on an added impetus.

What was so special about sixty-five in the first place? When Congress legislated the social security system during the Depression, it evidently decided upon sixty-five because that was the retirement age prevalent in European systems, even though the retirement age of civil servants was seventy. Perhaps another reason for choosing sixty-five was that the unemployment rate for those aged forty-five was higher and grew worse as workers got older.[1] But this rationale for age sixty-five as the retirement age has long since disappeared. Congress has already raised the age at which workers may be forced to retire to seventy, even though the retirement age for social security eligibility remains at sixty-five.

One of the reasons often given for failure of sixty-five-and-over

[1]Sylvester J. Schieber, "Social Security, Perspectives on Saving the System," Employee Benefit Research Institute, 1982, Washington, D.C., p. 19.

people to work is that workers look forward to living the rest of their days in leisure. Early retirement has clearly been a trend for the last two decades. In addition, the proportion of retirees working has dropped dramatically. In 1960, one-third of the men and 10 percent of the women who attained age sixty-five were in the work force. By 1981, these percentages had dropped to a little under 20 percent for men and 8 percent for women. But these trends probably will begin to reverse for all the reasons cited, including the fact that the earnings test will soon be eliminated from the law.

Older workers may be looking for a longer period of leisure, but the principal question is, With what? According to a 1977 survey by the Congressional Budget Office, 35 percent of households aged sixty-five and over had meager incomes either under the poverty line or only slightly above. If social security, welfare, and food stamps were taken away, nearly 60 percent of the retired households would have been below the poverty line. This study reveals that most retired people have to scratch for income and can't afford to go across the county, much less across the country, on their incomes.

Because of these factors, it seems probable that the number of people age sixty-five and over who choose to hang onto their jobs will increase sharply over the next decade. About 3 million out of the 6 million aged sixty-five and over are now in the work force, many of them in part-time jobs not related to the jobs they held before they reached sixty-five. By the end of the decade, it is estimated there will be 30 million people over sixty-five. If just another 5 percent of this age group decides to remain in the work force, 5 million elderly workers will clog the job pipeline. Older workers who decide to hold on to their jobs for a few more years freeze promotions and job opportunities down the line. There may not be one job opportunity lost for every single worker who chooses not to retire, but there is a relationship between the two.

Employers also will find that retaining older workers on the payroll, while more costly than hiring a younger worker, has a number of advantages. Older workers tend to be more reliable and more satisfied with their jobs. While they may seem to work slower, experience also means more efficiency. Older workers may not be as flexible as young workers, but that they cannot learn to do new things is a myth. A study by the Health, Education and Welfare Department (now Health and Human Services) in 1978 said that there was little evidence to back up the claim that older workers have a greatly diminished learning capacity. In fact, it said, the intelligence of most individuals remains constant until at least age seventy.

Can the older workers learn the new technology? It is highly unlikely that many computer programmers will emerge from this group, but using the new technology is not as difficult as it may seem. Many jobs that utilize computer technology actually have been simplified. Studies have shown that, after initial fear, veteran workers have learned to accept the new technology.

Finally, the move to a services economy where hard physical labor is not required is a benefit to older workers. As the nation's economy shifts further and further away from manufacturing, the aging service worker will be induced to stay on the job longer simply because the work isn't as hard. One reason often cited for early retirement was that workers who had toiled in difficult production jobs should be afforded an earlier release from the world of work. But these laborers are a declining percentage of the work force.

WOMEN: AT THE CENTER OF THE WORK REVOLUTION

Almost all of the new jobs of the future will require brains more than brawn. They will center around the office and involve the development and processing of information. They will require a good educational background and the ability to communicate. In other words, they are tailor-made for women.

Just as the switch from manufacturing to services has also made the older worker more viable, it has put the female right at the front of the job queue. It is not only because heavy lifting is virtually out. It is because women possess the unique qualifications for society's new smart jobs as equally as men. Indeed, in terms of sheer numbers, there will be more college-educated women entering the work force by the mid-1980s than there will be men. This in itself is a remarkable change. In 1960, 17.4 percent of the men aged eighteen to twenty-four were enrolled in college, compared with 10.5 percent of the women of the same age. By 1980, women had totally closed this gap and began to move ahead in college enrollment.

In 1982, women comprised 45 percent of all professional workers. Even though many of these were teaching positions, the number of women who had landed jobs in higher-paying professional positions increased. For instance, 7.4 percent of all women workers are now administrators or managers, compared with 5.2 percent in 1975. (About 14.5 percent of male workers are administrators or managers.) Roughly two-thirds of the nation's elementary and secondary school teachers are women. If the white-collar worker is the worker of the future, then women have the edge; 53 percent of the nation's white-collar workers are women.

Women are moving beyond the traditional occupations they held in the past as they gain more experience in the work force. After years as a school teacher in Fairfax County, Virginia, one woman decided to become an accountant. After several years of after-hours schooling, she quit her job and found a new higher-paying position. Women are increasingly moving into such occupation areas as financial advice, economics, computer programming, research, geology, and environmental science—some of the faster-growing job areas of the next decade. Xerox Corporation's appointment of Lynn Conway, an electrical engineer and a pioneer in very large integrated circuit design, to head the company's supercomputer effort is a harbinger of things to come.

Are men at a disadvantage in finding jobs in the work revolution? For all the changes brought about in society by women's liberation, the world of work is still male-dominated. Despite the strides made by women, their earnings still average only about 60 percent of men's. Part of this is due to the fact that women are in many low-paying occupations. The very highly paid professional and managerial occupations are still predominantly male. This is in part a holdover from the time when fewer women were in the workplace. Now, 52 percent of all women work, and by 1990 as many as 63 percent of all women will work, according to the Bureau of Labor Statistics. The sixty million women workers in 1990 (a high-growth projection) would be thirteen million stronger than the 1981 female work force.

Objectively speaking, a good case can be made that women workers will have a competitive edge over men in the job market of the future precisely because they accept lower pay. Any time there is a labor surplus—as there will be—job security will take primacy for workers, and employers will be able to perpetuate female wage differentials. Women might well be hired ahead of men as a matter of course. Ironically, if things get tough enough, the fact that women's pay has been held below that of men's could well drive men's wages down to a more competitive level in the future.

One of the most difficult questions to answer is whether women will be more or less at a disadvantage in the occupations that require science, math, and technical skills—areas women traditionally have not entered in large numbers. This is an issue confused by stereotype, emotion, and conflicting evidence. For instance, men achieve higher average mathematics scores on the Scholastic Aptitude Test (SAT) and other math tests administered at the high school level. Such performances have often been used to justify prejudice against women for jobs that are math-dependent. But to conclude that women are not qualified in math is to succumb to the tyranny of averages. Test score averages undoubtedly reflect the traditional lack of interest in math on the part of many women. Many women suffer math phobia because they themselves have come to believe that stereotype. But in workshops even average women have been "cured" of their math fear, and there are literally millions of women who perform equally as well in math and science as do the high-scoring men. It is these above-average women who are going to compete with men in the math and science job arena in the future.

Moreover, even though math and science will be important in the future, the work revolution is not entirely a technical revolution. In fact, it is more a revolution in communication and knowledge and organization and marketing. Women are excellent organizers and salespersons. Women are highly entrepreneurial. Women have superior small motor skills, so they are good on computers and word processors. Women are reliable and honest. These positive stereotypes will offset the negative stereotypes increasingly, as women prove they have what it takes to command smart jobs.

What is not greatly appreciated is that the revolution in women working is, from a historical standpoint, still in its early stages. It began with women manning factories in World War II. Then men came home from war and took their jobs back. The rush of women into the job market in the 1960s and the 1970s was a response to the pull of job opportunities in banks, insurance companies, telephone companies. Keypunch operators were in great demand to support the proliferation of mainframe computers. These machines ate up data encoded on cards and later on tape, and the women of America were the input experts. Labor saving aids such as automatic washing machines, dryers, and convenience foods helped women leave the home to work during the day, because now they could do the housework in their spare time. Initially, women went into jobs that were classified as traditional women's jobs, but in recent years they have been expanding into many occupations traditionally held by men.

Many economists (usually male) say that the influx of women into the labor force has peaked, since traditional values—the desire to nurture husband and children and tend the house and garden—will limit the number of women who could possibly want to work. This view (or is it wish?) led the Bureau of Labor Statistics to underestimate women's participation in the labor force in the late 1970s by a large amount.

The economists' conclusion is wrong on two counts. In the first place, the initial influx of women into the labor market put them into many historically low-paying jobs. But they fulfilled a valuable service to the country. When the nation needed workers as it shifted from a manufacturing to a services economy, women were there to fill the gap. The next logical step is for women to step up to higher-paying fields. This next phase of the work revolution for women may not take fire as fast as the first revolution, but it is occurring nevertheless.

To say that the influx of women into the work force is virtually over is wrong from another standpoint. According to the Bureau of Labor Statistics, women will account for seven out of every ten additions to the labor force during the 1980s. Because older women are returning to the labor force in large numbers and will continue to do so in the future, while younger women are staying in the work force longer, the labor force participation rate of women is still on the upswing. Figures show that presently, nearly 70 percent of women aged twenty to twenty-four are in the work force, compared with 67 percent for those aged twenty-five to thirty-four. Yet, as the current generation of women matures, they will not drop out as readily as women now in their late forties and fifties did. Seventy-four percent of the women aged twenty-five through thirty-four surveyed by *Working Mother* in 1983 intended to keep their jobs. A *Business Week* survey (May 24, 1982) showed that women who are in their thirties are learning to work around motherhood. Corporations are helping them to do so with "flexitime" and day care arrangements. Companies help because their female employees are a valued asset, not because management is altruistic.

These figures reflect what scores of women of all ages say about their career plans and what is happening among women of middle age, too. At Smith College in 1981, one-half of the women celebrating their twenty-fifth reunion were either working for pay or doing significant volunteer work. In the Yale class of 1981, 35 percent were female. Asked about their future, several of these young women say, "There is no question about it: We'll have to live with men who want to share family responsibilities so that we can continue to pursue our careers. It may not be easy, but there's no other choice for us." These young women are not only willing, but eager, to cope with the challenge of maintaining professional and managerial upward mobility. While many of the working women in these occupations who are now in their thirties have decided not to have children, the women now in their twenties are going for the brass ring—families *and* career.

IMMIGRATION: THE GATE WON'T SHUT

In Miami's Overtown, a black neighborhood where violence has erupted on several occasions, a thirty-year-old black man stood outside the union hall of the International Longshoreman's Association trying to get a job as a dockworker. He explained to a reporter that he had been forced to give up a job as an upholsterer because Hispanic immigrants had driven wages in the industry down to $5 an hour, without any prospect of raises. Nobody cared about his experience and efficiency, he said.

In Dade County, Cuban and other refugees have pushed the Hispanic population to over a half million and displaced thousands of black workers in the process. The same kind of displacement of black workers by Hispanic, Oriental, Caribbean, and/or Middle Eastern immigrants has occurred in most of the nation's big cities, with Miami probably the leading example.

As a result, a bitter rivalry among racial and ethnic groups seems to be growing, and the melting pot notion seems a bigger myth than ever before. This bitterness between groups has increased since the 1970s and the 1980s brought a new wave of both legal and illegal immigration into the United States. About 460,000 legal aliens entered the United States in 1979, after a surge in immigration of Southeast Asian refugees that brought the 1978 total up to over 600,000. But the failure of the government to release more recent figures on immigration is ominous. In any case, legal immigrants account for probably less than half the total and may account for only one-third of the total.

Estimates by experts such as the Environmental Fund and studies for the Select Commission on Refugee and Immigration Policy suggest that at least 500,000 and possibly 1 million illegal immigrants stay in the United States each year. The size of the illegal immigrant population in 1983 was variously estimated at 3.5 to 12 million. Leon Bouvier, director of demographic research at the Population Reference Bureau, said in a 1981 report that "perhaps 1¼ million persons may have immigrated to the United States during 1980. This exceeds the million entries recorded in 1907 and again in 1914. Thus, immigation now appears to be almost as important as fertility insofar as U.S. population growth is concerned."[2] It is plausible that both legal and illegal immigration will add from 800,000 to a million and a half people annually to the U.S. population. This flood of immigrants simply gives the lie to the optimistic view that the U.S. labor force will not keep pace with job growth during the rest of the 1980s and early 1990s, which would relieve the nation's unemployment problem.

Political and economic forces here and in foreign countries suggest that, even with new laws designed to curtail the flow of new illegal aliens, the number of illegal immigrants entering the United States will be large. The new laws will not prevent revolutions in other countries or political persecutions that our democracy will find hard to ignore. Continued war, political unrest, and poverty in Central America, along with deteriorating economic conditions in Mexico, will in particular cause many more immigrants to pour across a border that cannot be effectively controlled. The larger the number of a particular alien group, the stronger its political clout to oppose anti-immigration laws, as evidenced by the Hotel and Restaurant Employees and Bartenders International Union filing suit in April 1983 on behalf of Salvadoran workers' right to stay in the United States. Hispanics, who now officially comprise 6.4 percent of the population, could well be 10 percent of the population by the end of the decade. Orientals, though still a small

[2]Leon F. Bouvier, "The Impact of Immigration on U.S. Population Size," Population Reference Bureau, Washington, D.C., January 1981.

percentage of the total population, have taken over entire communities in places as diverse as Arlington, Virginia, Columbus, Ohio, and Jackson Heights, Queens (New York).

Do illegal immigrants cost Americans jobs? Many close observers note that illegal immigrants take only jobs most Americans would not touch. Thus, it is asserted, they are creating a market only for their own cheap labor. But this may be true only in a narrow sense. According to an estimate by the International Ladies Garment Workers Union, the average wage paid an illegal alien in a garment "sweatshop" was about $2 an hour, about $1.35 less than the legal minimum wage and only slightly more than one-third of the average hourly earnings of garment workers nationwide. Generally, sweatshop work is at least ten hours a day, six days a week, with no overtime.[3]

Although illegal immigrants work in many jobs most Americans have not taken in the past because of the low pay, that is no justificaiton for ignoring the economic impact of excessive immigration. Without illegal immigrants, U.S. employers would be forced to pay higher wages for American workers. Especially in the low-skilled service jobs, immigrant workers reduce choices for American workers. But not all displacement is by waiters, dishwashers, janitors, and busboys. Some is in jobs once considered good by any blue-collar worker's standards.

An example is the meatpacking industry. Once centered in Chicago, where the companies originally settled because of low-cost German and Polish immigrant labor, the industry gradually moved out as the union moved in and bargained up wages and benefits. To run away from unions, plants have been closed in the Chicago area and opened elsewhere, providing jobs for Indochinese refugees and Mexican immigrants. Although the work is demanding, starting pay at one of the nation's largest meatpacking companies was $7 an hour in 1983, hardly starvation wages. Here surely there are plenty of native-born Americans who would be willing to work at that pay. Every Mexican or Vietnamese who works in that plant is taking a job from an American.

It is difficult to discuss the economics of the immigration problem without sounding like a bigot. It is nice to think of the United States as a melting pot or salad bowl of opportunity for

---

[3]Sol Chaikin and Phil Comstock, "Toward A National Immigration Policy," *The Journal of the Institute for Socioeconomic Studies,* Vol. I, No. 7, Spring 1982, White Plains, New York.

the oppressed and the courageous. On the other hand, if we continue to serve that function for the entire world, it will inevitably drive down our standard of living. No other major industrial power absorbs as many immigrants as the United States does. Our northern neighbor, Canada, virtually prohibits any immigration, especially of dark-skinned people. Though idealism may dictate an open-door policy, practicality makes it necessary to examine that policy carefully.

There is no doubt that immigrants contribute much to the quality of life in America. And their contribution is by no means confined to picking our fruit or washing our dirty linen. Foreigners are earning doctoral degrees in science, mathematics, and engineering at a rapidly increasing rate, and they are putting those degrees to work in American industry and universities and hospitals. Many first-generation children are at the top of their class at school, and the prowess of Chinese children in math has awed educators and sociologists alike. It is inconsistent with the notion of equal opportunity and upward mobility to limit immigration to certain education or income levels, although we still manage country-of-origin quotas.

Yet on the face of it, it seems that different groups progress at different rates up the economic ladder. A good deal depends on the circumstances of their leaving their own country. Those who arrive as political refugees with a little saved capital or with relatives here who have some assets have been notably successful, so much so that they are the bitter envy of less prosperous groups. The Mexican migrant farm workers' stoop labor in California and Texas could probably not be bought for twice the price from American workers. Some immigrant groups have not gone to work for others, but have filled gaps, such as starting new grocery stores or photocopying businesses. It is said that almost every greengrocer's in New York City is owned by Koreans, while Vietnamese in the Washington, D.C., area have gone into almost every kind of local service business.

Of all the groups, it is the growing army of illegal resident Hispanics that poses the biggest potential problem, simply because of their vulnerability and their concentrations. Hispanic illegal aliens are, with the major exception of the middle-class Cubans who fled the Castro regime, generally uneducated or poorly educated and conversant only in Spanish. Like all illegal aliens, they live in constant fear of detection and deportation. Although they share these characteristics with other illegals, their concentration in certain cities of the Southwest does two things: It makes them an easy victim of employer exploitation, and it gives them a leg up on American workers in those areas.

Mexicans and Central Americans may, according to our standards, be an impoverished group, but from their perspective, have escaped their native lands to riches. Furthermore, over time many illegal immigrants are being assimilated, and many are climbing the economic ladder. In the Southwest, Mexican immigrants on average equal the earnings of native-born Mexican-Americans within fifteen years. Second-generation Mexican-Americans on average earned 9 percent more than those with parents born outside the United States.[4]

Immigrants are not necessarily relegated to the end of the job line, either. Where jobs are plentiful, as they were in the cities of the Sunbelt during the early 1970s, the typical long-term underemployed person is more likely to be a resident of several years rather than a new arrival.

Immigrants appear to make up a large part of the underemployed—a group, numbering from seventeen to twenty-five million people who work but, because their work is part-time and low-paying, live at the edge of poverty. The technological changes foretold here do not promise hope for these underemployed workers. If they are janitors or delivery persons or fast-food helpers, they may still have jobs, but they won't be paid better, and some of their jobs could well be eliminated by automation.

Given the crushing problems of failed economies, failed land reform, and massive debt facing so many developing nations, the number of victims of poverty, political oppression, and guerilla war will not quickly diminish. There will be more like the Vietnamese and Haitian boat people. And no matter how bad off our economy may seem to us, America is still the Mecca of safety and economic opportunity to all Third World nations. Short of police state tactics that most democrats abhor, it will be almost impossible to keep out the millions who will risk their lives to save their futures.

---

[4]Barry Chiswick, "The Economic Progress of Immigrants," paper delivered at a conference sponsored by the American Enterprise Institute for Public Policy Research and the College of Business Administration, University of Illinois at Chicago Circle, 1980.

A POSSIBLE CONFLICT SCENARIO

The working age population will be at least sixteen million and possibly twenty million people stronger in 1990 than it is in 1983. It will include larger proportions of women, immigrants, and minorities. There will be a smaller proportion of youth, but youthful entrants into the labor force will still number in the millions. There will be a larger proportion of elderly, many of whom will still be under seventy years old and still capable of work.

If the economy does not create twenty million new jobs in the next seven years, enough to provide work for the additions and reduce the unemployment rate to the range of 5 percent, there will be a sharp struggle over jobs. The old will refuse to give way to the middle-aged. The men will refuse to give way to women. The whites will refuse to give way to racial minorities. The young will have more trouble landing their first job.

If the relatively disadvantaged are willing to work for less pay and if they have good strong skills to offer, they may be able to bid their way into some good job opportunities. However, if the fit between jobs available and the number of people wanting them is unfavorable, many people will have to lower their sights. A smart job will be a bigger plum than ever, especially if it is a relatively secure one. And the need for credentials will not diminish, even though many people may have more education than they need merely to do the job they finally end up in.

7

The Displaced Worker: Social Dynamite

Joe's life was not all that complicated. A seventeen-year employee of the steel mill near Pittsburgh, he had followed his father into the mill after graduating from high school. With a salary and fringe benefits that paid the bills and supported his wife and two children, Joe was reasonably content despite two short layoffs at the plant.

Well liked by his fellow workers, Joe shared the camaraderie and that special blend of outward toughness and independence that seem to characterize steelworkers. He took his lunch pail and his swagger into the smoking city each day and emerged eight hours later tired and ready for beer and conversation at the bar across the street. There he talked about football, hunting, the miserable conditions inside the plant, the union, family, and life in general. Although the work was hard and not especially rewarding, it had given Joe a sense of economic and personal security and a well-developed support network of friends and associates. Joe and friends would rail against the company and its stupid practices (as they saw it), but there was always the union, the daily beer, and the job awaiting the next day. Although he often rebelled against it vocally, Joe felt a vague sense of belonging. Was it the job or his friends, his daily routine, and the role he played or the daily necessities caused by his family responsibilities? It was, in varying degrees, all of them. The job was not perfect, but it was a living, and he could fight to improve it.

That was all before the day they told Joe and his co-workers that the mill was being closed permanently. The news of the plant closure was shattering, even though it was not totally unexpected, given the fact that little new investment had been made in several years. Even though there were generous unemployment benefits, Joe knew that the future looked bleak, because the steel industry was shrinking all around him. The initial shock of the job loss left him deeply depressed and angry. He felt a deep sense of betrayal, and he blamed not only the company, but the union and the government. Gone was not only the job that supported his family, but also his sense of time and place and esteem, built as it was upon acceptance by his co-workers and participation in a rugged daily routine that they had conquered together. The trappings of the job had molded his character and burned into his psyche.

In the months following the plant closure, Joe developed a drinking problem and became even more embittered at the "system" that had cost him his livelihood. His marriage became strained. His job search turned up nothing that would even come close to matching his previous income. With few job skills other than those he had learned at the steel mill, Joe realized that the only way to find a well-paying job was through retraining. But how and for what? The newspaper classified ads were filled with help wanted ads for computer engineers and programmers and management consultants, jobs that seemed far beyond his expertise and the time he would have to learn the needed skills. These were not the blue-collar-and-beer jobs he knew; these were white-collar, white wine jobs that seemed unfamiliar and threatening. So Joe kept putting off retraining. The drinking increased, and so did the financial problems and the strains on his marriage. His health insurance was gone even as his health problems increased. How much longer would he be able to avoid foreclosure on his mortgage?

Joe is not one single steelworker, but a composite of many steelworkers we have interviewed. But he is a very real composite, and his tragedy is not exaggerated. These personal situations have in recent times repeatedly befallen highly vulnerable workers in this highly vulnerable industry. Joe was not displaced from his job by U.S. technology, but by new technology in new plants as far away as Korea. In the end, it didn't matter.

If by chance his old plant is reopened, it will be with fewer workers and with new automated processes. Since Joe's plant was shut down, the union has won some concessions on plant closings, including advance notification. But that victory is not really halting either plant closings or permanent layoffs.

America has long had difficulties with displaced workers like Joe, but in the past these difficulties have been much less severe. In the old pattern of a strongly growing industrial economy, a low-skilled worker engaged in goods production might lose his job in one industry, only to find another job in another industry in fairly short order. The transition required minimum retraining and little new education. But that has changed dramatically in the work revolution. The displaced worker has lost that flexibility to move from one comparable job to another.

The plight of the displaced worker is a national crisis and will become more so in the future. There are 200,000 or more workers laid off in the automobile industry who will probably never be called back. Hundreds of thousands of other workers laid off in newly automating industries will never get back to their old industries. But there's a new twist to the problem. Workers are not being displaced in manufacturing industries alone; many service-type jobs are being eliminated as well.

Estimates of the size of the displaced work force vary. Given the speed of installation and the pervasiveness of new technology, we believe most estimates are probably understated, as we said in Chapter 2. But even the optimistic estimates are staggering. The Congressional Budget Office, for instance, reported in 1983 that "the diffusion of microelectronic technology could cause the loss of three million jobs by the end of the decade—or 15 percent of the current manufacturing work force." Automotive industry sources report that 1.7 jobs are lost for every new robot installed. A study by Carnegie-Mellon University suggests a loss of 4 million jobs by the end of the decade as a result of the installation of robots in manufacturing alone. And this does not count job losses related to foreign competition or slower economic growth. Nor does it count the displacement likely to occur in the services area once new technology has been fully incorporated into service functions. The chances of displaced service workers being called back are also dim.

The poor performance of the U.S. economy between 1979 and 1983, caused by high interest rates and increased foreign competition, led to much of the worker displacement. This came at a time when the new technologies made possible the expansion of production and processing with fewer workers. James H. Evans, chairman of the Union Pacific Corporation, said in 1983 that the six thousand laid-off workers in his firm would probably never be called back. "We're running 40 percent more freight tonnage than we did twenty years ago—with half as many employees," he said. "If we had the same number of employees we had then, we would have priced ourselves out of the market. How have we done it? Automation."[1] This is precisely what many unions fear. William Winpisinger, the outspoken president of the International Association of Machinists, said that workers were laid off by recession and will not get called back because of automation.

Job displacement is nothing new in the United States. In fact, it is a normal process of the economy as it adjusts to new technologies and situations. Economists generally treat displacement indifferently, calling it an unfortunate and necessary transition that will take care of itself in time as the economy grows and more jobs are created in new ventures to absorb the labor surplus. Politicians have devised unemployment compensation, retraining programs, and trade adjustment assistance as ways to prop up the income of the displaced worker and help him or her move into a new job eventually. But these institutional crutches will prove insufficient as technological displacement picks up speed in the late 1980s. Congress accentuated the shortcomings in 1983 when it approved a jobs bill that included provisions for retraining displaced workers but failed to provide enough money to take care of the problem. The budgeted sum of $75 million divided among the 1.5 million displaced workers would provide only $50 for each.

Job displacement can no longer be treated with such great indifference. Several million veteran workers, including untold numbers with ten or more years of seniority, are going to be replaced by machines and foreign competition. The United States has never before been confronted with displacement of this magnitude in such a short period of time. What are the effects of widespread worker displacement, and how are we going to cope with it? Will the mere fact that the displaced worker pool will be so large force fundamental changes in the U.S. economy?

[1] *New York Times*, May 16, 1983, p. 1.

PERSONAL DEVASTATION

What happens to workers displaced in their jobs has been thoroughly documented. During the wave of plant closings in the late 1970s and early 1980s, study after study showed that veteran workers remained unemployed for long periods of time and, when their unemployment compensation finally ran out, they wound up taking lower-paying jobs. Their pensions were curtailed and their health insurance expired. According to a 1977 study by Herbert Parnes and Randy King of four thousand men over age forty-five who had served their employers for at least five years, nearly 5 percent had been displaced by their employers. Furthermore, the study showed that between one-eighth and one-fifth remained unemployed for at least six months before finding another job in another industry.[2] Besides wiping out savings and disrupting their lives, these job losses set a third of these men on a much more unstable pattern of employment in the future. Other studies show that the earnings loss suffered by displaced workers in subsequent years went as high as 50 percent, with the greatest losses naturally occurring among unionized workers.

RETRAINING—A FALSE HOPE?

What are the chances that a thirty-five-to-forty-year-old man who has toiled in a factory job all his working life can be successfully retrained and find another job in another industry? This is really the crux of the issue and one that needs to be examined.

In the first place, there will be only a limited number of new jobs for which these workers will qualify in the goods-producing sector. It is too much to hope that a significant number of them will qualify for the more sophisticated technical jobs of the future—those that require an extensive educational background in computer programming and operating. There will be too many highly qualified workers ahead of them in the queue. For the small number who will return to the factory, it will be in

[2]"Middle-Aged Job Losers," *Industrial Gerontology*, Volume IV, No. 2, Spring 1977, cited in Barry Bluestone and Bennett Harrison, *Capital and Communities*, The Progressive Alliance, Washington, D.C., 1980.

positions that involve the tending and maintenance of machines that do most of the work automatically. Some optimists believe that there will be vast new employment opportunities in the production and maintenance of robots. But these production lines will be automated in equal fashion, and maintenance of these new machines is not as labor intensive as widely believed, certainly not enough to absorb all those supplanted from their jobs.

In the highly unionized area of the economy where technological displacement is occurring, many of the workers were and are blessed with unemployment benefits that will tide them over for a year and sometimes longer, even though the benefits do not totally match their former wages. The existence of these income supports in many cases serves as a barrier to training. The displaced worker initially clings to the hope that he may be called back to his former job when things get better, even if there is no hope in an objective sense. The generous supplemental employment benefits tend to lock workers into a pattern of waiting, and why not? "No matter where I work here in Detroit, I can't equal the pay I earned in the automobile industry," said one laid-off Chrysler worker. "I'm going to wait it out for as long as I can." When General Motors set up a retraining program for workers laid off at two closed California automobile plants, only 1522 of 5400 eligible workers signed up initially, because many thought they would be rehired when GM and Toyota began a joint venture building small cars at the plant.[3] The number grew when Toyota officials issued statements saying that union workers would not necessarily be called back.

Denial is initially part of the process which prevents displaced workers from rushing into retraining or reeducation. Closely associated with this is the workers' own personal concept of the economic and social trappings surrounding their jobs and their long identification with that concept. It is not easy for a veteran denizen of a steel mill or an automobile plant accustomed to the daily routine of blue-collar life to imagine himself working in an office setting, wearing a tie to work and going "out" to lunch. It is equally difficult to figure out what it would take in the way of training and education to land one of these new jobs.

The displaced worker is thrown into a state of bewilderment by these sweeping changes. The concept of work that has sus-

[3]*Time*, March 18, 1983.

tained his life has evaporated, and he cannot fathom how to duplicate his old income in any new endeavor. He is not attuned to the white-collar workplace. He certainly doesn't have the network of acquaintances that could bring him, by word of mouth, into a new job market. People who see retraining as the answer to the dislocated worker's problems are thoughtless or frivolous. Displacement is a life-shattering experience, cutting the worker loose from his former moorings and often leaving him no safe harbor. Some do make the adjustment, of course, but it is not as painless as some policy makers in the nation's capital might suggest.

THE WORM'S-EYE VIEW

The displaced worker understands a few fundamental facts about today's economy, the first and foremost being that brains have replaced brawn as the determining factor in landing a job. Former manufacturing workers as a general rule have not invested heavily in their education. They know full well that the catching up they face is immense and expensive. At the same time, they have families and homes to pay for. How can they put the time and money into education and retraining when overdue house and medical payments are piling up?

The option of self-financed retraining is just not real for a majority of displaced workers. Studies of the displaced worker problem show that retraining programs are of greatest benefit to younger, better educated workers who have obtained some level of financial security.[4] But here's the shocking part: Even among these workers, only about 15 percent participated in retraining programs, citing lack of financial assistance during the training period.

There is an even more fundamental reason why retraining and education are not realistic options for most displaced workers: a lack of jobs that results in a lack of training slots. A young person in college is undergoing a speculative form of training and education in hopes of finding a job after graduation. A veteran displaced worker is not as interested in speculative training and education. Many analysts assume that the dis-

[4]See Jeanne P. Gordus, Paul Jarley, and Louis A. Ferman, "Plant Closings and Economic Dislocation," W. E. Upjohn Institute for Employment Research, Kalamazoo, Michigan, 1981.

placed worker problem is essentially a mismatch problem—that a worker who loses a job in one industry can be rehired in another once he has been retrained and reeducated. This assumes that there are and will be enough good jobs to go around and that the problem is simply one of the right amount of "job engineering."

Once again, this represents faith in the old industrial model—that economic expansion will take up the slack in joblessness. If there were or were going to be enough good jobs to go around, then there would be many more training slots available in all industries to take up the slack in the job market. The fact that there aren't is all the evidence needed to prove that the real problem is a lack of higher-quality jobs. Industries and workers both will go after what they need and want. There is no reason for industries to provide training programs for the many dumb jobs that will be available, and young people are already arriving at the personnel manager's door with the skills needed for smart jobs. The lack of training slots indicates one thing clearly: Almost all industries have cut back on their work force and, even with economic recovery, job openings are fewer.

WHAT WORTH COMPANY TRAINING?

General Electric's new training center at its Erie, Pennsylvania, locomotive plant is a model facility, with modern classrooms, comfortable surroundings, the latest educational techniques, and the newest technology used in its manufacturing process. It is in GE's interest to have this center, because it enables the firm to provide hands-on training for the new kinds of jobs in the automated factory being built in the giant complex close by. Throughout the company, GE's commitment to retraining workers appears to be high, and this would be expected of a giant multinational company that deals with the leading edge of technology every day.

But GE's commitment to retraining does not extend beyond its projected needs. Although the firm believes that new technology will create more jobs than it destroys, it feels no duty to retrain all workers that might be displaced if, in the normal course of business, it finds it does not need them. As enlightened as GE's retraining policy is, demands of economic efficiency and profits require that it keep its payrolls as lean as possible.

The Office of Technology Assessment, the scientific arm of Congress, surveyed more than five hundred companies in the electric and electronics equipment, industrial machinery, and transportation equipment industries in 1982 and found that only 22 percent sponsored or conducted education and training for new technology. In addition, among the plants not offering education and training, only 18 percent planned to do so in the future. The OTA speculated that the low level of in-house training for workers might be because the companies have not automated to a great degree as yet. Actually, another factor is at work. *Many of the automated facilities reduce the complexity of some of the tasks, and workers can be taught how to perform them without lengthy training programs.* It's roughly equivalent to fast-food restaurant employees operating computerized cash registers. They punch buttons showing pictures of hamburgers or Cokes, and the machine adds the total automatically. The cashiers don't have to calculate the change either, just to punch in the amount the customer gives them.

But automation has also created a demand for some new high-skilled positions in manufacturing. The Office of Technology Assessment reported that technicians who are trained in the use of computer-aided drafting systems are now in great demand in some industries; other technical positions that require two years of education are also becoming available. While this is encouraging, the number of new positions pales by comparison with the number of jobs destroyed. Firms in dire need of technical workers are providing in-house training to obtain them. What happens to the rest of the displaced workers left without any hope of company-sponsored training? Will they be left out in the cold?

The history of government-funded training programs has not been encouraging. The experience of the Comprehensive Employment and Training Act (CETA) left a bad taste. This government-paid training was often performed without coordination with industry and without regard to jobs available or the needs of industry. Training allowances often amounted to nothing more than a handout. CETA, of course, was aimed at helping the disadvantaged worker who had never held a steady job, not the middle-aged veteran worker suddenly thrown out of a job by a wave of new technology.

CETA was eliminated because of these and other problems, but Congress in 1982 provided for a new program, small in relation to the problem, that would put public funds into the retraining of displaced workers. If the program were expanded massively to provide retraining for all displaced workers, the question would still remain: Where would they work? A job training program for workers displaced by foreign trade met with little success. Because there were few jobs at the end of the line, few workers took advantage of it. According to studies, this program had no appreciable effect on the length of time unemployed or on subsequent wages.[5]

As a practical matter, retraining displaced workers is a good use of resources only if there are jobs available at the end of the line. For this reason, privately financed training is better; publicly financed retraining should be conducted in conjunction with employers. Public retraining that raises unrealistic expectations should be avoided.

Many other programs have been suggested for displaced workers, such as job search and relocation assistance. Both these ideas suggest that the government ought to help subsidize the displaced worker whose job search skills have grown rusty or who feels trapped in an area of high unemployment and needs help in meeting moving expenses. The public funding of job search skills is probably not a bad idea, but out of fairness, it shouldn't be limited to displaced workers alone. In fact, new entrants into the labor force are in greater need of job search skills than a middle-aged worker who has been around and understands how employers think.

Relocation assistance is based upon the notion that all the new jobs are being created in newly developed areas outside of the industrial Northeast and Midwest. This was certainly true during 1979–1983, but it may not hold true forever. In fact, as the installation of computer technology becomes more pervasive, worker displacement will occur almost everywhere. Does it make sense for taxpayers to subsidize the relocation of workers into an area where other workers are being displaced, too? In our view, it does not. The 1982 economic downturn brought numerous stories of families who left their homes in the industrial Northeast and Midwest and headed for the Sunbelt in their kid-packed station wagons in search of work. These modern-day

---

[5]George Neumann, "Labor Market Consequences of Trade Displacement," Institute for Policy Research and Evaluation, Pennsylvania State University, 1978.

Grapes of Wrath stories often wound up with an unhappy ending. Comparable jobs in the South had dried up, too.

DISPLACING THE LAND OF OPPORTUNITY

Many people tend to treat widespread worker displacement as an economic problem and nothing more. But displacing those comprising one of the most stable parts of the population from their jobs and jeopardizing their economic security have social and psychological implications far beyond the ability of economics to measure. It is highly destructive of the glue that holds American society together. It increases alienation up and down the line—alienation from our political and economic systems. It destroys confidence placed in employers and in the system of preparing young people for their careers. Over time, it could cause a more divided country and increase the tendency toward radical solutions and radical politics.

Studies of the psychological effects of unemployment suggest that it has a corrosive effect on the individual's self-esteem and health. Dr. M. Harvey Brenner, associate professor of health services administration at Johns Hopkins University, in a series of studies for the Joint Economic Committee of Congress, showed that there is a strong statistical link between unemployment and suicide, mental hospital admissions, prison admissions, and various ailments. Although initially highly controversial, Brenner's findings are receiving wider acceptance. Other research into the impact of unemployment turns up evidence that it destroys an individual's concept of his social and economic roles in society and increases political alienation, especially if the joblessness and financial strain persist. Louis A. Ferman, professor of social work at the University of Michigan's Wayne State campus, and John Gardner, economics instructor at Dartmouth College, wrote in a 1979 paper:

> First, career instability (successive and sudden job changes) can jeopardize predictable day-to-day living by creating constant anxiety about job tenure, income, and the meeting of essential demands. Second, unstable careers can make for unstable relationships with family and friends. The worker's influence in the family can decline if family members are faced with constant shifts in expectations about the worker's ability

to provide for daily needs. Finally, disruptive and frequent shifts in employment status can have a marked effect on the worker's self-esteem and self-image, since he questions more and more his capacity to control future events and his own sense of worth.[6]

In virtually all the research, job displacement is associated with negative feelings about one's self-worth, resentment toward and alienation from the economic and political system, and pessimism about the future. While the impact of displacement on an individual's life seems clear, little research has been done on how it affects the outlook of others about the world of work. But it seems clear that the threat of displacement itself will bring on many of these same negative feelings in workers who sense the same kind of vulnerability as those displaced. The fact that many union members voted to give up wage and fringe benefit gains is a sign that they, too, are lowering their expectations about the ability of the U.S. economic system to deliver. Aspiring workers who are sons and daughters or close acquaintances of displaced workers also pick up these negative feelings. And one cannot visit a one-industry, depressed town for long without deeply sensing the pervasive hopelessness and pessimism. It is in the stores, the schools, the churches, and the homes.

Americans more easily dismiss the problems of youthful workers and even of older workers nearing retirement. But widespread joblessness among workers in the prime of life, at a time when their earnings are supposed to be at a maximum and their economic lives the most secure, is no wave-of-the-hand matter. Their difficulties affect expectations across the board about the promises and capabilities of the American economy. The message is that no one is safe.

DOWNWARD MOBILITY

The displaced manufacturing worker who has several years of job experience is not necessarily at the bottom of the job queue.

[6]"Economic Deprivation, Social Mobility and Mental Health," paper presented June 1978, Conference on Mental Health and the Economy, Hunt Valley, Maryland, and published by W. E. Upjohn Institute for Employment Research, Kalamazoo, Michigan, December 1979.

Displaced workers are the perfect candidates for dumb jobs. When all the benefits expire and displaced workers finally take a lower-paying job, as many have, the likelihood is that they will displace others with lesser experience or will limit the opportunities for new workers looking for entry-level jobs. So a displacement in one industry can cause displacement on down the line, in ways that are not immediately evident. In addition, when a company establishes training slots, it is more likely to offer them to its own displaced workers, a process that also denies training positions to new job entrants. Thus the whole process of widespread displacement ripples throughout the work force, limiting work opportunities everywhere.

Since its first colonists struggled onto its shores, America has been known as a land of upward mobility. This sociological phenomenon was made possible because of tremendous job horizons and perpetually rising real income. Blue-collar workers have had a taste of upward mobility, too, seeing their standard of living and economic security rise behind a strong economy. Their children have enjoyed unparalleled opportunities, including the ability to move from the blue-collar to the white-collar world, because economic underpinnings provided by their parents have enabled them to get a college education. This ability of many children of blue-collar Americans to strike out on their own and escape any shackles of their family's class because they have gained solid educational credentials has been one of the distinguishing features of the U.S. society. The tragedy of job displacement is that it irreparably disrupts this whole process, because more of family savings has to go for survival and less for expensive college educations.

Even if the displaced worker finds a new job, the odds are that it will be a lower-paying dumb job that will not come anywhere close to replacing his or her former income. This is downward mobility at its most basic level. What goes through a steelworker's head when he is suddenly put to work stacking shelves in a grocery store is probably not positive.

The well-known social scientists Bruno Bettelheim and M. Janowitz have conducted research into the mental health of what they call "skidders," those who are downwardly mobile, and have come up with some alarming findings. One early study probed the attitudes of World War II veterans who had expected to be returned to their old jobs but found they had been bumped. It was discovered that this group generally was more hostile toward minority groups and had more interpersonal problems in everyday social relationships.[7] Another study tracked the job changes and attitudes of former Packard Company employees over a twenty-seven-month period after their job displacement. It was found that those who had been reemployed at a lower wage tended to have strong feelings of political alienation and individual isolation. Those who underwent more than one status change were found to have experienced the greatest alienation and the lowest social participation with relatives, friends, and co-workers.[8]

Many of these studies were performed at a time when upward mobility was a fact of life for the overwhelming majority of workers. Widespread displacement had not been foreseen, so to lose a job or take a lower-paying one perhaps was a greater blow to the individual than it is when more workers are in the same boat. The 1979–82 recessionary period resulted in downward mobility for several million workers, and the job trends suggest that the process of downward mobility is going to affect millions more for years to come. Although misery may be easier to accept when there's plenty of company, the previous studies suggest that widespread displacement and downward mobility will still hand the nation a social problem it can ill afford: an alienated class of veteran workers who have seen their dream go sour and who are faced with enormous adjustment problems—economic, social, and mental.

THE DEMANDS OF DEPRIVATION

The Great Depression brought despair and misery to many lives, but it did not bring revolution, despite some unsettling political moments in the midst of it. Many theories have been advanced as to why revolutionary conditions did not materialize. The most appealing one is that the United States responded to the demands of deprivation in a way that brought hope to millions. The New Deal did not solve all problems, but it did bring new income props to otherwise desperate people who might have starved without them. In the succeeding half cen-

[7]Bruno Bettelheim and M. Janowitz, *Dynamics of Prejudice*, New York: Harper, 1950.

[8]M. Aiken, L. A. Ferman, and H. L. Sheppard, *Economic Failure, Alienation and Extremism*, Ann Arbor: University of Michigan Press, 1968.

tury, welfare and other public assistance programs have grown dramatically with the political system's response to each newly perceived deprivation.

Economic deprivation on a wide scale in our society will always create a public "solution." The solution may not be perfect and may, in fact, be counterproductive, but deprivation will always prompt demands for a new "solution" if the previous one has failed to relieve the deprivation enough to reduce resultant political pressures. This is especially true in an age when political leaders have learned how to mobilize the deprived into political action. A refusal to accept continued deprivation was the driving force behind the effort by some black political leaders to register more poor blacks so that a black candidate could run for the presidency.

Worker displacement is being widely treated as a temporary "adjustment" problem by many political leaders and many economists. The belief is that it came about because many of the nation's basic smokestack industries are going through a fundamental restructuring that will settle down within a few years. These optimists hope that the displaced workers can be absorbed gradually into the services sector of the economy. After this one-time "adjustment" is over, the belief goes, the displaced worker problem will go away. The nation's current strategy for dealing with the displaced worker problem would be fine if this perspective were true. But it is not. Rather than dealing with a temporary problem, the nation is now entering an era in which worker displacement is going to be a long-term phenomenon in industry after industry, from the assembly line to the office. Deprivation—or the fear of it—is going to be felt by almost every family.

Studies indicate that worker displacement can affect physical and mental health and arouse feelings of alienation from the political system and friends. At the very least, the problem will affect the nation's health budget enormously each year; to pretend that the costs of these health problems can be borne privately is unrealistic. Any discussion of the displaced worker problem should take into account the potential costs that taxpayers will have to bear if the fundamental reason for the increased health problem—lack of jobs—is not addressed. If displaced workers lose their health insurance, then their ailments will have to be paid for by Medicaid, a program for which costs have already accelerated in recent years. This is not even to mention the other public costs that arise because of widespread unemployment—welfare, food stamps, social services. Displacement will strain public social budgets like never before.

But what should make politicians take note is the research into alienaton. Granted, the research appears to be somewhat nonspecific and perhaps easy to dismiss, especially during the early stages of the process of widespread displacement. Nevertheless, such shortcomings really do not invalidate the basic findings that unemployed workers who undergo a basic change in their expectations develop a bitterness toward the system. No one can predict how this bitterness will manifest itself if allowed to fester over a long period of time, especially among blue-collar workers who have been forced to accept lower pay and push aside the dreams they had for their children.

From the standpoint of possible solutions, displaced middle-aged workers should not be separated from workers of all ages who will be experiencing the bitter fruits of technological unemployment and fewer job opportunities in the future. But the plight of middle-aged workers, because there are so many of them and because the stability of society may be at stake, puts even more emphasis on the demands that grow out of deprivation. The solution is more jobs and more leisure, which will come about only with an enlarged public sector and shorter working hours. (We'll cover this in a later chapter.) The demands resulting from deprivation will drive the United States toward this solution, even though there will be a number of side tracks along the way as the political system experiments in an incremental fashion with various proposals. But, in time, we will get there—and the sooner the better.

8

Education for the Future of Work

Glimpses of a failing educational system:

- Kevin Ross, the not-at-all-fictitious star basketball player at Creighton University, found his reading skills abysmally deficient when he graduated from college. Ross went back to high school at the age of twenty-three to learn what he had missed.

- In Baltimore, John, a welder, age twenty-eight, a high school graduate, realized that he would never be recalled by General Motors and went to enroll in a computer programming course. But he flunked the entrance exam because he had never learned basic mathematical reasoning. He enrolled in a remedial community college course in elementary algebra.

Most of the 150 employers Dr. Schwartz surveyed in Milwaukee, the machine tool capital of America, said that the high school graduates they interview for jobs can't add or subtract, let alone read a blueprint. Many other employers the authors have interviewed echo this lament, as do reports for various education commissions and committees. One survey recently found that more than one-third of the nation's business corporations provide basic high school education for their employees. A survey of companies by the Center for Public Resources of New York showed that firms found their newly educated workers to be deficient in such grade school math skills as the ability to place a decimal point or read a fraction.

Enrollment in college remedial reading, writing, and math programs jumped by 72 percent between 1975 and 1980, and some educators estimate that as much as one-third of the faculty time devoted to college freshmen is taken up by remedial work.

Why so much remedial education in college and on the job? Because kids are not staying in school, and because those that are staying in school are not learning.

According to the National Center for Educational Statistics, only three-fourths of all eighteen-year-olds in the United States are high school graduates. And according to a recent Ford Foundation report, more than half of the population of the states of Kentucky, South Carolina, North Carolina, Arkansas, Georgia, Mississippi, Alabama, Tennessee, and West Virginia had not completed high school.

Only one-third of the nation's high schools require more than a year of mathematics, and only 50 percent of high school graduates take math or science after the tenth grade.

All these findings—and there are reams of statistics like them—are alarming, but they demonstrate one fact: America's educational system is preparing a large proportion of its young people to be excess baggage in the dumb-job market of the future. This is clearly not the intent of our schools, even though it is clearly the outcome.

And the results will be disastrous if something isn't done about American education soon. One way to assure that the United States loses its economic lead and falls irrevocably behind in the worldwide technological race is to continue to miseducate our young people. One way to lock in future failure is to lock out innovation and change in the education system, which needs an overhaul from nursery school to graduate school. Unfortunately, there is as much wrong as right with the recent attention that education has received—attention that may well prove to be shortsighted and misdirected.

SCHOOLS OF THE PAST—NEEDS OF THE FUTURE

Until a generation ago, the American school system served us fairly well. America was an industrial power, and brawn often fetched higher wages than brains on the job market. You could join the ranks of the prosperous middle class via a blue-collar job in the automobile industry or the steel industry, or as a printer or machinist. These jobs paid well and offered long-term security. They demanded at most a high school diploma, and no one cared much what kind of knowledge was guaranteed by the diploma. The promise of material security was so strong that in many steel towns, it was said, boys went to their high school graduation with a lunch box in hand, so they could join the next shift at the mill at the earliest possible moment.

No such security awaits today's graduates in Aliquippa, Pennsylvania—a steel town with unemployment above 50 percent—and other heavy-industry cities like it. Nor is it likely that we will ever again see the sure line of advancement to high-paying jobs based on muscles and hands-on experience. The jobs that literally made the blue-collar middle class will drift away slowly because of automation, and no other industry will be able to replace the lost opportunities for the minimally educated population. All students who seek any choice of work and career will have to have an education that prepares them for the jobs that will exist.

One-fourth of the population aged twenty to twenty-four lacks a high school diploma. Extrapolate this percentage to 1990, when there will be seventeen million labor force entrants aged twenty to twenty-four. If one-fourth of them also lacks a high school education, there will be over four million people surely consigned to dumb jobs, with no hope of escaping into a world of job choice or career mobility. They will be at the bottom of the heap of dumb-job seekers.

In an information- and knowledge-based economy, education is the primary industry, supporting all other industries. Beyond that, it is the key to national economic survival, because innovation and discovery are the only activities in which a rich nation can outperform poorer nations. Thus neither educators nor parents nor students can afford to be sanguine about the quality of America's educational system.

BASIC LITERACY

One of the first challenges of American education will be to deal with the basic literacy problem. Some experts estimate that one-fifth of the population is functionally illiterate—unable to read a job application, fill out the forms needed to get public assistance, or even follow instructions for assembling a simple toy. In addition, a million or more legal and illegal immigrants, many of whom are marginally literate or illiterate, are joining the work force every year. By 1990, 90 percent of America's population growth will come through immigration, because of low U.S. birthrates.

Whatever their origins, the functionally illiterate face a dismal future, and the rest of society will have to cope with the fallout. Even the semiskilled jobs, such as assembling integrated circuits, require ability to follow written diagrams and instructions. The number of private-sector jobs as messengers, delivery boys, janitors and cleanup personnel, miners, loggers, and agricultural workers available to the functionally illiterate is limited. Employers will always prefer to hire someone who can read and write, and one thing is sure about factory work: It will no longer be the haven of the marginally literate. With the elimination of many dumb factory jobs through world competition and automation, and with the upgrading of other jobs, factory work is going to go to workers with solid basic skills in reading, reasoning, and communication. So dumping millions more entry-level workers without high school graduate skills onto a base of poorly educated people will ensure a huge future unemployment problem, unless the nation decides to create public service jobs for the uneducated. A far cheaper decision would be to wipe out functional illiteracy, which is a drag on the nation's economic improvement.

SMART JOBS: CAN THE COMPUTER DO IT ALL?

Many studies have documented the failure of American education, but the solutions are more elusive. Two major questions loom: What should students do to prepare themselves for the work force of the future, and what should schools at all levels do to improve their programs? The questions are closely related, but the answers are much more complex than it would at first appear.

The debate is alive with cliché solutions. Here's one: computer literacy. This is the favorite catchphrase of the times, heard at cocktail parties, on television talk shows, and in congressional testimony. Those who advocate it vigorously often aren't sure what it means. Computer literacy is seen as the salvation of the economy and the ticket to higher-paying jobs. But, as with any phrase, this one is just a simplistic way to describe the process of getting a computer to work for you. As anyone with experience in computers will tell you, there are many levels of computer competency. You cannot compare the expertise of a professional programmer with that of someone who uses a computer strictly for word processing; the programmer is far ahead. That difference really defines the question for a student in the information economy: How computer literate does one have to be to obtain a smart job? It could be argued that a supermarket clerk is computer literate, as he or she uses an electronic scanner at the checkout stand. In many automated factories, the computer controls are not all that sophisticated; they can be taught in only a few weeks or months of hands-on instruction. Workers so trained are computer literate in only a limited sense.

Five years from now, anyone who is not computer literate in even this limited sense won't have much of a chance of finding a satisfying and stimulating job in an office, factory, or warehouse. The office will be managed by a complex electronics and telecommunications system in which all the mechanical tasks and all the repetitive, routine tasks are programmable. For jobs in support positions, as opposed to professional jobs, people will have to know how to choose the correct computer program for their needs, even if they do not know how to program. Managers and professionals will have to know how to write or adapt simple programs for specific purposes.

But that still does not answer the basic question of how computer literate one has to be to obtain the best jobs. Computer programmers and engineers will be in great demand in the new world of work, but not everyone can sign up for these two occupations. Some people do not have the kinds of skills required, and not that many programmers and engineers will be needed. In fact, most workers will be involved in some other kind of endeavor. But in these other fields, the computer will be pervasive. To be computer literate means to know how to use the computer most efficiently in your field. Anyone who operates a computer knows the phrase "garbage in, garbage out." A computer's enormous computing power relies exclusively on the knowledge and creativity of the user.

Knowledge of how a computer operates does not guarantee a student a smart job, but it will help. From the earliest possible moment, a wise student should combine at least one course per year in computer instruction with other courses. It would be wise to learn programming, even if you do not want to be a programmer. We have seen large companies virtually paralyzed when they bought a new computer system, because their management included no one who could intelligently question obvious weaknesses in the software. A well-educated person who expects to be in a responsible position in the future cannot be the unwitting slave of the computer technicians. The technicians need not dominate every endeavor, though this will happen if students do not foresee the demands of a knowledge-based economy.

This means that computer courses and programming instruction will only be part of the ticket to a smart job. The computer is only a tool. Every smart-job seeker will still need a field or fields of expertise. Then, combining that expertise with the ability to use and apply electronic capabilities, those who are geared to the real work of the future will be able to come up with all kinds of new opportunities. Rather than merely responding to want ads, they will be able to create jobs for themselves or even to go into business for themselves.

This is already happening. Based on the miraculous fast-growing technology of the personal computer, there is flowering a network of specialists in programming for personal computers—specialists who combine substantive knowledge, in fields like accounting or business finance, with programming knowledge. A decade ago no college or high school counselor could have advised a student to prepare for this exciting career opportunity, but computer scientists and even hobbyists who saw the coming boom of the personal computer a few years ago have positioned themselves for rewarding and often highly lucrative careers. Opportunities will abound to combine educational expertise, scientific expertise, health care expertise, and professional expertise of all kinds with programming for the personal computer, which no successful smart-job holder will be without by the end of this decade.

THE RENAISSANCE STUDENT

Sarah de Lone is a Yale undergraduate who is majoring in economics and electrical engineering. Ms. de Lone is positioning herself for a smart job when she graduates in 1987. She is the kind of person who may well become a "renaissance worker" with the kind of mixed education needed to succeed in the work revolution.

You might think of the renaissance student as one who builds the greatest possible amount of flexibility into his or her curriculum, not starting in college but starting in elementary school. This doesn't mean a scatter-gun approach to course taking, or being the dilettante who knows a meaningless little bit about a lot of subjects. To the contrary, it means planning a curriculum more carefully, integrating disciplines in which one has talents but also specializing in two or more substantive areas. It means sharpening the ability to relate these areas, as well as the ability to communicate the knowledge that one has.

If we were to select one word that holds the key to job security, it is *synergism*. By mastering two or more skills that, combined, can accomplish what neither can alone, the renaissance student will be in a position to get a job, to move to another job if the first is destroyed by technology or changing economic conditions, and even to invent his or her own job.

Synergism is also the key to keeping computers and robots a tool, not a master. Some people looking at the reality of the technological future will, like the Luddites who resisted the introduction of weaving machines in the nineteenth century, try to resist modern technology to protect their futures. But this would only postpone the inevitable and make eventual adjustment harder. Embracing the technology will throw open the opportunities, and one thing is certain: Computers cannot yet do what a human being with creative energy and adaptive skills can do, which is to think of something that has not yet been invented or programmed. Computers are still the artificial, not the original, intelligence systems.

Honing the Skills of the Future

But synergistic skills don't just emerge; they are nurtured. The ability to analyze, to think "beyond the field" being examined at any one time, and to articulate are all part of the development of synergistic skills.

What does the student do to enter this synergistic arena? He or she does not have to devote years to science and math, as some educators are now recommending for just about any competent student. But some math and science beyond the elementary level ought to be part of the broad education that prepares one for the substantive areas that will be the focus of so many future jobs.

Important as math and science are, they are not more important than logic, problem solving, and an understanding of how organizations, including society itself, function. The renaissance worker will be prepared to adapt to quickly changing events, including the fast changes that can occur in the workplace or the system by which work is organized. The work revolution will not eliminate friction between groups and individuals, so the adaptable worker will have to know how to recognize friction and handle it.

Education for Better Leisure

Tomorrow's workers might spend as much time off the job as on it. That is because there is likely to be too little work to employ everyone forty hours a week. So when we think of what we want from our education system, we have to think about education for off-the-job time as well as education for work.

People will need a broad education just to be able to enjoy extra leisure. They will have more time to contemplate, to read, to study. So they will need to have study skills. Beyond that, they will be regaled with information from many different sources about what they ought to do, so they need to learn in school how to sort out all the information. A recent national assessment of education showed a declining ability of high school students to understand the hidden purpose behind what they are reading. This is ominous indeed, because it suggests that we are educating people who can read but not think.

FACTS, INFORMATION, AND KNOWLEDGE

The facts demonstrate that America's educational system needs an overhaul to prepare students for the new world of technology in the job market. The nation's school system is tradition-bound, beset with many budgetary problems, and decentralized. Is it starry-eyed to believe that, as a practical matter, much can be changed in a short period of time? The hopeful signs include a new introspection that was not present only a few years ago. And while educators may not totally perceive it, the means are becoming available to correct many of the shortcomings that now permeate the nation's schools. Just as it is revolutionizing the work force, the computer can also revolutionize education. Here are some examples:

Many reasons can be dredged up to show why our school system is failing our people and our economy, but no shortcoming has been greater than the failure in the classroom to distinguish between facts, information, and knowledge. The work revolution will demand that the educational system sharpen the distinctions between these three and put the emphasis where it belongs.

Almost from the beginning, the American educational system has been obsessed with facts, from important dates in history to the chief exports of nations. There are many statistical facts and there are also events, such as the fact that Franklin Delano Roosevelt was the only U.S. president to be elected to four terms. School children have traditionally been bombarded with facts. With varying degrees of emphasis, they are exhorted to learn dates, quantities, phrases, and slogans.

Facts are an important crutch for U.S. teachers, who have used them almost exclusively to judge the performance of students. The teaching of facts consumes an enormous amount of time in our classrooms and contributes to what most everyone agrees is the most wasteful aspect of American education—the endless repetition. Yet in the electronic society, facts can be stored and retrieved in a few seconds. Each child in school will be able to own a cheap computer, in which all facts about a particular subject can be stored for retrieval in an instant.

Information is distinguished from facts in that it includes uncertainties. Information may depend on facts, but it also depends on probabilities and possibilities. Information includes estimates. It is when we get into the information realm that we really begin to think—gathering facts and memorizing them is a mechanical task, while gathering information is an analytic task.

But knowledge goes a step beyond information. A pocket thesaurus helps provide the distinctions. The synonyms for *information* include *communication, communiqué, bulletin,* and *dispatch.* There is a strong element of transmission associated with information. It is an active concept with a physical component. The synonyms for *knowledge* include *cognizance, comprehension, enlightenment,* and *information. Comprehension* is the key word. Knowledge is experienced. Whether one has it depends only in part on the transmission of information. It depends on the creativity of the person using the information and on his or her ability to integrate new facts and estimates into the knowledge already retained.

When we talk about a knowledge-based society, we are setting a goal for ourselves much bigger than the pop expression implies. Now, we have an information society, not a knowledge society. We have no standards for every citizen learning to comprehend, be enlightened, or understand what is going on in the physical, political, and social worlds.

Ezra Pound once said that "real education must ultimately be limited to men who insist on knowing; the rest is mere sheepherding." Our present educational system is set up to prepare intellectual shepherds, nothing else, with the emphasis on the rote learning of facts. This is one of the prime reasons for so many failures. We are in great danger of compounding that problem because of the big new push to educate everyone for technical skills. Technical skills require the learning of facts and the absorption of information, but they do not require the evaluation of information or exercise of judgment. Not that more technical education is bad, but an overemphasis on it will inhibit the United States in its effort to develop an educational system that will properly train students for the work revolution. A knowledge economy demands analytic skills, and analytic skills must be taught to students in elementary and high schools before they go on to higher education.

Suppose a high school teacher assigns an essay on World War I. The student will need facts—when did the fighting begin, which were the critical battles, who was in charge, and so forth. Obviously, there are hundreds of thousands of facts the student can draw upon. But why is he studying World War I at all? Is it not to learn why nations go to war, under what circumstances war is avoidable, and how the technology of warfare has changed these circumstances? If the student's understanding of what happened in World War I is to be of any use to him as an adult thinking about the merits of a future war, he will need not just facts, but information. What objectives did the leaders of each country pursue? Did the armies have enough equipment to fight a long war?

In the past, few high school teachers could know enough about all the subjects to teach at such an analytic level. This was a matter left to the colleges, where professors specialize in narrow fields and can pursue the matter in depth. But the computer can change that. The computer's ability to store and retrieve information speedily will make possible the development of educational information systems that would, for example, summarize the major schools of thought on the origins and causes of World War I. The works of scholars like Barbara Tuchman could be made known to the student in one or two paragraphs. The student may not be able to reach an informed judgment on which interpretation is accurate—a knowledge process—but a valuable lesson will have been learned: that there are many different interpretations.

Analyzing the advantages of computers in education, David W. Bray, dean of Clarkson College's Educational Computing Center, said they "can aid the student in obtaining more insight into scientific principles that are being studied. Once a student has obtained a solution to a problem that has been calculated by a computer, there is very little effort involved in obtaining more solutions to the same problem with different input parameters. The ability to obtain many solutions to a problem within a matter of a few minutes can provide the student with intuition about the subject matter that is generally not possible without a computer."

At the Stevens Institute of Technology in Hoboken, New Jersey, educators found that they could more easily take students beyond rote calculations into theory and abstract concepts. As a result, course offerings were strengthened. Some colleges are finding that they can bridge the chasm between facts and information and a higher level of knowledge with the computer. But elementary and high schools, and many state-supported universities and colleges, are still a long way from putting computers in the hands of every student so that this is possible across the board.

COMPETING AGAINST COMPETENCE

The U.S. educational system uses a rather primitive method to judge how well schools are doing their job: comparison. National norms are generally used to compare the effectiveness and outcomes of education. Standardized tests compare students to one another. Classroom tests are merely an extension of this system of comparative education.

A far better system would be what has become known as

"competency-based learning." This tongue-twisting phrase means that at every level of education, each person is allowed to proceed at his or her own pace. Because each person is different in skills and talents, competency in a subject is not always achieved in the same chronological order. Chicago's public schools tried a form of competency learning, and test scores among sixth graders in some of the city's poorest areas jumped a full grade level.

Though ideal, competency-based learning has always been difficult because it is costly and demanding. In the first place, the curriculum must be based on measured competencies. It is a lot easier to give a test than to specify and measure the desired outcomes of the learning process. In the second place, it is extremely difficult to administer such a program. If Mary gets 75 on her arithmetic test, she can move on with her class to the next lesson, even if she cannot multiply by 12. But in a competency system, Mary has to keep practicing until she knows how to multiply by 12. For teachers to keep track of each student's competency, testing and retesting every pupil is generally too time-consuming and prohibitively costly. In addition, some teachers do not wish to deal with students on an individual basis because it requires constantly shifting gears to deal with discrete bits of each child's work program.

Almost all the negative elements of using competency teaching and learning can be eliminated by computers. Computers can evaluate the outcomes of teaching by administering self-tests to students, who can take them and score them without help from the teacher. All the teacher need do is record the results. The student can take many such tests in a short time to establish the competencies needed in each subject. The computer can even design a work program for each student in each subject area based on an initial screening of the student's competencies and a ranking of those abilities. Moreover, the computer can group students by their levels of competency in each subject, helping the teacher know exactly what to teach. With a few key strokes, a teacher can plan lessons for any time period, revise lesson priorities, and keep track of who knows what.

The revolution in the work of teachers is only beginning now, and many teachers remained frightened of it. But as the electronic age matures, more and more school boards will experiment with this type of teaching.

This will raise a basic question: Who should decide what levels of competence are necessary to finish a certain level of education? Home rule for public school is a cherished tradition in this country, but some good arguments can be made that the U.S. needs minimum national educational standards. According to the National Science Foundation, American youngsters fall far behind the Soviets, Germans, and Japanese in science and mathematics. In the Soviet Union, sixth and seventh graders learn algebra and geometry and eighth graders take trigonometry. In the United States, many high schools do not offer trigonometry at all and algebra is not generally taught until the eighth or ninth grade. In Japan, a quarter of the time spent in junior high school is devoted to math and science, and a third of all students take four math and three science courses. But in the United States, in many schools, students in academic programs proceed only as far as elementary algebra and get by without any "hard science" at all.

The reason for teaching more advanced courses in these subjects is not to equip every citizen with skills that might never be used, but to educate a cadre of workers who can function well in a technological society. In the information-knowledge economy, where services relying on brain power will rule, the more new ways we can think of doing what has always been done in the past and the more new services we can think of providing, the better off we will be economically. This requires a large pool of highly educated scientists and technicians. To create such a pool, the nation has to start developing them young.

The best way to bring about this goal is to set minimum competency standards for every high school graduate. Educators should get together to draft the basic competencies for math, science, social studies, and English. Once adopted, these standards probably should not be mandatory at first, because the tendency would be to lower them to the lowest common denominator. They should be advisory and, if adopted by the nation's educational establishment, would go a long way to giving the public the information it needs to monitor school performance. Minimum educational standards could close some of the gaps between the U.S. educational system and those of overseas competitors. In a highly decentralized educational system, the sense of national urgency associated with this issue will be lost, and many different standards, less rigorous than needed, will flourish.

EDUCATING THE EDUCATORS

"I have no more patients with this disorderly class," a teacher recently wrote on the blackboard. The fact that spelling deficiencies among teachers abound is no secret to students and parents and many educational professionals. But these deficiencies are symptomatic of a broader problem. Today's teachers lack the training and, in some cases, the basic knowledge to prepare children for a rapidly changing, technological society. There is a nationwide shortage of qualified teachers in science and math. Applicants commonly fail the math and science questions on the National Teacher Examinations prepared by the Educational Testing Service. Teachers and aspiring teachers score poorly on general competence, too. In California, one-third of the nearly seven thousand prospective teachers flunked a minimum competency test.

Teachers display shortcomings in social studies as well. A high school teacher in one class recently described a recession as an event "caused by unemployment." Another teacher explained the stock market as a "place where people buy and sell shares of corporations in the hopes of making profit," without mentioning what happens to the proceeds of the stock sales and their real purpose.

The crisis in teacher preparation is long-standing, but now it is more crucial that it be solved, because inadequately trained teachers are inflicting profound damage upon the economy. Despite that need, the nation is amazingly long-suffering, unwilling to take the steps that will turn the situation around. The United States has a teaching staff of last resort. Teachers are in the lowest quartile of their class in college and university. Education majors ranked twenty-sixth in scores on Scholastic Aptitude Tests for 1982. College-bound seniors preparing to be teachers scored the lowest on SAT tests. Education students widely report that their classes and their professors are too easy. Education departments in colleges and universities often are seen as backwaters.

America is getting what it is paying for. The average starting salary in 1983 for teachers was $12,800, about the same as that for a clerical worker with a high school education. Society has always expected teachers to be so dedicated to their profession that money could not entice them away. The shortsightedness of that view is highlighted by the fact that the U.S. shortage of math and science teachers is caused by the fact that qualified individuals can fetch higher salaries in private industry. Maximum salaries for teachers with the highest rewardable level of education in the states paying the highest salaries range from $33,000 to $38,000. These salaries are more than twice the national average.

The first step is to inject some flexibility into the teacher reward system. Currently, most teachers are paid for longevity and not much else. In every other occupation, there is merit pay for a job well done. Excellent teachers should be paid more than bad or even fair teachers. Excellent teachers should also be given the chance to share their excellence with other than their own small classes—with other teachers and teachers of teachers. But the unions are resistant because they are afraid that these rewards will undermine the status of ordinary teachers and eventually hit the unions in the pocketbook because boards of education will prefer to hold general pay down in order to increase merit pay. The argument often advanced in opposition—that no fair system can be devised for evaluating teachers for merit pay—is specious. This problem can be worked out quickly.

It won't be enough to make teaching more financially attractive unless national standards for teachers are adopted. Only six states now use the National Training Examinations to test minimum competence. According to the American Association of Colleges for Teaching Education, only half the states plan this minimum-ability screening, despite the fact that states that do use it have a powerful tool both for selecting and training teachers, because the tests show where the trainees are most deficient.

The irony of this situation is that the nation's education colleges are training teachers for jobs that pay dumb-job wages, so that they can teach students to go out and qualify for smart jobs.

TEACHING AND THE WORK REVOLUTION

Many states currently reward teachers who take additional courses with higher salaries, but they do not necessarily ensure that the courses taken have improved the teacher's competence. Competence testing should become more pervasive in the whole process of training and retraining and evaluation. Before getting past the first year as an education major, a prospective student should be able to demonstrate certain basic skills required in teaching (including people skills) or wash out. In addition, educational institutions should adapt more of an analytic approach to learning, rather than the rote system of "instruction." If this happened, education colleges would have to change their curricula and screen applicants for different skills than in the past.

Ironically enough, the work revolution itself will provide some hope for the teaching profession. Many qualified young people, discouraged by the prospect of shrinking work opportunities, will find an incentive to go into education. Computer technology will give schools a wider choice over whom they employ. Teacher training institutions will be more selective and more rigorous in their demands. It will be possible to improve the quality of the teaching profession over a fifteen-year period. Teaching will probably be more attractive because the work revolution will eliminate some competing job opportunities, reduce the skill levels in others, and put a downward pressure on wages and salaries across the board.

It is mandatory that computers be worked into the teacher training curriculum as soon as possible, so that teachers can take maximum advantage of computers introduced into the classroom. But teachers will not only have to be taught how to use computers, they will have to get over the fear of computers. Many teachers believe the computer will replace them, when in actuality it will free them from rote and drill. But, freed from rote and drill, many teachers will feel helpless, because that is their stock in trade. They will need group sessions, counseling, and retraining, just as blue-collar workers do when their jobs have been destroyed.

THE CLASSROOM COMPUTER

At Clarkson College in Potsdam, New York, Union College in Lincoln, Missouri, Drexel University in Philadelphia, and Stevens Institute of Technology in Hoboken, New Jersey, incoming students will be required to have computers in their rooms. Now that the cost of the personal computer has come down dramatically, it is going to be the most pervasive tool in higher education in a matter of two to three years. Preliminary reports on the performance of students using computers are astounding. Students who use them tested 15 to 25 percent higher than students without such equipment and used one-third less study time.

But the college level and the elementary and secondary levels are different. Even though a study by the Educational Testing Service shows that a computer drill will increase the performance of poor elementary school children by 15 to 40 percent over those who do not have such a drill, school boards are still not rushing out to buy computers, primarily because of a lack of funds. But the realities are harsh. Schools without computers in 1985 will be as useful as schools without textbooks in 1895.

Because the budget problem is real, schools will have to come up with creative suggestions for getting computers installed in the classroom. One way would be to buy computers and hire computer aids, just like those now present in colleges teaching computer science, to help students use them. Teachers would be involved in selecting the educational programs they want the children to use, but they would not have to learn computer operation or programming. This approach could greatly improve both the productivity of teachers and the quality of their teaching experience. Over time, fewer teachers would be needed to teach the same number of students. But teachers currently employed would not be in danger of being forced out. In the future, as teachers develop computer literacy, the ratio of teachers to students might even increase. The quality of education would be greatly enhanced because children would spend more time on their own or in small groups with computers, supervised only by a teacher's aide or computer aide, freeing the teacher for more discussion and creative work.

Teachers will not be asked to work harder. They will be given the chance to work better, to have a more interesting daily routine, to expand their own horizons and gain much greater reward from their work. Teaching is probably the one single occupation in which the quality of work will increase by 100 percent because of technological change.

THE FORK OF THE ROAD

The U.S. system of education confronts an important crossroads in the next few years. Will it take the road of sharply stepped-up technical training, or will it go the route of knowledge-directed education? Nothing is assured. As many communities face the pinch of the work revolution and see many jobs disappear, they may come to the conclusion that the answer lies in pumping money into technical education to the exclusion of most everything else. This would be a mistake, but mistakes have been made before.

While educators face the enormous challenge of how to obtain computers for their classrooms, school boards across the nation will be facing decisions of an entirely different nature. The major political question will be how to add capability without breaking the bank. If the funds cannot be found from local tax revenue, then it is imperative that school boards look elsewhere—to Congress, to large private donors, to new arrangements with computer manufacturers in which computer equipment is donated or leased in return for tax breaks—to finance the equipment so necessary for the world of work tomorrow.

Usually people get what they demand and are willing to pay for. The merits of a knowledge-based system of education seem clear enough in today's tumultuous job picture. It will bring hundreds of thousands of new jobs in the schools and related to the schools—computer aides, master teachers, educational programmers, and jobs related to computer manufacture, repair, and service. The nonprofit educational institutions will add more jobs because sharing information on the fast-changing hardware and software will become more time-consuming. Teachers' colleges will hire more teachers to train and retrain classroom personnel. Even principals and superintendents will go back to school to improve their skills. With the exception of the actual manufacture of the computers, these jobs are all in the service sector. The quality society of the future must have them.

9

The Vocational Education Alternative: Ifs, Ands, Buts

College may be the best way to prepare for the smart jobs of the future, but it is not the only way. Vocational education has been the traditional alternative to college. Because vocational training is very skill-specific, it has many appealing aspects, not the least of which is that it is less expensive than a four-year college program and takes less time. So many youngsters currently entering the labor force have looked to vocational training as the best way to get skills that employers would be willing to pay for. But will that hold true in the future?

On the face of it, vocational education and training seem to offer a fairly good payoff, especially for persons for whom college is not an immediate option after high school. A study prepared by Wen Lang Li for the National Center for Vocational Education at Ohio State University in the late 1970s showed that throughout their lifetimes, people who had received vocational education in a formal school setting earned 12 percent more than people who had not had that additional training. We can expect that in the future the earnings gap between the well-trained and the untrained worker is likely to be even greater, because the smart jobs will demand better skills and the ability to relearn on the job.

When we look past the surface of earnings power, however, to see whether or not vocational education is a good bet, the answer is a resounding "maybe." While vocational education can provide a person with skills, a particular course is worthless unless there are actually jobs out there that match the skills learned in the course. If the skills a student has after completing vocational training don't sell in the job marketplace, then the program he or she has been through hasn't been worth it.

The purpose of vocational education and job training is to prepare people to get a job *and keep it*. But a student can't rely on just any vocational education program to fulfill this mission. It takes a lot of effort on the student's part to make sure his vocational education dollar and his training time are well spent. But making the effort to determine what to study and where in order to get the desired result—a job—is well worth it.

Since there are at least four different types of vocational training institutions and hundreds of different courses offered at thousands of institutions, there are obviously no easy answers. And there will be different answers for different people. Who you are, what your talents are, where your interests lie, and where you live and what the local labor market conditions are all must be considered in coming up with the right answer. But there are some pitfalls to beware of and some ways of telling a good opportunity from a bad one that apply to everyone seeking vocational training.

We've all heard horror stories about the young women who enroll in private schools for "executive secretaries" with the promise that at the end of the training line there will be a luxurious office, lunches with the boss, and glamorous people to deal with, only to find six months and $3000 later that the best job for marginally competent typists is a far cry from that dream. And skills training should certainly be more relevant than that still dished out to hundreds of thousands of youngsters in high school vocational education courses. When those young people are subjected to hours of "training" on hand-turned lathes or World War II vintage aircraft, their "vocational education" is worse than nothing at all, because it raises hopes that are almost inevitably going to be dashed when they start job hunting.

While a chilling enough tale could be told about irresponsible and even fraudulent vocational training, it is useless to lay blame. Rather, we turn our attention to ways to avoid such situations. Of course it would be very nice if training institutions would guarantee that all courses would lead to jobs. That promise would require their courses to be designed with the future in mind. But wishes are only wishes, and sensible parents and students will take the initiative with a lot of checking to make sure that the vocational education program they choose will indeed be worthwhile.

WHAT TO LOOK FOR AND LOOK OUT FOR

The four basic places to get career-specific training are secondary schools, generally in the vocational education program or track; independent post-secondary schools, which generally teach one cluster of skills, such as medical-dental assistant, secretarial, auto-welding, or plumbing and heating; community or junior colleges, the two-year post-secondary schools that combine liberal arts courses and applied, skill-development courses; and apprenticeships, on-the-job training run either by an employer or a union or jointly by both. Each type of institution has some special characteristics, but some offer much broader choices than others.

The choice range is an important element of the decision process, because the traditional distribution of vocational education courses, by general subject area, does not fit well into the future labor market. Reflecting only partial changes since vocational education was developed as a way to quickly train World War I veterans for an emerging industrial and mechanized agricultural economy, vocational education tends to be compartmentalized into agriculture, trades, home economics, technical education, health, business, and one or two other categories that are defined by the work sector, not by the skills themselves. So in addition to the problem rampant in many communities—overtraining students in the trades and home economics and agricultural areas—there is the problem of discovering what is actually taught in these programs that can be useful in many job settings.

A useful way to approach the latter problem is to think not only of the type of business or public service enterprise that would make an interesting place to work, but also to think of the specific competencies you would like to have when you finish your training. For example, you might want to be an inventory control manager, and you might be willing to work anywhere from a small business to a large government agency. The skills you need will be the same in either setting, but they may not be neatly listed under course headings marked "technical." Indeed, a useful course in buying might be found in home economics, while valuable courses in using computers to manage information might be found in the technical department. Few vocational education systems now offer the kind of information that matches skills and training opportunities to the jobs market (although five states are making progress in this area), which means that the vocational education student has to let his or her fingers do the walking through a lot of information about specific course content.

Assuming that a student has given some careful thought to his own abilities and eliminated from the field of his search jobs that clearly demand skills for which he has no native ability, the search for appropriate vocational education should start with a survey of the job market. A person taking vocational training is generally going to enter any career or job sequence at the entry level, but there is no law that says one has to stay at that level. If the main idea is to advance out of that first job as fast as one can, the innovative vocational education student will look in his own labor market area for job openings not only at the entry level, but also at higher levels, to see what kinds of skills are needed to advance. Perhaps a student can't get all of these skills in a training program, but by knowing what they are he or she can be sure not to miss those that are available and will be useful in the future.

Another recommendation that vocational education students don't always consider is to examine the curriculum offered very carefully. Catalogs and brochures may be thick and beautiful but be backed by very little in the way of really good instruction. It is perfectly legitimate to ask to talk to the instructor before enrolling in a course and even to ask to sit in on a session.

It's a good idea to check out the equipment used in a course, too. If a school's equipment is old or damaged or obsolete, training on it is obviously a waste of time. Equipment obsolescence is a very serious problem in most public high schools and in many community colleges. In Pennsylvania, for example, a 1983 survey found that the bill for bringing the vocational education system's equipment up to state-of-the-art standards would be $77 million. But plenty of independent schools, too, get by on outdated machinery—machinery that a worker would never find on the job and so is of no use in a classroom.

A person who has defined some job opportunities, identified the skills needed to get those jobs, and found a program that looks as if it promises to teach those skills still has one more task ahead: to determine whether graduates of that program in that school have been successful in getting jobs. One way is to study the placement figures in the school's placement offices. Another is to check with employers. The best is to contact graduates of the program to find out from their experience how successful their training was.

There are some guides to vocational training selection that are not very relevant to the quality of the training. Cost is not always an indicator of quality, and duration of training is not always an indication of value. However, these factors, in addition to the breadth of choice in curriculum, are what *appear to differentiate* the training institutions from one another—plus the fact that independent post-secondary schools are profit-making, while the other training institutions generally are not. A training course in a profit-making institution can cost as little as a few hundred dollars and as much as $6000; it can last for as little as three weeks or as long as two years. Similarly, one can get vocational training in a community college either by enrolling as a degree candidate and taking a full course load, which would cost in the range of $3000 per year, or by taking individual courses that seem to offer just the skills needed. While an associate degree is probably a valuable asset, someone who cannot afford the time or money to get a degree is still not completely out of luck.

The point is, though, that value per dollar spent will not be uniform across any type of institution. It will always depend on the management, the instructor, the equipment, the time devoted to practice, and the teaching methods. As the competition for jobs becomes keener and the value of training in order to get just the right job goes up, it will pay well to examine *all* these factors very carefully before launching into a training program.

VOCATIONAL EDUCATION SKILLS RIGHT FOR THE WORK REVOLUTION?

Whatever school or program a student is interested in, that student will have to have mastered basic skills before the vocational training will do any good. Many community colleges, and even some independent vocational education schools, teach remedial math and English, and anyone who is marginal in those basics would do well to improve them.

With the basics under control, the vocational education student has to bear in mind that traditional vocational education is not, like college, a well-rounded curriculum encompassing more than the major subject. The vocational education student today can expect to learn specific job performance skills, period. For example, students who have successfully completed a course in computer repair will know how to identify the source of trouble when a computer breaks down, how to take the computer apart to get at the offending part, and how to use the right tools to install a replacement part. While knowing these skills is the first and fundamental step to getting and keeping a job as a computer servicer, that's not all there is to it. The person who wants job security and advancement prospects also has to know how to write a report, fill out a requisition form to secure needed parts and supplies, and pass along information about computer failures to those who manufacture the computers. If he or she is really ambitious, the student will also start thinking about companies' organization: Where can a serviceperson move to, and what organizational and management skills will he need to rise in a company? A vocational education student would do well to pay attention to quality control and efficiency issues. As an ambitious repairman, for example, can he figure out ways to reduce the time costs of service or to route the service calls more rationally? In other words, even though credentials will be important in the work world of the future, not everyone will have a Ph.D., and the vocational training student, just like the college student, can plan to acquire needed skills for upward mobility.

Let's call these job-functioning skills generic skills. They have more to do with decisions about what to do and how to do it than with the actual doing of tasks. They are useful in many settings, and they are a supplement to the specific skills taught in most vocational training classrooms. But they are even more important than the job-specific skills for the work of the future because they are readily transferable from one occupation to another and from one occupation in one industry to the same occupation in another industry. As mobility will be the main requirement for the work of the future, the successful worker will have to be ready to move quickly—sideways as well as upwards. Moves between job slots in the same firm may come quicker than in the past, just as moves from one job slot in one firm to a similar job slot in a different firm may come quicker. Here are seven generic skills that will serve most workers well.

- Following instructions
- Transmitting information accurately
- Anticipating outcomes of decisions and actions
- Recording
- Reporting
- Making a decision and knowing why it was made
- Innovating

This is not, as might first appear, a list of the obvious, because almost any employer will complain that at least half of the job applicants and nearly as many of the firm's employees are blissfully ignorant of these skills. But they are absolutely essential to an effective and efficient organization, and if humans are to be as valuable as robots, it is in these areas that they must excel.

As more of the mechanical and repetitive tasks are handled by electronics, organizational and work-arranging aspects of an enterprise become more important—and perhaps more complex. In our look at the workplace we observed that there will be many new ways to work together, and workers will have to know how they relate to other workers and other units. Thus decisions about what to do, when to do it, and at what cost may fall on many more workers than formerly was the case. Just knowing what was done and communicating it to others who need to know is a key element of performance in many jobs. Knowing how to avoid mistakes and how to deal with mistakes once they are made is equally important—and rare in today's work force. Dealing with the unexpected is one skill successful workers will have that computers and robots won't have.

The ability to innovate is also a smart-job skill that will be even more in demand in the future than at present. The ability to innovate includes the ability to think of new products to make or new ways to make old products; new services to provide or ways to offer existing services more cheaply; and new clients for everything. To capture the specialized markets that will be America's forte in the future, firms are going to have to be innovative—to formulate and sell new ideas—because with the pace of change in the future, the entire marketing system will be speeded up and competition will develop faster than ever.

Of course there is value to the worker, too, in having these skills—value other than the promise of advancement. Those who work will know they are productive and feel good about themselves. They will not fall into the trap of today's dislocated workers, who had one skill and one skill only and are now discarded vestiges of a former work world.

In a work world where substitution of machinery for human labor is an ever-widening option, employers will be able to be far more selective than they were in the past. They will not tolerate indifference and irresponsibility, and they will not need to accept inferior quality, either in goods produced or in services rendered. And, since so many first jobs will involve working with expensive equipment, these generic skills will all be important not only for advancement, but to get and keep that first job as well. The old system of tolerating mediocrity will go the way of the old production system, as employers insist on staying "lean and mean." As long as there are more job seekers than jobs, employers will be able to pick the cream of the crop and choose workers who can demonstrate all the necessary job-related skills.

The generic skills we've listed are not generally offered in the curriculum of vocational training institutions. Most of these institutions are training for entry-level positions, and they do not waste time on other than the bare essentials. They may teach record keeping for the dental assistant—appointments, billings, etc.—but they are unlikely to teach bookkeeping for the repairman. And they certainly do not teach general management.

It is to be hoped that vocational training schools will respond to the changing needs of the job market with more relevant and complete training to include these generic skills, not as add-ons but as elements of the regular curriculum. For example, students in the computer repair course could be taught to take the call for service, dispatch the servicer, write up the service report, summarize the results of all service reports, and write a report on failures that will then be delivered to the provider of the equipment.

In the meantime, there are places to get such supplementary education. One could combine two vocational training courses at two different types of institutions—for example, one for office workers and one for repair and maintenance workers. Or a student could enroll in the local community college or business school to get some of the management and record keeping training that isn't taught in his or her vocational training program. Another way is to read books. One could also take advantage of educational seminars offered by the U.S. Small Business Administration or by other government agencies. Yet another way is to attend seminars put on by management consultants and others whose job it is to teach these skills through employers. Such seminars are periodically advertised in local newspapers.

CHANGING HORIZONS FOR VOCATIONAL EDUCATION ITSELF

So far we have been talking about what the individual who wants to find a good training opportunity should do to get it—or what the parent of a youngster in vocational education should look for. Ideally, since the vocational education institutions comprise a sort of mini-marketplace, if all vocational education students could and would exercise a rational choice among them, all of the programs would improve in quality and their relevance to the real job world. This would happen because their directors would try hard to provide job-relevant training at a reasonable cost and to change their curricula quickly to meet changing needs.

Unfortunately, however, the notion of an unfettered market does not apply to the education and training system, and there are many built-in obstacles to self-generating improvement in the system. The obstacles include the usual impediments, ranging from bureaucratic ineptness to plain old-fashioned greed.

Bureaucracy

That old culprit, bureaucracy, contributes its fair share to a somewhat muddled and often inadequate vocational education system. For example, there are many states in which no school can offer a course without express permission from the state department of education. There are other states, such as Maryland, where every high school accredited to teach vocational education courses has to include a specific set of courses. Since the prescribed course list can be changed only by committee, regulations or legislative provisions such as these virtually guarantee that a school cannot constantly adjust its curriculum to train to the job market needs of its community—or of other communities, which might sometimes be appropriate. Even where local option exists, many schools are slow to change. For example, in Pennsylvania, where Dr. Schwartz has evaluated the vocational education system, there were five times as many high school vocational education students enrolled in home economics and trade courses as were enrolled in technical courses and business courses, even though the jobs will be in the latter two related areas. With the shortage of funds available to spend on education, it is a tragic waste to divert resources from important growth-oriented fields to fields where there are no jobs. Yet, nationwide, it appears as though secondary school vocational education programs have turned out two or three times as many people with skills as lathe operators, carpenters, roofers, and bricklayers as they have people prepared to become computer servicers, robot maintainers, laboratory technicians, or any of the other workers likely to find interesting jobs that do not require a college degree.

Another form of bureaucratic drag is caused by the hustle to get federal funding for secondary school vocational education. The federal government has put about $625 million per year into vocational education for the last decade, much of it going to programs that do not lead to jobs—like home economics. States can spend the money on whatever training they want to spend it on; some states leave that decision to the locality. In 1983, the Vocational Education Act was up for renewal, which gave Congress a good opportunity to see whether the monies it appropriated were being spent for needed and valuable services. Like many other federal programs, the funds provided are avidly supported by special interest groups, including the vocational education teachers themselves. But these groups, like most others who benefit from federal expenditures, do not want the federal government to set any standards for performance in the service it is paying for. Since there are no national standards, the debate over refunding is pretty irrational—there are no uniform measures to determine whether past funds have been well spent or to help choose between alternatives.

The Question of Focus

There is one unique dilemma in trying to teach job-related skills in secondary schools: Should vocational education students be treated like kids or like future workers? They are after all, kids, deserving of their carefree youth. Yet if they are going to be successful in the work world, they have to learn the work world's responsibilities. Many vocational education teachers do try to create a work world within their classrooms. Then they run into conflict with the students, who want to skip class for basketball practice or stay home "sick" the day after a big test. And sometimes they run into conflict with the school administration, too. Being easy on the students does not really help them in the long run, especially when they are competing for a dwindling number of work opportunities. And much too often vocational education courses are viewed by the schools that run them as dumping grounds for kids who have been labeled troublesome or hopeless; no serious effort is made to launch the students into the tough world of work reality.

A good argument can be made that the work habits young people learn in vocational education classes are more valuable than the specific skills. If they develop nothing more than a sense of responsibility and the ability to follow instructions, they will have the best leg up into the work situation.

The Problem of Greed

Another factor inhibiting quality vocational training is simple avarice. And this is by no means limited to profit-making institutions. Publicly supported institutions have very similar incentives for bringing in as many tuition-paying students as possible, even should this mean flooding the job market with trainees in excess of the jobs available. Where for-profit institutions seek profit, the public institutions seek capitation payments. The net result can be bad for the community and a minor tragedy for individuals. When training schools advertise auto welding as a sure-fire future occupation and scores of boys and unemployed men hand over a few hundred dollars to learn that skill, the schools are cheating both the trainees and the community, because auto welding is by no means a secure skill to have. By the same token, if a community college accepts hundreds of young women in the bookkeeping course, even though book-keepers are in no demand on the local market, it is doing a disservice to its students and its community.

Yet such situations are hard to avoid. There are no rules saying only so many students can enroll in specific programs. If there were, objections would be heard loud and clear. Many individuals, even if told that a field is overcrowded, will tend to say, "So what—I'll be the best in it, and I'll get a job even if the market is tight."

Training more workers than there are jobs for is not opposed by employers, of course, because it enables them to choose from a large, qualified pool, and a labor excess tends to keep wages down. So there are many institutional forces working against a well-balanced relationship between supply and demand for labor.

Pressures from Displaced and Older Workers

One of the immediate problems to be faced by the country as a whole is that the demand for vocational training is soaring as a result of the displacement of so many workers from the traditional basic industries. Many of these people are being shunted into vocational training without careful consideration of the generic skills they will need to use in addition to specific vocational skills on the job. But this new market for vocational training should force most of the training institutions (except secondary schools, of course) to adapt more quickly to the demands of the new job marketplace. As trainees get older on average (in community colleges, the average age is now thirty), due to the shrinking of the youth population and the greater willingness of older people continually to upgrade their skills, the institutions will be challenged more strongly than they have been in the past. And as vocational education consumers get wiser to the needs of the work world, they will demand broader and more through training.

KNOWING WHAT THE CHOICES ARE

While there is no good way to manage the training market, the balance between supply and demand could be improved if more people had better information about it. If we could walk into the local library, sit down at a computer terminal, and call up a list of jobs that are likely to have openings in the future, together with a description of the skills required for them, we would be light-years ahead of where we are now in terms of job market information available to individuals. Most such information is now obtained either by word of mouth or through employment services or newspaper advertisements.

Word of mouth (or in the case of small manufacturing operations, a "help wanted" notice on the door) is, as a rule, limited to a network of individuals in the same general line of work. For some jobs word of mouth pertains only to local opportunities, although for others, especially technical and professional jobs, it can be international in scope. But it is slow and cumbersome, and it tends to restrict information about job openings to insiders and individuals with many friends, while withholding that from persons who may not have an immediate network connection but do have valuable skills.

Employment services for blue-collar jobs and many relatively junior white-collar jobs are notoriously underinformed, because they depend on employers to give them job-openings information voluntarily, and those data are often outdated by the time they are passed along to a job seeker. When jobs are in short supply, employers have no incentive to provide information. In fact, the only time they have such an incentive is when labor is in short supply.

Employment services also have a lot of power over the job seeker in that they can, and do, parcel out interview opportunities on criteria other than first come, first serve. This is as true for entry-level positions as it is for the senior management and professional positions filled for large companies by the so-called headhunters—employment services working for employers, not for job seekers. Employers like this, because the employment service screens applicants for them. But job seekers would be better off if they had access to more information than that gained through employment services.

As for newspaper advertisements, they are often misleading. The employers may already have candidates for the jobs advertised and are advertising merely to see if a better candidate comes along. But ads are still useful in describing the general skills needed for specific jobs in specific fields and so provide a good source of general information for the person trying to decide what kind of training he or she needs.

For people who want to train or retrain themselves, a much better and more efficient information system is needed—one that relies on modern technology to provide up-to-date information about both the job market as a whole and job-training systems, and that can be used by an individual without making him or her the victim of an information-rationing system. Those seeking training need to know where the job openings will be. They need to know in what fields the openings will occur, and what general and specific skills employers will be looking for.

They need to know where to get the training for these skills. And—an important feature that no job information system now has—they need to know what the competition is, in particular how many people now in the labor force already have the needed skills. In a work-scarce world, the last feature will be perhaps the most important feature of all, because it could prevent overcrowding and ward off wasted investments in training for the wrong field.

This ideal system is a far cry from what now exists. Our research has turned up only five states that have any job market information in their information banks. Only twenty states have computerized systems. Even where they do, the information in the systems is not comprehensible to the ordinary person. Nearly all of the thirty-six states that operate occupational information systems with federal aid under the National Occupational Information Coordinating Committees/State Occupational Information Coordinating Committees (NOICC/SOICC) still rely on the technical jargon devised for vocational educators—jargon that defines jobs in the arcane language of a personnel officer, not in terms of skills required. The *Guide for Occupational Exploration,* published by the U.S. Department of Labor, did not as of April 1983 include any description of jobs related to robots. The job descriptions in the industrial section described manual skills that will be totally useless once robots and computers are installed in any factory. No substitute skills were described. It is one of the ironies of the work revolution that the last people to be informed about its effects on them are the workers.

There is no technical reason why the information all workers need cannot be provided. The mechanical capability is certainly there. The means of gathering the information are there. The only thing lacking is the insistence of the public. That insistence will come with the realization that the jobs workers are prepared and preparing for are going to disappear and, as things stand now, no one will be able to tell them how to prepare for replacement jobs.

SEIZING THE VOCATIONAL EDUCATION OPPORTUNITIES

Vocational education offers many opportunities, both for youngsters who need to start earning money at an early age and for older workers who seek to upgrade or expand their skills. But vocational education does not always come well packaged to meet all the needs of a person aspiring to a smart job and job security. Just like the college student, the vocational education student will have to take stock of all the options and do some innovative planning to fashion an array of generic and specific skills that employers with real jobs to offer will like. Keeping an eye on the changes down the road is as important to vocational education students as to all of us. To meet the demands of the future, institutions will have to change some of their approaches to vocational education and training, and students will have to shop around carefully for the right training opportunity.

And while vocational education offers an attractive alternative to people who feel that a college education is unnecessary or too expensive, it probably will not be the end of the line for anyone seeking a smart job. In the short run, a two-year certificate or a special training course may be just fine, but as job shortages emerge in many areas, top-notch credentials will become increasingly important. So the first vocational training course will probably be a stepping stone to more education and training. And in that regard, vocational education makes a valuable contribution to the country's education system—it helps workers into an income-producing situation that will permit them to work and learn simultaneously and continually.

10

Leisure and Work: Work Sharing

The average work week in the United States is still 37.5 hours long, and it has shortened only 2.5 hours since the end of World War II—a 6 percent reduction. Productivity—output per hour of labor—has risen by 165 percent. Logically, one would expect that the more productive workers are, the less time they would put in on the job. But the statistics show that has not been the case. The 1983 work week is still the standard five-day week, and the majority of organizations work off a 2080-hour year. There are several reasons for this.

In the past, both management and labor preferred to have fewer workers work longer hours than to have more workers work shorter hours. From management's perspective, it is less costly to do this, because the fewer the workers, the fewer the people for whom fringe benefits such as health insurance, unemployment compensation insurance, and social security taxes must be paid. Also, management would rather supervise and train fewer people to do more tasks, as a rule.

When management wants to reduce its payroll only temporarily, it reduces hours or shortens shifts (for jobs that are compensated on an hourly basis). But when permanent labor cost reductions are to be made, management prefers to drop employees from the payroll, rather than to shorten the work week, even if employees would agree to less pay for less work.

During the 1960s and 1970s, especially in the large industrial unions—the United Auto Workers, the United Steelworkers, and the Teamsters—the work year was shortened through longer vacations and more paid holidays, but compensation went up as the unions negotiated guaranteed minimum wages. This led to soaring production costs. For example, the hourly cost of steel production labor came close to $23 in 1982, of which about $12 to $14 was hourly wages and the balance fringe benefits. Automobile workers, miners, and many members of the Teamsters Union were compensated at a roughly equal level, with miners being the highest-paid of all workers.

Even before the recent recession, output of American firms in these high-paying industries was slipping, and foreign competitors were gaining large shares of the domestic market.

From the perspective of the labor unions, the fault was not to be laid entirely at their door, and the problem was not one to be solved on the backs of the workers alone. And indeed they had a valid point. It is a perniciously inaccurate view that labor costs have caused the current crisis in all industries. Labor costs have not risen nearly as fast as profits, depreciation, interest, rent, and indirect taxes. In real terms, compensation for labor was 1.2 points lower in 1983 than in 1977, while business and industry payments for the non-labor costs of doing business were 45.3 points higher.[1] Moreover, in 1983 American workers earning the average nonagricultural wage had $3 less to spend after an hour's work than they would have had in 1977, and their wages had risen only 3 cents an hour in the preceding year.

The power of unions to push wages and benefits up faster than in nonunion industries has been shrinking in the last two years, as is evidenced by the AFL-CIO's report on the outcome of collective bargaining. Still, in 1982 unionized employees' cost of wages and benefits for the basic work week, excluding overtime and bonuses, rose 7.2 percent over the previous year, while those costs for nonunion employees rose 6 percent.[2] The problem the unions faced was how to abandon their traditional positions in the face of massive layoffs without losing all of their bargaining clout. Until 1983, both the private-sector unions and public-sector unions such as the American Federation of State and

[1]Bureau of Labor Statistics, "Productivity and Costs," USDL Bulletin 83-247, May 26, 1983.
[2]Bureau of Labor Statistics, "Employment Cost Index," USDL Bulletin 83-48, February 3, 1983.

Municipal Employees (AFSME) had generally preferred to allow payroll cuts rather than to accept any reduction in wages and benefits—including shorter work weeks. Situations where work weeks were cut but compensation was cut less—which would reduce costs for employers less than would layoffs, while retaining more work for employees than layoffs—were difficult to find. The reason for this is logical and economical: Union leaders fear losing the approval of all members if they support a reduction in the standard of living for all members. If a union loses members because they are laid off and no longer pay their dues, at least the remaining members will be satisifed with what the leadership has gotten for them. At least that is how it has worked up to recently. Now that the reality of a reduction in the labor force as a result of layoffs and plant shutdowns is so great in many industries, labor has been forced to beat a reluctant retreat and to inch up to work sharing. In the late 1970s, for example, the United Auto Workers proposed spreading overtime work by paying half the overtime in time-and-a-half wages and half in compensatory time. Although this amounted to double-time pay for overtime, it was a baby step in the direction of work sharing. Recently the AFL-CIO has strongly supported a national thirty-five-hour work week law, which would increase the costs to employers of paying overtime and make it more attractive for them to hire more workers at regular pay.

Work sharing is easier to negotiate in unions where compensation is based on output rather than time. It is also easier to negotiate in industries in which the employment can foreseeably be stabilized at an irreducible minimum. In the steel industry, modern technology can virtually eliminate the need for steelworkers on the production line, but in the apparel industry, operators will always be needed to put garments together, no matter how automated other tasks may be. That is the major reason why work sharing has been a policy of the International Ladies Garment Workers Union since 1935. ILGWU members work a thirty-five-hour week, and have for many years. The philosophy that it is better for more workers to have jobs is of course easier to sell to women, who often prefer a shorter work week, than to men, especially men who are the sole breadwinners in a family.

The ILGWU and the Textile Workers Union have also encouraged technological advances in the apparel and textile industries, in the knowledge that without it, more and more production would emigrate overseas. Since most of the apparel manufacturing companies are small, this means that an ILGWU local makes arrangements on a case-by-case basis. When an employer has added some labor-saving equipment, the union—which retains its own production engineers—conducts a time and motion study to see just how much productivity has been increased by the equipment. Then the union bargains with management to set wages at some midpoint between what workers were earning before the technology was introduced and what they would earn if they were paid the same piecework rates as they received when using the old equipment. The union's position is strictly pragmatic. If it were to insist on doubling the wages, the result would inevitably be a shrinking of the work force. The approach adopted benefits both labor and management, as the firms with higher technological capability turn out more volume and ultimately can increase their work force—or at least retain the same complement of workers they had before they upgraded their equipment.

Two unions that went through the tough period of adapting to new technology are the International Longshoremen's Association and the International Printing and Graphics Communications Union. The general policy in these unions has been to accept technology but to exact from management guaranteed annual incomes for the union members employed at the time the technology was put into place. For the longshoremen, the technology was containerized shipping, which over a period of ten years made the stevedore obsolete. For the printers, the technology was electronic typesetting and photographic reproduction, which eliminated whole categories of work. The cost to the companies installing the new equipment was high in the initial years but diminished as older employees retired and were not replaced.

Paying people for not working was a bitter pill for both management and labor to swallow, but it made more sense than enduring a prolonged strike or loss of productivity owing to labor–management hostility. It was the only immediate choice when the choice over the longer term was between reducing labor costs or going bankrupt. As the number of people replaced by technology begins to escalate, however, guaranteed annual incomes may become prohibitively costly, and such vast numbers of workers may well be replaced that unions find their bargaining power diminished, compared to the power they commanded in the shipping and printing industries. Organized labor might then fight for a shorter work week to keep more people on the job, because this will be one way to keep union membership large enough to support the union's activities through dues.

One of the likely events in the future is supplementing of these traditional approaches to work sharing and income preservation by new forms of work sharing, including part-time jobs and two-for-one jobs. So far, when this has happened, it has been more of a quality-of-life experiment than an economic necessity. But in the future, if there are not enough jobs to go around in a given industry or field, we may have to move to job sharing as a way to prevent widespread disaffection. It's easy to imagine this occurring first in the communications industry—for example, in the telephone companies, where automated equipment and modular phone systems are steadily reducing the number of repairmen, operators, and clerks needed even as the volume of telephone calls handled goes up. Telephone companies do not like to lay people off, because the entire public is a potential critic. It is also possible to envision a switch to job sharing in some of the financial institutions, which, when the next two years or so of automation are completed, will require far fewer personnel for much more volume than is now the case.

Work sharing is actually made more feasible by automation, since there are fewer skills to be applied by an individual. The more automated a task is, the more easily different people can perform it. It is easy to imagine two secretaries, two machinists, or two economists, aided by computerized technical support, sharing one job. To make shared work possible takes only a little organization and communication, so that each party knows what has been done and what needs to be done. As long as the tasks are defined clearly, there need not be any loss of productivity through work sharing. Indeed, in the creative aspects of the tasks, two minds might enhance the quality of the work.

Work sharing is, of course, more than just a way to slice up the income-generating pie. It is also a way of permitting people who do not want to work forty hours a week the opportunity to contribute their skills and gain work satisfaction. Parents with young children, for example, more and more often look for part-time jobs so that they can spend time with their children. It is hard to know how many people—men as well as women—actually share a single job, either working together or separately in coordination with another person, but every now and then you read about such cases in the newspaper.

Nevertheless, the impetus for work sharing will be economic

hardship generated by unemployment, not the quest for a more humane life-style. One harbinger of things to come is the state-subsidized work sharing that has been instituted in California, Oregon, and Arizona. These states subsidize work sharing by allowing workers who are working partial shifts to collect unemployment for the part of the work week they are not actually on the job. A company that is cutting man-hours by, say, 20 percent, instead of laying off one in five workers, reduces the hours of all workers by 20 percent, and all workers collect unemployment compensation for one day per week. This experiment is five years old in California, where officials say that it has been a success, keeping the jobless rate lower during the recent recession than it would otherwise have been. The state's Employment Development Department reports that about 3 percent of the $2.4 billion paid out by the state in unemployment compensation during 1982 was for work sharing.

But in this case as in other cases, California's impulsiveness may prove to be its Achilles' heel. This work sharing subsidy is inherently unfair, and if practiced on a large scale, could cause firms that do not expect employment to shrink to look twice before locating or expanding there. The subsidy ultimately shifts to the employer with a steady employment record (whose insurance rates are relatively low) the costs of subsidizing employment by firms with a more volatile unemployment record (whose insurance rates would, without the subsidy, rise). A January 1983 *New York Times* article indicated that companies participating in subsidized work sharing saved $16 per worker per month in insurance contributions. For subsidized work sharing to be equitable, we would need to overhaul the unemployment insurance system nationally—which will eventually be necessary in any case, because it is vastly underfunded and over fifteen states, including California, are millions of dollars in debt to the federal government for borrowed funds to pay unemployment compensation.

Still, work sharing—with or without government subsidy—is a better solution to mass unemployment than the solution so often suggested by many traditional labor economists, who say that if women would stay out of the labor force, or if older people would retire earlier, or if teenagers would be forced to work at below minimum wage levels, there would be no unemployment problem. Such solutions are simply a way of rationing jobs in favor of certain groups. Nothing could be more undemocratic. While we may eventually use subsidies to persuade individuals to voluntarily give up their right to work, everyone inherently has an equal right to hold a job.

UNIONS AND THE RIGHT TO WORK

"Job rights" is a notion that gained popularity as the recession deepened and the longer-term effects of structural unemployment began to show through the false promises of recovery. But the notion that every individual has a right to work is a serious concept indeed, and there is no powerful group of advocates for this notion at the present time. The reason is simple enough: If I guarantee you a job, I may be guaranteeing myself only half a job.

One might think that organized labor would be the natural proponent of a true right-to-work law, one that guarantees that everyone who wants to work can work. But even if they were—and so far, they have not seriously fought for this concept—they would probably not be able to get it into legislation. Unions have other concerns, and they are losing their ability to promote their bread and butter causes.

Work sharing may be in the cards for the future, but the larger unions' response to structural unemployment or the threat of automation has been to secure termination benefits (also known as employment security) and wage increases. The Communications Workers of America, for example, in 1983 negotiated a contract with General Telephone and Electronics (GTE) in California covering twenty-one thousand union members, a little more than half of the GTE workers represented by the union. That contract provided for retraining expenses, relocation allowances, and termination pay benefits, and it extended health insurance benefits in the case of threatened reduction in the work force. To call these benefits employment security, as the union does, is somewhat of a misnomer, since they are in reality security contingencies in case of unemployment. Still, they are new benefits responding to the threat of layoff, primarily job elimination resulting from automation, and as such foretell the future role of labor unions: to fight for security as much as for wages and current benefits.

In some of the older industries, the promise—or the illusion—of job security has been won only at the price of "give-backs" of previously won benefits. For example, in the contract negotiated in 1983, steelworkers gave up a week's vacation, a paid holiday, and the thirteen-week vacation every five years to which senior workers had been entitled. This give-back, which the United Steelworkers Union had initially protested vigorously, was permanent, although the 9 percent wage cut, which the union also agreed to, was to be restored during later years of the contract. The agreement of the United Steelworkers to cut costs in the steel industry was long overdue, in the eyes of some observers, but to those on the side of labor who recalled the pioneer role steelworkers played in unionizing American industry—including the infamous battle between strikers and Pinkerton men at Homestead, outside of Pittsburgh, almost one hundred years ago (1892)—the decision was too soft on management.

The Erosion of Union Power

One of the factors inhibiting the work sharing option is the erosion of labor unions themselves. Whereas in 1970, 30.8 percent of the work force belonged to unions, in 1980 only 25.2 percent were union members. Of course the labor force itself has grown in the interim, so while the percentage of the work force has shrunk, the actual number of unionized workers has increased from 21.852 million to 22.811 million. Still, this increase was not nearly as great as the increase in the total number of employed workers. The power of organized labor has been undermined not only by the work force reductions in the highly organized industries, but also by the proliferation of nonunion factories in southern states.

Just take a look at the membership figures for the large labor unions—the AFL-CIO and all unions with 100,000 or more workers in 1980—between 1968 and 1980. Membership has fallen by this much: machinists, 149,000; auto workers, 116,000; steelworkers, 114,000; carpenters, 10,000; clothing and textile and garment workers, 186,000; hotel and restaurant operators, 59,000; electrical workers, 91,000; railway and steamship clerks, 100,000; rubber workers, 53,000; oil and chemical workers, 19,000. Many of these losses were suffered by the unions that first organized labor in America.

Of course, membership has risen in many other unions: by 136,000 in the Teamsters Union; by 248,000 in the food and commercial workers unions; by 677,000 in the Brotherhood of Electrical Workers; by 194,000 among communications workers; by 40,000 among office employees, and by many thousands of government and postal workers.

With the national average of union membership at 25.2 percent in 1980, compare the averages for these primarily southern states:

Arkansas, 16.0	New Mexico, 18.9
Arizona, 15.8	North Carolina, 9.6
Florida, 11.7	Oklahoma, 15.3
Georgia, 17.5	South Carolina, 7.8
Kansas, 15.4	Tennessee, 19.1
Louisiana, 16.3	Texas, 11.4
Mississippi, 16.3	Virginia, 14.7

All of the states listed above—except Louisiana, New Mexico, and Oklahoma—have "right-to-work" laws that make it difficult for labor leaders to organize workers, and in recent years there have been bitter battles over unionization. Even though several western states also have right-to-work laws and, therefore, low rates of unionization, they have not attracted as much industry and business as the southern states.

Other odds are heavily against unions. Right-to-representation elections are bitterly fought by many companies, and union organizers report that the variety of ruses used to discourage workers from participating in representation elections is growing. For example, an article by Guillermo Gernier in the May 14, 1983, edition of the *AFL-CIO News* concluded that Johnson and Johnson was using quality circles, supposedly formed to increase productivity and the quality of output, to weed out prounion sentiment in its Ethicon plant. A study of North Carolina textile industries by a student of Dr. Schwartz in 1981 reported the lethargy of workers in face of the long battle to exercise the right to representation won in legitimate elections at J. P. Stevens Company. Martin Berger, who has organized for the International Ladies Garment Workers Union (ILGWU) in many southern states, complains that the National Labor Relations Board (NLRB) in any administration, but especially under the Reagan administration, takes unconscionably long to deal with cases brought before it by the unions, especially when unions have already won a representational vote but employers still refuse to bargain, on various pretexts. Some cases, he says, have been stalled for as long as twelve years.

There are no published NLRB statistics that would support or refute this assertion. The most recent data reflecting the outcomes of union activity are for 1980, and we could obtain no summary of the duration of cases before the National Labor Relations Board. The outdated statistics show that approximately the same number of elections were held in 1978, 1979, and 1980 (a little over eight thousand) and that unions won representation in approximately the same proportion each year (46 percent), while approximately the same proportion of workers in the industry came under union representation each year (38 percent).

Many of the newer technology-based companies also have instituted so many employee benefits that unions have a tough time defining a grievance that would induce workers to join them. No conspiracy is implied here; it is merely the case that the more management offers employees in the way of "flexitime," fringe benefits, and participatory democracy, the fewer grievances are left to persuade employees of the utility of collective bargaining.

However, labor leaders have by no means given up, and there has been a proliferation of organizing activities, in some cases under unlikely circumstances—such as an ILGWU local in Pennsylvania organizing a word processing shop. Many unions are going after the high technology industries and the office-based services, which have traditionally been difficult to organize because women are more reluctant joiners than men and because white-collar workers do not see themselves as union members as readily as blue-collar workers do. Further evidence of job shortages should help unions advance their cause, even in the southern states. The question will be whether management preempts unions by providing job security, work sharing, or post-employment benefits voluntarily. As long as companies can decide to send the work to other countries and can still sell the final service or product at a competitive price in the United States, labor is at a substantial disadvantage both in organizing and at the bargaining table.

Organized labor will have to decide where work sharing fits in among other priorities, which will primarily include health care and retraining. Different benefits will appeal to different worker groups. For example, older workers will benefit least from retraining and education. As the work force is in fact aging, this might mean more votes in favor of a guaranteed job—even one entailing only twenty or thirty hours of work a week—as preferable to any other benefits, since with a guaranteed job a worker could purchase his or her own education, training, health care, or mortgage.

It is virtually certain that the tremendous pressure on jobs that will be caused by automation will force labor unions to take a new look at their collective bargaining objectives. If there will not be enough jobs for full-time employment for half of the industrial work force—as certainly seems likely by the end of the 1980s—then some very difficult choices have to be made. The numbers of lost union members are potentially so large that labor leaders may well change their views about what is most important. And with alternative jobs scarce in other industries, union rank and file may be more willing to work shorter weeks for less pay than to risk long-term unemployment.

SPREADING THE WORK

There is a very real possibility that the work revolution will create a situation where some people work a full week and others do not work at all, no matter how much they want to or how hard they try. If the average work week remains at the present 37.5 to 40 hours, and if the labor force is as large as is presently expected, there will not be enough jobs to go around. Even if the work week is reduced to 35 hours, there is no promise that there will be enough full-time jobs to allow everyone in the projected labor force to have one. But work week reduction is a good start. Imagine for a minute that the number of jobs increases by a very optimistic 5 percent per year and that there are 110 million 37.5-hour jobs in 1985. Assume that the work week is reduced by law to 35 work hours per job. Then 7.8 million more people could be employed. Reduce the work week to 30 hours, and today's equivalent of 110 million jobs could translate into 127.5 million jobs.

Now imagine that the U.S. economy does not create more work for people to do, because machines replace people. At today's work week, about 100 million people can work. If the hours on these jobs were reduced from 37.5 to 35, 7 million more workers could be employed, and if hours were reduced to 30, 25 million more people could be employed. In other words, work sharing could wipe out the unemployment problem completely.[3]

---

[3]Number of current jobs here is based on the Bureau of Labor Statistics household survey, which indicated in May 1983 that 100 million people were at work. This estimate included part-time workers, self-employed persons, volunteers, and farm workers, as well as full-time wage and salary workers.

Of course these are only numbers, and that part of the unemployment problem caused by the jobs-skills mismatch would not be solved by reducing the work week. There would still be many people who would not be employable without intense (re)education and training. There would still be industries with excess workers and industries begging for workers. But work sharing would be particularly effective in reallocating shrinking work opportunities in industries going through technological change and reorganization of the production process.

Without serious consideration of work sharing (an idea, incidentally, which has been advanced at other periods in our history by sociologists and others), there will surely be a very inequitable division of work opportunities. Some people will work and others will not. The work sharing option would let everyone lead a leisure-rich life, working a pleasant thirty- or thirty-two-hour week. Unemployment, involuntarily leisure, is not much more socially desirable than involuntary servitude.

There are many other ways to continue to shorten the work year other than reducing the work week, of course. In 1983 the AFL-CIO unions that were renegotiating contracts added one day of holiday to most of their contracts, bringing the total paid holidays up to eleven or twelve.[4] German workers are accustomed to as much as six weeks a year of paid vacation. The main difference between shortening a work week and shortening a work year is its impact on pay—both base pay and overtime. A reduction in the work week would have to be accompanied by reductions in one or the other form of compensation for employers to pay attention to the proposition.

What are the alternatives? Some workers can have 37.5-hour-a-week jobs and others will have none. That has been the traditional way we have dealt with job shortages, primarily because we always considered them to be temporary. But now it is clear that they are not temporary, that job shortage is endemic to the advanced industrial economy. Should we therefore share the work? If that would be our aim, how would we do it? Who is going to decide who works? On what basis? Shall we decree that only one person per household may hold a job? And if so, how will we define a household, and how will we police the employers to find out if anyone is cheating? Or shall we decree that only those over twenty-five or under fifty can work? That is easier to police, if harder to legislate. In contradiction to law,

[4]*AFL-CIO News*, May 14, 1983.

America has been operating for years under a very efficient and effective "market" rule that allows more whites than blacks to work and, further, almost guarantees that only three out of ten young black males will work. In a work-short society, the easiest course of action would be to let such illegal rules perpetuate themselves. It remains to be seen whether our democracy is resilient enough to provide a superior alternative.

11

The Future
Workplace

Because technology is changing the tasks that are done in factories, offices, warehouses, and stores, it will also change the way the workplace is organized. In the process, it will alter many of the traditional roles of workers and supervisors. The importance of decision making and planning, compared to manual or technical tasks, will profoundly change the way we work together with co-workers. And technology will make the work site less important than it is now. Cottage industries of one or two people working at home making things with inexpensive robotized machinery or providing services via electronic equipment will become ordinary. The telecommuter will be on the scene—a person who works a good part of the time at home, communicating with colleagues and reporting via video and telecommunications.

THE FACTORY

At 7:30 A.M., the first shift of five hundred or so workers at the new Nissan truck plant in Smyrna, Tennessee, gathers, wearing Nissan uniforms, for calisthenics in the company recreation area. After the warm-up, they gather in work groups to discuss the plans and problems of production that week. When they break for lunch, they will be joined at the company cafeteria lunch table by their foreman. The foreman's position in management—the fifth tier—is one-third closer to top management than in most American automobile companies, which have twelve to fourteen layers of management. On the job, workers will work on an assembly line that anyone of them can stop at any time, and they will be encouraged to stop it—no defects are tolerated in a finished vehicle. When the plant is finished, there will be a complete recreation facility and a day-care center. Some of the workers have visited Japan, courtesy of Nissan, to see how Japanese factories work. The plant's management, in promoting participatory management practices, hopes that the workers and the company will come to regard each other as "family."

Does this sound like pre-1900 paternalistic capitalism, the kind that built company dormitories for the farm girls who worked the textile mills of New England? Well, it is and it isn't. There are no company houses at Nissan, and the American operation will probably not emulate all of Japanese industry's well-documented attention to workers' satisfaction. For instance, Nissan will not give workers in the United States low-cost loans to buy houses or cars, and there are as yet no plans to guarantee workers a job for life, or even for a year. Still, participatory management is gaining ground in this and many other, home-grown corporations as a way of attacking the problem of poor quality and of reducing absenteeism, sabotage, and loafing on the job.

In one automobile plant of an American corporation in Detroit, the sabotage rate is reported to make three hundred cars a week rejects. At the Baltimore GM plant Dr. Schwartz visited in 1981, foremen tried with notably little success to get work teams to come within five points of the target Quality Control Index. "You'd be nuts to trade your 1977 Chevy for a 1981 model," one of them confided after work over a pitcher of beer. An assembly line worker in the same GM plant thought the visitor was a physician. "I hope you do a better job on people than we do on cars," he joked. A 1983 study indicated that two-thirds of all retail, manufacturing, and hospital workers engage in counterproductive behavior, ranging from sloppy work and absenteeism to theft of the employer's goods.[1]

---

[1] John P. Clark and Richard C. Hollinger, "Theft by Employees in Work Organizations," University of Minnesota Sociology Department for the National Institute of Justice, Washington, D.C., reported in the *Los Angeles Times*, June 11, 1983.

These kinds of problems have led GM and other automobile manufacturers to set up "quality control circles" modeled after European and Japanese systems, the purpose of which is to bring supervisors and workers together in a team approach to production. These meetings of labor and management now take place in over six thousand corporations, but they only affect a small fraction of America's workers—about 275,000, according to Darius Van Fossen, executive director of the International Association of Quality Circles. The subjects these "quality circles" deal with cover the wide range of concerns anyone would have on the job, all of which—besides quality itself—affect quality: morale, safety, efficiency, cost, absenteeism, condition of equipment, and training. A *Chicago Tribune* article quoted a union leader's satisfaction with the changed attitude of management. The union leader said that since quality circles had been instituted, he no longer felt he had to check his brains at the entrance to the plant. It was evident that management realized he could think and solve problems as well as or better than management itself. But many workers feel that management tries to subvert the purposes of quality circles, hoping to turn them into a way of preventing union activity and controlling workers.

The federal government has put its stamp of approval on this innovation as a way of improving the business climate. In 1978 Congress passed the Labor Management Cooperation Act to help finance such committees, and former Senator Jacob Javits, in a *New York Times* "op ed" article (January 21, 1983), claimed more financing was needed to end "unnecessary" antagonism between labor and management. Since it is in the interest of both parties to end that antagonism, it is difficult to understand why the federal government needs to pay for it.

Quality circles in factories are not the only form of cooperation being introduced on plant floors. To help improve the standards of cars, GM introduced team production in several of its plants, modeled after the Volvo production process in Sweden, where instead of an assembly line, each team builds a complete car. GM's current tooling does not allow it to go as far as Volvo has gone—in effect the Swedish company produces signed final products. But having the same group produce more of each auto is another attempt to undo the damage that boredom on the job, dissatisfaction with working conditions, and fear of the future have brought to the factory floor.

Eliminating job titles is another avenue to job satisfaction and, with it, to better-quality products. In 1983 the Lee Company, a small firm in Sharon, Pennsylvania, took over a large plant abandoned by the Koppers Corporation to keep it running for the workers. Its owner reported that the venture depended on high productivity, to be gained by flexible assignments and good communication between management and labor.[2]

Perhaps the most well-known of the pioneers in flexible manufacturing assignments was Edwin Herbert Land, designer of the Polaroid camera. In 1944 Land determined to make his company "a new kind of social unit," in which "all will regard themselves as labor in the sense of having as their common purpose learning new things and applying that knowledge for the public welfare. . . . The machinist will be proud of and informed about the company's scientific advances; the scientist will enjoy the reduction to practice of his basic perceptions."[3] Polaroid followed the precept, convinced that loyalty depends on more than money. It also rewarded loyalty in bad times, refusing during the 1982 recession to lay people off, instead giving them large bonuses for voluntary severance.

This kind of freedom from status and pigeonholing is not always favored of course. Some workers are not comfortable with not knowing where they stand and with fuzzy lines of demarcation between responsibilities. But of the alternatives, "flexi-jobs" and fixed jobs, the former should be more successful in keeping people's interests fired.

THE OFFICE

Factories are not the only type of workplace in which experiments in organizing work and allocating responsibility are going on. Some of the larger financial institutions, utility companies, and telephone companies include quality circles among their many management approaches. Boredom and frustration are not foreign to the office workplace, which will take on more and more attributes of the assembly line. Preventing boredom is becoming a career in itself. Some companies work with individuals carefully to find out exactly what each worker wants to do, and will sacrifice volume of output for worker satisfaction.

[2]*Pittsburgh Press*, April 10, 1983.
[3]Michael Blumstein, "Ideas and Trends," *New York Times*, August 1, 1982.

Coping with the boredom induced by the de-skilling of work via electronic technology may involve forgoing the use of technology itself. For example, Jane, who works for the New York Telephone Company, hated her computer-aided job as clerk analyst. She preferred her first job, at lower pay, which required her to make judgments, do arithmetic on a calculator, and copy data accurately. The telephone company gave her back her calculator but let her keep her higher title and higher pay, betting that although she would not work as fast as she did with the computer, she would work more faithfully and steadily. But in the future, younger workers coming up the ladder won't necessarily be given these choices, because it may become too costly for management to customize work procedures.

A large international bank has found that two account managers working on the same accounts give better service than if each has his or her own account portfolio. Why? Because the account managers want to be able to talk about their work, preen themselves on successes, and have an understanding co-worker to complain to when things go wrong. So job satisfaction is not limited to the type of work, but also embraces the way work is organized and the way people interact with one another when they are doing it.

A new work-related illness has hit office workers. It's "CRT fever"—the dizziness, blurred vision, and sometimes cold sweats that word processor operators complain about after sitting in front of the green screen for eight hours without stopping. There are physical and mental limits to the productivity increases that can be gained through new technology, but no one yet knows what that limit will be, because the equipment has not begun to reach all the places it will eventually wind up in.

The potential for problems is obvious. The new equipment makes it physically possible for one person to type one hundred pages a day. How long any worker can be expected to type even half that many pages every day is another question. Office managers will have to find innovative ways to encourage productivity via job satisfaction, and it will not be in volume alone. Although presently the trend is for individuals to specialize in word processing—a speciality, by the way, that commands a very high salary (upwards of $20,000 in the Washington, D.C., area)—in the future it is likely that office managers will try to rotate the tasks of workers. Word processing is a novelty that soon wears off, and unless the tasks are varied, it is doubtful that many people will be happy to work at it without ceasing for years on end. With rotation, if a worker puts out a hundred pages in one day, she or he will perhaps be assigned a task other than word processing the next day.

One of the attributes of computer technology is that it is a boon for the person doing his or her own work, because that person is highly motivated to complete a lot of work in a short time. But it can be seen as less than a blessing by those who are working for others. The manager and the secretary will have an entirely different relationship in the future, and that relationship will depend in large measure on how computer competent the professional or managerial officer is. If he or she can use a computer, operate a word processor, and utilize electronic mail—all tasks which are relatively easy to learn—he or she will be less dependent on a secretary. This independence will give a manager more control over the secretary.

By the same token, if a secretary is computer competent and can operate managerial software, such as accounting packages, she or he will no longer be separated from the boss by a gulf of substantive knowledge. And these programs are not difficult to learn or use. So technology will generate new kinds of relationships between categories of workers and eliminate some of the basis for hierarchical relationships. Without the power of superior knowledge or skills, the boundaries between support staff and professional-managerial staff will tend to blur. The major differences will be in salary and in the social distinctions set up in the company itself.

Firms will react differently to these opportunities, depending on their own management's style. Some will embrace a new kind of office democracy, while others will try to perpetuate distinctions artificially. But workers in both support and professional and managerial positions will face a much different workplace than we know now.

The potential for technology to free people to enjoy life more than was ever possible in the past is also there. One sees hints of what we all will be able to get in places like Research Triangle Park in North Carolina or the cluster of high-technology-based communities south of San Francisco. These areas have no heavy industry. They are like oversized think tanks—their economy is based on research and finding, analyzing, disseminating, and storing information. Some workers are on fixed schedules and staggered work hours, but many others have a good deal of freedom in terms of when they arrive at work and when they leave. They are provided with recreational opportunities in or near their job site, often by their employers. They can take a break during the day to jog or swim or otherwise relax— anything to make their thinking time more productive.

Many workers in the future won't even go to the office, at least not every day. The new technology makes it possible to work from remote sites. There are advantages. A person does not have to get up early, does not have to dress a certain way, does not have to meet people, and can take as long a lunch break or golf break as desired. So the vision conjured up by Toffler's "electronic cottage" has some basis in reality.

On the other hand, people like company. Social interaction is a very important part of work. Psychologists note that social interaction takes up from one-fifth to one-fourth of the average work day. So many people will go to the office for fun.

Competition in the office hierarchy might also preclude people working at home. Middle managers, especially, might think twice about leaving their "turf" untended while they work at home. They might miss hearing some important information or rumor. Or their absence might give rivals an opportunity to undermine their efforts. Putting aside the cost factor, which is also important—companies are not going to pay for two computers for every worker, one in the office and one at home—there are good reasons why the electronic cottage will not become reality for very many workers very soon.

The electronic cottage is a reality for one group of workers already, however—those entrepreneurs who have seen the potential offered by the personal computer and who are cashing in on their particular technical skills in the marketplace. All over the country, individuals are busy creating software for personal computers. They work at home, and they generally work alone. They help each other out, and they even distribute free software so users can test it for them. Some sell their products to big companies, and some market it themselves. They are the Horatio Algers of the 1980s, because right now it doesn't take a particular genius to do well in this area—just a competent programmer. Although some of these new workers will become very wealthy, others will just enjoy a life of comfort in which they are the boss. They can set their own work schedules, they can decide what to work on, and they can determine the degree of perfection they want to obtain.

THE ORGANIZATION PERSON

This is the ideal of independence for those who crave independence, but most people's choices will still be bounded by the interdependence of one worker's tasks on those of another. Breaking into the dependency chain to make sure that the tasks are done properly is what many of the current quality-of-work experiments are all about, but they aim at making the workplace itself of real interest to the workers.

The most famous U.S. experiment in improving quality of work and work life began at Harman Industries in Bolivar, Tennessee, in 1972. The Bolivar experiment, conducted in a factory that made rearview mirrors, included much more than quality circles. It also included work quotas, which, when fulfilled, allowed workers to leave early; education and training at the plant for hobbies as well as job-related skills; even worker participation in bids on contracts.[4] Widely viewed as highly successful, the experiment did not prevent Harman Industries from ultimately closing its doors, a victim of economic forces that even these efforts could not overcome.

If quality of work is to be an antidote to labor–management strife, it has to be more than an experiment. And old attitudes die hard. Few managers really believe that workers should have a say in making business decisions. Few workers trust management's interest in their welfare to be anything more than a way to get more work out of the rank and file. There are few politicians, corporate executives, or union leaders who would support a European-style policy of codetermination, in which workers in key industries are included on boards of directors in substantial numbers (although the deciding votes still rest with management).

While employee ownership through stock-option plans is spreading more widely every year, there is no proportional increase in employee-owner participation in management decisions. A study completed by the University of Michigan's Institute of Social Research found that employee-owned firms had higher profits than conventionally owned firms in the same industry.[5] But the few scientific studies of worker participation in management and productivity have not produced conclu-

---

[4]Bruce Stokes, "Worker Participation—Productivity and the Quality of Work Life," Paper 25, Worldwatch Institute, Washington, D.C., December 1978, p. 14.
[5]Stokes, Ibid., p. 34.

sions powerful enough to persuade the skeptics that it makes much difference. And it is difficult to draw these kinds of conclusions under any circumstances, because one has to study the same firm with the same workers before and after participatory measures are introduced and over a long period of time.

Many observers still feel that there are no economic gains to be gotten from worker participation in management. Unless there is a conviction that worker participation is economically beneficial, most experiments will remain just that, and worker participation will not become an integral part of the production process, whether the products are goods, information, or services. Humanists who want to make the worker happy for happiness's sake will not get far with the people who watch the bottom line.

South Bend, Indiana, presents a prime example of the futility of worker ownership under less than ideal conditions. In 1980 employee-owners of South Bend Lathe struck against themselves. Until then, the company had been touted as a model situation. In its first year of employee ownership, productivity had jumped by one-fourth.[6] But when profits fell and there were no more bonuses, workers—who had failed in their attempt to claim half the seats on the board of directors—got mad. Eventually the strike was settled, but it remains a vivid illustration of the fact that employee stock ownership plans are not always fair to all the workers and are often used just as a way to bring new capital into a firm that can't get it anywhere else. The white-collar, salaried workers at South Bend Lathe got more stock than the blue-collar, hourly workers because stock distribution was based on income.

THE REWARDS OF WORK

The central fact about the quality of work life is that sometimes it won't be possible to improve it very much; workers will have to find their satisfactions in just doing the job well. In other cases, it will be possible, but "soft" incentives to workers, like quality circles, won't have lasting effects unless there are "hard" incentives also, like bonuses and dividends.

Without the hard incentives, productivity and quality may go

[6]*Business Week*, September 22, 1980.

up temporarily but fall again shortly thereafter because of what psychologists call the "Hawthorne effect." The name derives from a famous experiment that showed that workers would try harder temporarily regardless of whether their working conditions were being improved or downgraded, as long as management showed an interest in them. But the increases in output were not sustained over time when no tangible rewards were forthcoming. The Hawthorne effect makes it safe to predict that you can't fool a worker into putting more effort into a job unless the worker sees a real economic and social reward ahead.

The jobs in which all satisfactions—financial, status-related, and intrinsic—can be found will be the smart jobs. More satisfaction than ever before will be experienced in many of those jobs, because each person will be able to accomplish so much more with the aid of technology. Technology will liberate us to use the best of human nature: originality, compassion, creativity, and even humor. Washington Roebling, the construction engineer for the Brooklyn Bridge, that technological wonder of one hundred years ago, marveled that, in just a few hours, one mind could plan enough work to keep a thousand men busy for years. With the new technology, one mind will be able to *plan and execute* the work formerly done by ten minds or more. This is an inspiring thought.

12

The Individual and the Work Revolution

All the institutional changes we've mentioned are necessary for America to survive in the next decade and in the next century. But it is too optimistic to believe that many of them—especially guaranteeing publicly supported jobs—will be enacted quickly enough to help all those who will be affected in the immediate future.

American workers will be left in a cold new work atmosphere, competing with robots and word processors and illegal immigrants even as jobs are being destroyed and deskilled.

THE NEW GROUND RULES

What to do? How to survive? These are the central questions for everyone who wants to work.

The first thing to remember is that the rules have changed dramatically.

Change Is Continuous

The rule that you prepare in youth for the job or career that will last a lifetime has been turned on its head. Survival will increasingly mean changing occupations continually, especially if you are interested in smart and challenging jobs. The twenty-year-old student may find this rule easier to follow than the experienced worker of forty-five. But the experienced worker will not escape it any more easily. If you are an alert worker, you will be ready to learn and relearn throughout your lifetime, whether you are in a blue-collar, white-collar, or pink-collar job.

You May Have to Do What You Don't Do Best

The next rule is that the kinds of skills we will need will not necessarily be those we would prefer to develop. We won't always have the luxury of following our preferences. What you do best isn't necessarily marketable. Those who think it's clever to say they can't understand computers as well as their five-year-old may be telling the truth, but they may be dooming themselves to be outpaced in the career development system if they don't develop an understanding.

The Rewards Have Changed

The rewards for work may stack up differently than they have in the past. If there are many people seeking the same jobs, employers can change the reward systems radically. Take the example of the Chrysler Corporation. Workers there gave up wage increases to help save the company. Those still on the job wanted them back when the firm began to make profits after a government bailout, but those on indefinite layoff were willing to work for less pay than their colleagues at General Motors or Ford. Job have-nots suddenly develop different values from job-haves.

In the work revolution, lower pay may not be the only change for some jobs. Workers may have to accept fewer hours of work. They may have to accept fewer fringe benefits. They may have to change their expectations about the long-range financial rewards that work will offer. Rather than higher pay, they may find themselves negotiating for more leisure or more flexible hours at the same pay or for a work sharing arrangement to protect job security.

Education Is No Guarantee

A college education no longer guarantees a good job. It is useful to a thinking person, but many graduates now are struggling to find a job. There will not be enough jobs that demand college educations of the kind that people now have, and it will take special planning to see to it that college-educated individuals have the right skills and experience and knowledge that employers want.

The specificity of needed skills becomes more important with the rising number of degree holders. The class of 1983, the largest ever, had almost twice as many members as its parent class of 1963—965,000 compared with 500,000. The number of graduates has been rising fast but will taper off somewhat in 1986 as the last of the baby boom graduates. Even so, the Scientific Manpower Commission predicts that by 1992 there will be 3.3 million more college graduates than there will be jobs requiring a college degree.

But this doesn't mean avoid college. It means more education beyond college. Only the particularly qualified candidates will be able to compete for the jobs that require college degrees. The race for getting credentials for a job will escalate.

The race will not necessarily be won by those who hold advanced degrees. It's the combination of abilities and knowledge suited to the job market that will be the key to coping with the work revolution. For example, chemists who can assess the costs and benefits of alternative ways to manage toxic wastes will be in short supply and will command high salaries. Political scientists who can devise new ways of securing voter participation in polls and referenda by using electronic communications will be assured of a job for a long time. Unique combinations of education will help people survive in the work revolution. Math can be combined with child development, philosophy with engineering, or biology with computer systems analysis.

Each college graduate, though, will have a leg up on the nongraduate when it comes to finding a job at all, even if he or she cannot find a smart job.

BASIC JOB MARKET CONCERNS

All America Computer Competent

The point cannot be overstressed: No one who is not computer competent can legitimately expect to be a candidate for a smart job, with the possible exception of some of the helping professions that involve working with people exclusively. So the first essential and irreducible step toward a smart job is to buy a computer. By 1984 almost no one will be able to claim poverty as an excuse for not buying one. Step two, however, is a little harder: Learn to use the computer.

With every month that passes, more easy-to-use computer programs hit the market. Instructions are more clearly written now than they were last year and will be far more understandable next year. Anyone of any age can easily learn to use a computer to do something. Whether it is calculating one's income tax, making and keeping a household budget, or keeping track of a gourmet recipe collection, just about anyone with average intelligence can learn use of the computer with packaged software. High school students can learn to do math, sort quotations for literature papers, or track results of science experiments. There are a few basic computer capabilities that are readily transferred from one field to another, and a few basic terms that have to be incorporated into the user's vocabulary. Beyond that, however, "user friendliness" is taking the drudgery out of learning to use these electronic wizards, and computer competence does not require understanding any of the hardware or even any of the principles of programming.

Educational Basics

For young people and their parents, there are a few other steps that can be taken to guarantee access to smart jobs. The obvious one is to choose a school system that uses computers, if the choice presents itself. But another, not so obvious step runs counter to the received wisdom of the day: Do *not* concentrate on math and science. Study those, and study them extensively, but remember that making decisions in a complex world is going to be what most smart jobs are about. So other subjects are equally or more valuable in preparing people for the new world of work. History, philosophy, social studies, English— these courses, if taught well, help students learn to reason, to solve problems, to relate cause and effect, to understand events, and to plan ahead. Technology will make rote learning unnecessary as well as uninteresting, so today's pupils can have a lot more fun than their parents, learning only the facts that are relevant for a particular purpose knowing where to find more facts when they are needed.

A youngster finishing high school who cannot go to college for financial reasons, or older workers who have not had college educations and do not want one, should shop for the best available combination of skills training and general education they can find. The same principles will apply to them in the job market as apply to college graduates: Employers will want some unique combination of skills and learning that is out of the ordinary. So vocational training should start with specific skills that are in demand now and promise not to be obsolete in two or three years—for example, laboratory technician, medical assistant, financial information compiler.

Once on the job, workers can build up their backgrounds with study in other areas that make them more desirable than the run-of-the-mill person with the same skills. If they study management at a local business school, for example, or learn about particular applications of their knowledge, such as epidemic control for medical assistants or accounting for word processors, they will have more marketable skills than their competitors. Again, they will be following the new rule: Look beyond the first position, prepare for change, and expect no continuity of demand for any set of skills.

As for not finishing high school at all, that is a form of deliberate self-destruction. Young adults without a high school diploma will have no choice as to what kind of work they can get. They will be sure candidates for perpetual joblessness. They will have to obtain high school equivalency certificates even to enter the job market. They will also have to be sure that they can compete on other grounds—they will have to be well-spoken, agreeable, reliable, neat, etc. And this does not apply merely to disadvantaged youth who may not have been taught the niceties of everyday life. Plenty of independent middle class youngsters also face closed doors when they go looking for jobs, because they will not conform to the establishment's expectations as to how they should look or talk.

The Displaced Workers

The most visible and voluble group within the labor force today is comprised of the displaced blue-collar workers who will never go back to the auto plants and steel mills they expected to employ them for years. Their problem is severe, because they don't have either credentials or skills for white-collar or pink-collar work, and they don't have experience that is valued in many places other than those where they formerly worked.

But even as these words are written, the situation is changing, and displaced workers are learning to cope with the new rules, too. Whereas in 1982 there were no peer counselors available to dislocated workers, as of 1983 there were volunteer programs in many communities. Whereas in 1982 the only types of people to try to help displaced workers were charity groups and welfare workers, as of 1983 there were a myriad of special assistance programs run by union members and outsiders to help workers get over the grieving period that follows layoffs and plan a future.

The larger problem of displaced workers will be finding a set of competencies they can master and then mastering them well enough to get a different job in a different work setting. All of the suggestions about how to do this that apply to vocational training students and undergraduate students apply doubly to displaced workers. They cannot risk another failure, so they must choose their next set of skills very carefully. Computer competence is no more beyond an ex-auto worker than it is beyond his son or daughter, if he can stand the thought of sitting still all day. Dislocated blue-collar workers have got to think beyond their experience to new fields and new work settings. In doing so, they will set the example for others to follow.

Upgrading on the Job

Finally, there is that largest group of all, of workers who are for various reasons dissatisfied with their present job or fearful that it will not last, but uncertain as to whether or not they can do other kinds of work. These workers might follow the same paths as college students, learning enough about a new field to combine knowledge of two diverse areas. They could also follow the lead of vocational education students and learn a few applied skills that will make them more desirable as managers or supervisors. They could enhance their skills at existing professions, as did a math teacher we know who enrolled in a Master's program in computer-based math education. For many people, the threat of losing a job or finding oneself in a dead-end job may be just the catalyst that is needed to open up whole new areas of self-fulfillment.

For people who want variety, responsibility, and challenges, there are not as many choices openly offered as they might desire. People who get variety, challenges, and independence go looking for those rewards. And they often pay for them, by giving up other rewards. There are not very many smart jobs that pay the highest salaries, offer the most power, provide the greatest status, and permit the most autonomy. In the past, what we sought was generally what we got, and we stuck with it. In the work revolution, what we seek may not be what we find, so we'll have to keep on looking.

Beyond these general thoughts about how individuals can cope with the work revolution, there are the usual admonitions for job hunters: Dress well, write a good resumé, spell the words correctly, learn to conduct an interview with ease. There are plenty of how-to books on the market to teach the tricks of job hunting, and the serious worker will use them. The serious job seeker might also complain, in the right quarters, about the lack of job market information, adding another voice to a chorus demanding more and better quality job data. To drum up job opportunities, the serious job seeker will also follow all informal leads—through friends, mentors, jobs clubs, electronic bulletin boards, and other networks. By no coincidence, computer-user groups are an excellent source of job information, because the members work for companies that are using new software, which generally means companies that are expanding job opportunities.

WHERE DO WE GO FROM HERE?

The work revolution is here. The future job market in business and industry is going to be a buyer's market for some time to come. The potential for greater tension in American society is high if the nation—and individuals—fail to realize the seriousness of a constricted job market. The way to defuse that tension is to create and pay for more jobs. These are jobs that are highly desirable for maintaining the quality of life of our society, even though we have not been willing to pay for them in the past.

The efficiencies of the work revolution in the factory and in the office will raise the productivity of labor and business to the point that national income will remain high, even as joblessness is high. This paradoxical situation will demand that more attention be given to finding work for the victims of efficiency.

Those who oppose putting higher taxes on this efficiency to provide badly needed, publicly supported jobs cite the sorry history of past pump-priming efforts—the temporary, real make-work, countercylical jobs programs that we had during past recessions. But a permanent, deliberately planned system of creating needed goods and services is not at all in the same class with the old failed programs of the past. Once a program for such a system is approved, America could put a lot of its job anxieties behind it and concentrate on demanding the types of goods and services it wants most from publicly supported jobs.

Those who oppose putting higher taxes on new efficiency cannot also sit back and rail against welfare, food stamps, and unemployment compensation—unless they enjoy seeing people starve or suffer. And these programs are a less efficient way of helping the job have-nots than publicly supported jobs. It is frightening to contemplate the consequences of doing away with all these support mechanisms at a time when millions will be denied work opportunity in the private sector. Many have argued that reducing these programs dramatically would free up more private capital and provide many more jobs in the private sector. That argument, used by its adherents to buttress demands for investment "incentives" but not for work, is alluring because of the past successes of new investment in creating jobs. But this argument will lose much of its force in a real world where it will be demonstrated that investment in technology, as well as other forces, are destroying jobs and job opportunities.

The United States will once again be the most productive nation in the world as the work revolution takes hold. The big question is how the new efficiency will be shared: by everyone or by the lucky majority that might be tempted to look the other way? This is the dilemma of the revolution.

13

Matching Work and Workers

In 1983 business, government, and individuals spent an estimated $210 billion on education and job training—a full $930 for every man, woman, and child citizen.

We are not getting our money's worth from this investment in people. Proposals being put forth in Washington to invest in "human capital" tinker at the edges of a system that needs a major overhaul to cope with the demands of the work revolution. Many of these proposals, well-disguised as assistance to displaced workers, would further polarize the United States into a nation of job haves and job have-nots.

Let no one be fooled into thinking that the apparatus that educates, trains, and places workers in jobs runs on the fuel of altruism. It is a business worth money, and it is subsidized now by federal, state, and local governments. Whether federal government training funds subsidize training in private firms or by community groups or by government via educational institutions, we are talking about $10 billion per year. (Budgeted expenditures for 1983 were far below the previous years' levels. Federal Jobs Training Partnership Act authorizations were only $3 billion in 1983, as compared to $11 billion in 1979 and about $8 billion annually from 1980 through 1982.) Little wonder that the great training pork barrel has generated energetic lobbyists in Washington and self-serving entrepreneurs on the local scene who bypass professionally designed plans to match training to job opportunities and successfully manage political patronage through control of the training funds.

No matter what the current variation on the mechanism by which Congress doles out training funds to firms, community groups, or state and local governments, the fact is that the supposed beneficiaries get short shrift. The only way to unravel this net of favoritism, which is also burdened by bureaucratic definitions, restrictions, and reporting requirements, is to get rid of the apparatus itself and bring the worker, the education and training opportunities, and the job opportunities into direct contact. The following are some suggestions as to how this can be accomplished.

BALANCING SUPPLY AND DEMAND

For workers to be able to prepare themselves for work and find the right work opportunity, they need complete and consistent information on both current and projected job openings. By the same token, for employers to know how many workers are going to be available, they need information from the training pipeline. And for training institutions and educational institutions to provide the right kind of preparation, they need to know what kinds of skills will be needed when, where, and in what quantities.

If such information were available, then the interaction of job seekers and employers would work like the ideal market. The supply of workers in given occupations would match the demand for them, because when jobs in certain fields were not available, workers would stop looking in those fields. The more information on wages, working conditions, and advancement opportunities available, the more easily the number of would-be workers in a given field would adjust to the number of probable job openings. The more information about potential workers employers were provided, the more readily employers would adjust wages and benefits and working conditions to attract job applicants.

Of course there is no such thing as a perfect fit in the labor market, any more than in most complex markets. Imbalance will always exist. One source of the imbalance, which is often ignored in rosy forecasts, is the reluctance of would-be workers to face defeat in a job market they think is unlikely to give them a break. Discouraged workers just do not go looking for jobs at all, or else look so sporadically that their likelihood of finding one is minimal. Many discouraged workers are impoverished and skill-less, and there is no way to estimate how many such workers there are, because they are alienated from the larger society and would not, even if surveyed, be willing to answer questions about their work experience. Others are people who have worked but who are now immobilized by the sudden and dramatic reversals in their work life. And yet others are people with education but no work history, caught in that revolving door: You can't work without experience, and you can't get experience without work. The housewife who wants to return to work but has no specific skills, the poor black kid who has knocked on a hundred personnel-office doors and never landed a permanent job, and the over-forty-five manual worker who has been collecting unemployment insurance for nearly a year are all part of the vast army of discouraged workers.

The discouraged workers are grossly undercounted in official government statistics. The official estimate of the number of such workers in mid-1983 was 1.8 million, but some analysts place the figure at closer to 15 million. Certainly it is reasonable to guess that a substantial portion of those who are listed as "not wanting a job"—56 million people—are so listed because they have never been offered a job they want at a wage that seemed reasonable. In addition, there are an officially estimated 6 million involuntary part-time workers who would prefer a full-time job. Add to these the officially unemployed, and there were in 1983, officially, 18 million people unwillingly unemployed or underemployed—and possibly as many as 25 million.

The underlying unemployment rate—that is, the difference between the number of jobs available and the number of people who would like to work—could well be twice the official unemployment rate. The ebb and flow of workers into the labor force moves with the number and type of work opportunities, but not at the same time. It takes a little while for would-be workers to see and believe that they can find a job if they go looking for one. So after a recession, when the employment rate goes up, for a short time the unemployment rate goes down, because there are more jobs being filled relative to the previously counted labor force: those working and those actively seeking work. Pretty soon, though, people who had previously not been seeking work start looking for jobs. Then, unless the number of new jobs created continues to increase faster than the number of actual workers and work seekers increases, the unemployment rate goes up again.

To plan for the matching of work and workers, forecasters must pull their heads out of the sand. An estimate of the potential work force should form the basis for planning. This potential work force consists of all those of working age, eighteen to seventy, who are physically and mentally able, minus the people pursuing education full-time and minus women and men out of the labor force to raise children. This work force was numbered about 186 million in mid-1983—10 million more than the working-age population on which government unemployment statistics are based.

Imbalance in the labor market comes from another source, too: the information gap. Only 15 to 20 percent of the smart-job seekers can find out easily where the jobs are. The rest cannot do so because most of the players want to keep the information under their control. Employers don't want to be flooded with too many applicants or the wrong kind of applicants. Job seekers themselves are closed-mouthed in the face of fierce competition. Private employment agencies want a monopoly on the information so that they can keep themselves working. Public employment agencies know only what employers choose to tell them.

Despite the pages of ads in the Sunday newspapers, the vast majority of jobs available are not known to the public at large. Luck and whom you know play a big role in getting a job, especially a smart job. This lack of information helps ration jobs inequitably. Female would-be professionals and managers, and minorities whose networks don't overlap the majority's networks simply never hear about the good jobs available.

The first step in an ideal system to match jobs with job seekers is to make sure that skills are defined in relation to real demand, as distinguished from need. *Need* is what firms or institutions think they would like to have in the way of workers, but *demand* is how much labor they will buy and of what type and at what price. There is an important difference in job creation. For example, the Social Security Administration has long "needed" more programmers and systems designers, but because government regulations prevent it from paying competitive salaries, the agency cannot exercise economic demand for such personnel.

Skills relating to demand for workers should be listed in a job information system that is useful to the job seeker, but this is often not the case. What should be offered is a comprehensive inventory of jobs listing required competencies by industry and industries by geographical location. Then a worker or would-be worker could go job-hunting by answering many different questions about skills needed in specific industries and occupations in specific areas.

Unfortunately, a job seeker today finds something quite different. The state occupational information coordinating committees subsidized by the federal government offer the best systems available, but only twelve of them are computerized and these only allow the user to search for occupations, not for skills. And some state systems are better than others. There are differences as to the type of computer system used, how simple and "user-friendly" the system is, and how specific the information is relative to a given labor market. Data are poor and not updated frequently enough. Assumptions are often incorrect, and projects for the future are based on history that will never be repeated.

So far, attempts to organize and centralize job information for the benefit of workers and educators have not worked well. The best data are on topics such as earnings and work settings, the very type of information most readily available to individuals anyway; little useful job-opening data are available. But the promise is there. Here is an area where technology will be kind to workers. Once in place, it will solve many of the current job-search problems. Before that happens, schools, counselors, and individuals will have to clamor for it. They will have to insist that the ideal information system reflect:

1. Professionally approved, uniform data collection procedures;

2. Standardized estimating procedures for both short-term and long-term projections, made from the bottom up;

3. Uniform definitions of occupations and skills;

4. Accurate data on the number of workers in the occupational job market.

Having this information will give an individual the basics to find out where to get education and training to prepare for specific job categories. Ultimately, complete up-to-date information on education and training should be included in a job information bank. In the interim, all states should first speed development of job-skill information. One way to reduce costs is to eliminate historical data, using only current and projected job market data.

The primary effort should be to make sure that the system provides more realistic projections of demand by occupation and industry, updated at least every six months, and accurate information on the number of workers with needed skills. From this information, it will be possible to maintain a "gap estimate"—a moving measure of the difference between demand for and supply of workers. The gap estimate will be the important final product of the system, because it will help prevent overtraining in certain skill areas and shortages in others.

HOW DO WE GET THERE FROM HERE?

Literally dozens of organizations are involved in creating and distributing current state occupational information data. That is one reason why it is so difficult and costly to organize an adequate national job information system, despite the available technology to do so. And Congress does not help, because instead of fully supporting what was basically a good idea, it has set the scene to destroy what it created in 1976 under National Occupational Information Coordinating Committees (NOICC). The Jobs Training Partnership Act of 1982, which provided federal funds for state-directed training programs operated in cooperation with business and industry, permitted governors to set up alternative information systems even if federally funded state occupational information systems were already effective. It would have been far preferable for the Jobs Training Partnership Act to require states to improve their state occupational information systems and make their information more widely available, and to extend the funding of those systems. When the two laws come up for review, it is hoped that Congress will see the waste inherent in its uncoordinated legislation. To ensure this, educators, business leaders, parents, students, and workers need to become more vocal in insisting on the importance of a single, uniform, complete information system.

The federal government should follow through on its initiative to consolidate labor market information by matching state funds on a fifty-fifty basis, at a high enough funding level that states have the resources they need to set up first-rate occupational information systems. The ideal system outlined by NOICC would cost an estimated $6 million to $10 million annually to mount and maintain. Federal support for all states now totals $1.4 million annually, and the amount has been decreasing during the most critical period in recent history in terms of need for education and job training information.

But government money necessarily comes with government controls if it is to produce useful results, and job information is no exception. Right now a number of private firms acquire government statistics, computerize them, and sell them, in effect offering reruns of government numbers. It would be more useful for private purveyors of occupational information to create original systems for using and understanding the information. States should not purchase from private vendors computerized raw data or data that are presented in the same form as published government documents. Rather, they should force vendors to produce more useful and forward-looking analytic and descriptive tools.

Communities should insist that such creative computerized systems be available *and publicized.* Community groups that do all sorts of fund raising for worthy causes have neglected this subject, but what could be more worthy than helping to provide critical labor market information to the residents and workers in the community? Community groups can also help the state occupational information systems to update their data base with employer-generated local data to make the information more relevant to particular locales. Businesses hate to be surveyed, and the state systems have to be careful not to overburden them. But business leaders should volunteer their time to provide data as a community service. The all-important information on skills and competencies could be added to government-generated occupational information.

If all these things were to happen, individual workers would have a gold mine. They would probably be willing to pay a nominal fee to use it, but they should not have to. Even with such data available, individuals should supplement the official information with books and articles about careers and with talks with placement offices at local universities, colleges, and community colleges; personnel officers at major employers in the area; and jobs clubs.

No one should expect to be spoon-fed all the answers. Since all of us had better get accustomed to the idea that the work we do today is not necessarily the work we'll do tomorrow, being on the lookout for new opportunities is a responsibility each person will have to take on for him- or herself.

OVERHAULING EDUCATION AND TRAINING

More of us will have to get used to the idea of seeing skills grow obsolete and of subsequently preparing to move on to new opportunities. Education and training will be lifelong processes, not one-time accomplishments. The revolution in work will bring about a revolution in education and training, not only because the nature of work is changing, but also because the student population is changing. There are ever-increasing numbers of older students in the classrooms of colleges, community colleges, and training schools. There has always been a small percentage of such students, but there will be more in the future. More women than ever will go back to school to get the training they missed earlier, which will also push up the average age of students. Mature people with work-oriented learning needs will place different demands on teachers than younger students who have not had their hard knocks. Even younger students are beginning to shift to a more work-oriented curriculum.

And there is a new class of students that will grow bigger—the displaced blue-collar and clerical workers. These men and women come into retraining reluctantly as a rule, forced to do something, anything to rejoin the ranks of the employed. They are often bewildered and resentful. Although things will change in the future, right now most of these displaced workers haven't budgeted either the time or the money to allow themselves to attend classes. They need quick answers and job-specific training in growth fields that are least likely to lead to the same type of dying-industry casualties.

With a student population this diverse, it will be a real challenge to provide education and training-delivery systems that meet the full range of critical needs. But consciousness that more forward-looking approaches are needed to deal with the changes that can now be foreseen and with the unexpected dynamics that the work revolution will bring on is the first requirement.

A number of quick-fix solutions to the displaced-worker problem were proposed when observers became aware of the problem in late 1982. One is a voucher system, by which workers would be given, instead of their full unemployment compensation, a chit entitling them to be trained or retrained in a private firm or in a classroom. The trainer would get part of the foregone unemployment compensation as a fee for providing training services.

The presumed virtue of this proposal is that the burden of paying for training would be on the employee, not on society at large or on the company that will employ him after retraining or on the company that laid him or her off. But the advocates of the voucher system remain silent on the question of how an unemployed worker would also be able to pay the rent or a mortgage or health insurance and buy food with what was left of his or her unemployment insurance check.

Another proposal was to establish a new tax gimmick, called an Individual Training Account, to which both employers and employees would be required to contribute. The proceeds would be available to the employee needing retraining. If an employee never used the money for training, his or her contribution presumably could be recovered at retirement. Business economist Pat Choate, who proposed this, believes it has the virtue of sharing the cost of retraining equally between current employers and current employees. But the proposal does not deal with the bigger question: What happens to people who have never been employed? Besides, it would be a roundabout way to get employer-employee financing, which, as we shall see, is not really necessary.

A quick-fix proposal described in an earlier chapter was to reduce the hours of individual workers and compensate them for time not worked through the unemployment compensation system. This technique, however, did not apply on the same terms to all firms or all workers and, over the long run, would tend to deplete the unemployment compensation fund.

Another suggestion was to offer broad and deep corporate income tax credits to firms that agree to retrain workers. Presently employers can claim a business expense for training or retraining their workers; a tax credit would be even more valuable if employers had a substantial income tax liability. However, broad and deep tax credits could also eliminate completely the tax liability of many firms. So this so-called costless means of financing retraining would really mean that nonbusiness taxpayers, who would have to pay more to make up the tax revenues lost through the training credits, were indirectly footing the bill. The workers who were being retrained would have no responsibility for paying for their own skills upgrading, and the employers who benefited from a more highly trained work force would not be paying for the benefit.

All of these proposals are aimed at financing retraining but distribute the burden of financing it in very different ways. Each tries to avoid the appearance of taxing the public directly. Each reflects an underlying philosophy or at least an unspoken objective concerning the role of business and labor in paying for skills upgrading. Each has a more profound limitation than that, however: All assume that the problem is how to finance training and that if that issue can be solved, the job problem will be solved, too.

In other words, these so-called solutions are aimed at the wrong problem. While rapid retraining is desirable in many industries, there is no evidence that firms will not retrain workers when they need to, nor is there evidence that workers will not find a way to get retraining when they want to. Indeed, all of the evidence suggests the opposite: When there is a sudden surge in demand for particular skills, people go out and get those skills. For example, in the summer of 1983, record enrollments in computer programs at colleges and community colleges were achieved. To deal with the retraining issue in isolation from the bigger question—what all the trainees will work at—would merely worsen the problem by pretending to solve it and is an excellent example of the "law of public policy": that for every problem there is a solution that is simple—and wrong.

Most of these proposals to finance training are somewhat disingenuous, in that they shift the cost of training away from the firms who will benefit from it. Investment tax credits and accelerated depreciation (ACR) for business and industry have already just about wiped out the tax contributions of business and industry. There is almost no tax liability left against which training tax credits could be used. Will proponents of such legislation propose a refundable tax credit, as they did in the case of the accelerated depreciation allowed on capital investment—so that a firm without a tax liability this year could get a check from Uncle Sam in the amount of its earned but unused credit?

We do not accept this approach. We believe that business and industry, which will be more productive and more profitable when the fifth technological revolution is complete, will be able to assume more of a share of providing tax revenues, not less.

There are serious questions of fairness involved here. There

are also questions of simplicity and efficiency involved in deciding what mechanism should be used to provide financing for
training and retraining. If the burden is to be borne by employers and workers only, an additional payroll tax is the simplest
mechanism. This is what the training account proposal is, under
a different guise. The social security tax could be raised for both
employer and employee if it was determined that lifelong training and retraining opportunities are as essential an element of
security as are retirement benefits. Or a reformed unemployment insurance compensation law could include, say, $1000
worth of training for every unemployed person. This would be
roughly half the average value of unemployment compensation
collected during the 1981–83 recession. This would be cheaper
than setting up a new program and a new bureaucracy and
could be a spur to an overhaul of the entire unemployment
compensation system, which is needed in any case to deal with
the states' excessive debt to the system.

As of 1983 states owed the federal government some $12.9
billion because the insurance premiums they had been charging
were not sufficient to meet the large payouts that had to be
made during 1982 and 1983, and the federal government bailed
them out. Either the federal government will have to forgive
this debt, or the insurance premiums will have to be raised to
pay it off, or the benefits paid to future unemployed persons will
have to be reduced. Or some combination of the above options
will have to be arrived at. Since future demands are likely to
throw the actuarial estimates out of whack, it is a safe predic-
tion that unemployment compensation reform will soon be on
the political agenda.

WHO'S IN CHARGE HERE?

Individuals always have found and always will find a way to
prepare themselves for real work opportunities, if they believe
those opportunities lie ahead. Indeed, we find somewhat dis-
tasteful the notion that an unemployed steelworker who has
been socking away part of $25,000 to $35,000 per year earnings
for several years is so helpless that he can't figure out for himself
how to prepare himself for a different work life.

All in all, the training and retraining system will work best if
approached on a market basis. Those who seek training for a
specific purpose should prepare themselves. Those who want

trainees to have specific skills should continue to provide the necessary on-the-job training and classroom training, as they have in the past. Government should intervene in this system only to assure that no individual is deprived of an opportunity to get education and training because of a lack of funds. But all individuals are no more deserving of subsidized training than all individuals are deserving of government-subsidized housing.

The tried and true, simple way to help people acquire services they cannot afford to pay for all at once is to lend them the money. The best way to encourage people to invest in their own future is to lend them the money at interest rates they can afford to pay back. The United States already has a good deal of experience with loans for education. The same philosophy can be extended to finance retraining, training, or education. The cost in bureaucracy is minimal. The individual's responsibility is maximal, as he or she will not retrain unless the training seems to promise an avenue to being able to repay the loan.

The only argument against a low-cost education-and-training loan system is the specter of default, which has plagued some of the student loans of the past. There are easy ways to ensure repayment if the political will to do so exists—through the income tax withholding system. Research on mortgage defaults shows risk of nonpayment is relatively low among blue-collar workers, anyway. A 1983 study of unemployed Pennsylvania workers by Garfield Schwartz Associates showed that only a very small proportion of mortgagors were at risk of default on their mortgages.[1]

Revenue for a massive education-and-training loan fund can be raised in the traditional way: through general individual and corporate income taxes. Or it could be raised by "mortgaging" the future earnings of individuals and issuing training debentures guaranteed by the government. A guarantee is far less costly than a direct loan fund, and if it is accompanied by a subsidized interest rate, would attract a substantial amount of private capital into the loan pool. The rates would have to be competitive with alternative returns on loaned funds to induce lenders to participate in a substantial way.

To set up a pilot education and retraining fund would cost

[1]Lawrence Swanson and Gail Garfield Schwartz, "Mortage Foreclosure: A Risk of Structural Unemployment," working paper for Majority Leader Pennsylvania House of Representatives, Garfield Schwartz Associates, Washington, D.C., May 1983.

relatively little, and the market for it could be tested quite easily. All it would cost the government in the short run is the debt service plus the publicity and administration costs. If administration were made the responsibility of an organization that already manages government loans, those costs could be kept to bare bones. To set up a loan guarantee fund of say $10 billion, which would be enough to lend $3000 to 3.3 million people, would cost, at current rates, in the neighborhood of $1.5 billion per year. (The actual cost depends on the terms, interest rates, and volume anticipated in the first year.)

This is really a very simple old idea: Increase the demand for high-quality education and training, and you can reduce the unit costs of providing it. While improving the quality of the labor force, you allow individuals to choose their own future at a price they select for themselves and on a timetable of their preference. If that is done, the supply of training should meet the market.

To ensure that the supply of education and training opportunities is the right kind at the right price, government can also help reduce market friction by subsidizing an adequate information system. Individual consumers of education and training will be encouraged to find the best value for their investment because they have to pay back the loans. The purveyors of education and training will be encouraged to provide the best courses in order to attract the best students and the most tuitions. The employers will naturally be encouraged to select the best-trained persons. The value of the human capital "in circulation" will increase over time as people are better prepared and retrained. All other things being equal, wages and benefits should adjust to reflect that value, as it is translated into higher productivity for employers.

FILLING THE NEED TO KNOW: EDUCATION

With the work revolution, our attitudes toward the overall educational and vocational training system will change. We will no longer think of education as something young people do and training as something manual workers do. It will be a case of everyone doing something somewhere to improve his or her job prospects. Some will retrain to change fields, others to get higher pay, others to move into new occupations, and others just to enjoy mastering new skills. Many people will retrain and reeducate themselves many times during the course of their working life.

If the educational and vocational training system is to meet the new demands placed on it by all different types of students in all different stages of development, it will have to overhaul itself. The first step in what we have called the market-oriented approach to that process, as we have said, is the gathering and disseminating of the necessary information about opportunities for jobs after training. But enabling trainers and educators to know what to train for is not enough to promise employers that an adequate supply of qualified workers is in the training pipeline. Curricula and processes also must be changed.

Educators call it competency-based instruction. We call it a need-to-know approach. From the list of skills described in the discussion of the information base needed—which is to be provided by employers—new curricula can be devised, which include the basics needed for particular groups of occupations. *These basics may not be the basics now normally taught.*

Contrary to the popular received wisdom, the old-fashioned basics, presented in the old-fashioned sequence, may not be the right prescription for the classrooms of the future. Logical reasoning may be taught not through geometry, but through programming first, with geometry and higher math coming in later. The reason for this is that the way people go about solving problems with computers helps them absorb in a very concrete way the abstractions usually associated with learning math. Not that the entire traditional curriculum should or would be thrown out overnight. But as educators become more familiar with the way the computer aids learning and school children become at-home with keyboards, symbols, and sequences, new approaches will be inevitable. It will be wise not to insist that old approaches are necessarily the best, whether in teaching math or any other subject. Think how happy countless students would be if spelling were to be relegated to the arena of frills by computer dictionaries.

Skills Centers

Making the best use of available training equipment in the most cost-effective manner is another major goal. Right now, most manpower training and education is client-group centered, with different institutions offering the same kinds of training and education to their particular market segment. Client groups include public school students, apprentices, the handicapped, post-secondary school students, displaced workers, disadvantaged youth, housewives returning to work, retirees, and many other special groups. Duplicating programs at various institutions is a very costly way of imparting the desired knowledge to the interested groups and creates a competitive atmosphere among learning institutions as each seeks to maximize enrollment to increase tuition revenues (private schools) or per capita subsidies (public schools).

Such duplication of effort might seem at first glance to be beneficial to the student, who gets to choose the best from the lot. But another outcome is that such a group-centered system produces too many trainees in some areas and too few in others. In preparing for future work, such overlap and duplication will become prohibitively expensive, because more and more of the applied training will demand expensive equipment such as computers, robots, or laboratory equipment. As technology races foward, it will be necessary to update equipment on a more frequent basis. State-of-the-art equipment must be used in training to produce well-qualified workers, and this equipment should be used to its maximum capacity to justify the investment. It can most effectively be provided in skills centers that are used at least eighteen hours a day by different students under the authority of different organizations. In the early day, for example, high school students could use the equipment, and in the late day and evening, working people and adult trainees could use it. Costs of purchasing and maintaining the equipment would be minimized to each institutional user because fewer items would serve more people.

Educational institutions should adapt the same centralized approach for remedial math and English courses, which are now offered at all educational levels at great waste. From apprenticeship programs to four-year colleges, educators lament the time and effort spent on teaching skills and competencies that should have been learned before the student entered their particular program. Remediation could more efficiently be handled through community centers, to which many different institutions, both public and private, would subscribe. Such basic learning centers would attract the best teachers and allow other institutions to spend their time and money on substantive subjects.

Preparing for the Best Smart Jobs

In the technological and scientific fields, demand for labor has temporarily outstripped supply, and we are faced with a challenge to train and retrain a cadre of elite scientists and engineers fast. The number of graduate students in engineering, physical sciences, environmental science, mathematics, and computer science has either been dropping or rising very slowly. Many of the related professions are "graying" as their members age, and if the older professionals don't reeducate themselves regularly, they become useless employees. The problem has been noticed most in engineering. Forty percent of the existing engineers are over fifty-five, and many leave the profession because their skills are obsolete. The number of graduates now being trained is insufficient to replace them. But upgrading will be continual in life sciences, too. And mathematicians are also in very short supply, with an especially acute shortage in secondary-school math teachers. Only one thousand persons received doctorates in math in each of the last ten years.

It is generally agreed that if the United States is to regain the lead in innovation and applications of new discoveries, we need to increase the number of entry-level personnel in the science and technology fields by a factor of five to ten. But adding to the supply of new, well-trained scientists and engineers is the easier part of the answer. Providing for life-long knowledge upgrading is much more difficult. The higher levels of skills are generally obtained in university settings, but universities are not prepared to deal with older, part-time students. Again, overlaps and gaps can be prevented through cross-crediting, shared personnel, and shared facilities. Cooperation can lower costs, which will be high over the lifetime of the average student, and expand opportunities.

The number and distribution of learning centers are a matter for local determination—on the basis of considerations of accessibility, economies of scale made possible by purchasing equipment and supplies in bulk, availability of space at relatively low cost, and proximity to needed support such as laboratories or materials suppliers. By bringing the discipline of a profit center into the education and training system, it will be possible to help more people obtain the skills they need in a rapidly changing work environment, at a lower cost, and more quickly than under the present chaotic system.

Education of Teachers

Without adequate personnel, the nation's industries cannot develop the innovative adaptations of existing technology that will enable them to capture new markets and reduce the costs of goods. To educate and reeducate the needed scientists and technicians, we need top-notch teachers. But it's not only scientists and technology students who need highly competent teachers familiar with the latest uses of technology. All teachers from elementary school through the Ph.D. level need basic computer proficiency to prepare all citizens for the twenty-first century.

The quality of teachers and school administrators is not a pop subject to be headlined today and forgotten tomorrow. We need a long-term commitment to quality control in education. Ways to gauge the quality of teaching should be encouraged, but more important, communities should act now on the basis of knowledge available as to what makes a good school. Basically, it's sound leadership in an atmosphere of creativity. Research on good schools is not needed; action is.

Some schools now require tests that establish a basic standard of achievement and if students do not pass such tests, they receive a certificate of attendance instead of a diploma. This is a step in the right direction, but to it we need to add more challenges and better rewards to attract the brightest people into teaching. After all, our children are our most precious resource.

ORGANIZATION AND DELIVERY OF EDUCATION SERVICES

The fragmentation of the American education and training system is so profound that the growing debate over who should be in charge of improving education is literally without significance. Many educational institutions have jurisdiction over small parts of the education and training system. State agencies with control over funds and programs include departments of human resources, labor and employment, commerce and industry, and economic development. Realistically, centralizing education and training seems out of the question, given such bureaucratic chaos.

The only sensible thing to do is to insist upon more coordination among agencies and institutions—a tall order because of the mores of bureaucracy. Only the enduring crisis in education and training will force changes in the scope of services each institution can and should provide.

Specialization by educational institutions in providing training and education is a prime goal; the educational and training system in the United States is rife with duplication. One way to eliminate some of this terrible national waste is for institutions to establish stronger communications links. They should jointly plot their central strategic goals and try to make them conform to the areas and the industries they are serving. Giving up some individual autonomy and power will yield greater efficiency. Institutions will survive by specializing.

Information on Education and Training Opportunities

To guide both institutions and potential students through the maze of available offerings, a description of all education and training opportunities in each state is needed. The list should include all the institutions in a labor market area that provide instruction in each area of competence. For each one, at least the following information should be provided: course titles, time offered, duration, cost, prerequisites, kind of placement offered, and number of program completers placed. Then students, teachers, and administrators can find more information as needed from catalogs and actual course descriptions.

It is not likely that educational and training institutions would bar students from courses with a low career relevance, but they can offer responsible guidance as to the utility of various courses of study in the job market so that students can make intelligent decisions. Colleges and universities should help liberal arts students study practical subjects such as programming, management, or accounting to supplement their other course work and make them more competitive in the job market. Skills-training schools should help students find supplementary education opportunities. Special efforts should be directed toward helping people with science and math "phobias." And financial suport of occupational training that is in high demand should be provided.

Help Wanted from Business and Industry

Business and industry leaders hold the key to unlock an improved education and training system. The demand for labor makes or breaks a community economically. To improve the matching of workers and work, educators and business have to start talking the same language. Business personnel should work closely with educators to design courses to fit the needs of the future. They should work with test designers to develop competence measures. They should make their anticipated skill needs as explicit as possible and update them frequently.

An important role for business and industry is to help trainers and teachers evaluate competency. While most competency evaluation can be done by computer—with word, number, symbol, and logic problems—some competencies are "hands-on." Educational institutions do not have and should not have enough personnel to assess these competencies, but the private sector can send qualified people to perform the evaluations.

Business can also boost education quality by offering part-time employment for teachers. This not only supplements teaching pay, but also gives teachers practical experience so they can plan lessons in a real-world context. When business leaders agree to a highly visible and continual involvement in education and training, they will not only get the benefit of tax write-offs and good will, but the long-term gain of a well-qualified labor force.

THE MOVING TRACK

Matching work and workers is the end of the line of a long process that involves many actors. It begins at home with the education of toddlers, becomes institutionalized in nursery school and preschool, and will end in life-long education and retraining for the worker. It is dynamic, because the needs for education and training will always be changing, and the opportunities for getting education and training will be fluid, too. So getting on the education and training track is something like boarding a moving sidewalk. Because conditions will probably change rapidly, many people will become confused and make mistakes. These can be costly and disappointing and discouraging, and in the transition to the new technological society, there will be some bruised individuals. Still, people are very adaptable. Once they know where they want to go they can usually figure out a way to get there.

Workers deserve some help in the transition, as do youngsters coming up the ladder and people who have never yet had a chance to work. It will benefit everyone if as many people as possible adapt quickly to the new world of work, even if it means a massive education and retraining effort. But it is the worker, not the employer and not the training and education establishment, who needs the help. Any government assistance should go directly to the worker, so that a real market for education and training will be guaranteed.

This market should be discriminating; workers should look the field of offerings over carefully before placing their funds at the tuition window. This cautious consumerism will make education and retraining more effective and more efficient. Government can help in this process two ways: by providing information that helps match people, skills, and work and by helping individuals finance their own education and training if they need aid. The responsibility for doing this lies with the federal government, because local and state governments in areas with the highest rates of unemployment and the greatest need for change do not have the fiscal resources to do it.

There is one element of the match between workers and work that the individual, no matter how energetic and forward looking he may be, has no control over: the number and nature of jobs to be sought. Unless the nation attends to both sides of the equation—that is the supply of jobs as well as the supply of skills—all the education and training in the world won't solve the basic problem: too little work for too many would-be workers.

$$14$$

Coping with the
Work Revolution

America has never been psychologically ready to accept a pessimistic view of the future. Perhaps it is not in us to do so, and that may be an important foundation for the sanity of the nation. The political system is attuned to problem solving, and every economic failure in one administration brings on a counterwave of new ideas in another. The recurring cycle of proposal and counterproposal stirs hope, then disappointment, then new hope. The nation's history of attempts to smooth the ups and downs in the economy and to protect those who are hurt the most by them amounts to a series of actions and reactions that have left us a layered social welfare system and a confusing array of private subsidies that, taken together, no longer stand the test of reason. Yet this wavelike structure of our economic life—from failing program to new proposal, from recession to recovery—mesmerizes the nation into accepting the belief that employment losses today will be made up tomorrow.

Because recoveries follow recessions according to the natural flow of the business cycle, many Americans cannot shake off the spell of shortsightedness long enough to see the work revolution dogging them at every step. The changes they see are dismissed as inevitable, part of the cyclical adjustment that will somehow work out to the benefit of all. But this viewpoint has long since reached its limits, because it applies primitive theory to vastly more complex situations. The new complexities virtually guarantee that, although the unemployment rate will fall somewhat after the 1981–82 recession because of the business cycle, it will not fall by very much—and certainly not as low as the 7 percent it was before the recession began.

The underlying unemployment rate is creeping up. Scholars and politicians alike are now ready to accept 6 percent permanent unemployment, and some accept rates even higher than that. That is a more sober view than a few years ago, but compared with what is really going to happen, it represents excessive optimism. The optimism reflects nostalgia for what can never be again; it projects an almost romantic image of a simple world of small businesses and transparent business transactions.

On closer examination, it is clear that the work revolution has been chipping away at these romantic notions for years. The romantics are finding they have less and less room to prove their view of the world, because each cycle brings a higher unemployment rate than the last. Even the theoreticians have come to realize the inadequacies of their approach to explain and predict what is really happening. In 1983 a prominent group of international economists announced intentions to take another long-range look at economic theory on grounds that the old theories haven't worked and that economics had failed to consider the impact of the new technology in an adequate fashion.

Not only have times changed, the very nature of time itself is changing, too. Technological changes have wreaked havoc with many of our fast-held notions of time as it related to work. Tasks can now be completed in less time than it formerly took to plan how to execute them. Technology is also destroying concepts of human limitations. The new machines are making the impossible possible. A few years ago, it took sixteen days to make a locomotive engine frame; now it takes only sixteen hours, with a drastic reduction in the number of people required to do the job. Speed in mental work has been accelerated. It takes one microprocessor less than ten seconds to recalculate every number on a work sheet with a thousand entries on it. It would take a researcher using a calculator at least one day to do that work.

Like all its predecessors, the new technology is a double-edged sword, offering great promise while also setting the stage for many new problems. The very benefits of the speed and effectiveness of machines strike a realistic fear in our hearts: Human power may not be needed at all. Human ingenuity will surely create new work opportunities, but the new technology, coupled with international competition, will displace more workers than it employs. There will be a mismatch not only between the unemployed and the number of available jobs, but also between the unemployed and the types of skills required for the new work.

The new unemployment will be different. Many more Americans will become "structurally unemployed," because in many occupations fewer workers will be able to produce much more work. In industries with many such jobs, layoffs will not be a temporary phenomenon attributable to a recession or inevitable business cycles. Rather, they will be permanent. In other occupations, changing demands for skills will increase the number of jobs for which there are not enough applicants and the number of jobs for which there are too many workers. Thus so-called frictional unemployment—the result of the inability to match job seekers with job openings—will also rise. Some people will be jobless for longer periods and the periods of high unemployment will be longer. This revolution's victims already include millions of displaced workers and millions more disrupted lives—and there will be many more.

Widespread unemployment is a threat to the health and safety of the nation in many ways. It is a corrosive agent when it comes to political stability. It affects the physical and mental health of the country in many overt and subtle ways. It raises public costs as social budgets are strained. It renders meaningless many government support programs that rely on high employment. Not the least of these are the social security and Medicare systems. When Congress approved the social security bailout in 1983, it thought that the financing problem had been solved at least until the baby boom population reaches retirement in the year 2020. But the truth of this assumption rests on a higher level of employment than now anticipated, so the security we all look for in our old age as a reward for hard work may not be there.

Another victim of the revolution could be the degree of stability among economic classes in the United States. Social tensions are bound to intensify as technology splits the work force between good, smart jobs and dull, routine jobs. Beyond the social strife, Voltaire's statement still holds true: "Work keeps us from three great evils—boredom, vice, and need."

The developing technological and economic situation demands a more comprehensive "solution" than the old cyclical attempts of the past. Elaborate economic programs designed to manipulate the economy in the short run with tax cuts or new social programs now have been exposed as inadequate to the task. Presidents Nixon, Ford, Carter, and Reagan, for all their other differences, all tried this incremental path to prosperity. At the end of all the tax cuts and other growth incentives were prosperity for some, riches for a few, and unemployment for many. None of the last four administrations fully appreciated the challenge of foreign competition or the effects of the blooming technological revolution.

Where we go from here depends, of course, on whether the nation is willing to accept that the work revolution will bring further adverse consequences on individual lives. The danger is that we will ride through two or three more business cycles with hope and still find ourselves left with double-digit unemployment, wasting precious national resources in the process. To avoid that danger, people must realize that the technological revolution will be an unprecedented boon to many workers and an unprecedented threat to many others. The trick for the nation will be to reap the rewards and avoid the individual tragedies. There are never any easy answers, only difficult choices. Here are some of our difficult choices.

JOBS FOR THE COMMON WELFARE

On June 28, 1983, near Greenwich, Connecticut, a massive section of Interstate 95 spanning the Mianus River collapsed. A week earlier, a dam in Utah burst from the heavy rains. And a few weeks before that, officials discovered a huge concentration of dioxin in Newark, New Jersey. There's a common thread in all these events. They reveal neglect; they reveal jobs that need to be done but aren't being done. They also reveal a potential solution to the joblessness that will be spawned by the work revolution.

Technology will make it possible to do much useful work that is not now done, financed through productivity gains in the private sector. For want of a better phrase, we need "quality of life" workers who can build and repair roads, railroads, airports, water systems, waste treatment plants, parks, and recreational facilities. They can renovate historic buildings. They can monitor power plants and toxic waste disposal and air and water quality. Undersupplied services—day care, health services, mental health care, geriatric care, rehabilitation of criminals and the physically and mentally handicapped, beautification, and arts and cultural projects all can be provided in abundance. That is the promise of the work revolution.

The only way to provide these jobs is through an expansion of the public sector. Publicly supported jobs have received a bad press, partly because our first experience with them was so limited in scope and in mission. They were designed to help only the disadvantaged, and sometimes they amounted to little more than a handout. But in some cases, they did a lot of good. Although many people think of such jobs as demeaning and useless, that doesn't have to be the case. It's how you label the work, not what the actual work is, that demeans it. "Make-work programs" is a phrase that conjures up jobs that are useless to society, even though the term itself is virtually meaningless. For example, you will not find many businessmen calling an investment tax credit a "make-work program," even though it is as much a subsidy as a public-service job might be.

Publicly supported jobs would be as valued as private-sector jobs if Congress decided that it is public policy to provide meaningful work for everyone who wants it. A national Jobs Declaration is necessary to begin to meet the challenge of the work revolution. The declaration would have five parts:

1. If given permanent financial and psychic rewards, people will work. They are interested in productive work.

2. Government has a responsibility for ensuring that everyone who is able to work can obtain useful work.

3. Publicly supported projects will enhance the quality of life for everyone and improve the economy.

4. Publicly supported jobs should encompass a wide scope of skills, not just menial tasks.

5. A match is feasible between the skills of unemployed people and publicly sponsored jobs.

The most important of the five is Number 2, of course. Such a declaration, if it carried the force and teeth of law, would be a dramatic change for the nation. But the opponents are legion, asserting that any kind of publicly supported job would merely redistribute income and sap the strength of the private sector.

This argument is based on two false premises. One is that the private sector would create the jobs if the public sector did not, which is clearly not the case. The other is that publicly assisted jobs are economically worthless—that they just give away government money which would not otherwise be spent, without creating any value.

Publicly assisted jobs create income and wealth just as private-sector jobs do. They are not merely a drain on the economy. For example, publicly supported jobs that improve the nation's highways, bridges, water and sewage facilities, and public buildings spur economic development and increase the value of both public and private facilities. Every dollar paid a worker from tax revenues is turned over in the economy just like dollars from private-sector workers. It's spent on food, housing, clothing, appliances, and services. On top of that, the workers are doing enormous good, providing needed facilities we don't now have.

Those who oppose government-guaranteed, publicly supported jobs also cite the high cost and budgetary problems. To be sure, these jobs are expensive, but the opponents miss a basic point: The gross cost of a permanent Quality of Life jobs program would be largely offset by the contribution Quality of Life workers would make to tax revenues, the social security system, savings in unemployment compensation and health care and welfare costs, and the value added to the economy and society by their labor.

This point is so vital that it's worth a close look. Suppose the government's *lowest* projection is correct, and there are only 122 million people in the 1990 civilian labor force. Suppose there are 115 million jobs available through growth in the private sector and constant employment in the public sector. This would mean that 7 million able workers were without jobs. Assume next that 5 percent of these unemployed workers are between jobs or frictionally unemployed—that we don't have to worry about them. This would mean that 6.65 million workers who are able and willing to work are available. Suppose that there were a wide range of Quality of Life jobs for them, ranging from construction projects at minimum wages to paraprofessional jobs such as nursing home attendants to technical jobs like toxic-waste inspectors, so that the average wage paid for each job was $15,000 (an amount equivalent to $12,000 in 1983, assuming inflation at 4 percent per year for the rest of the decade). The gross cost of the Quality of Life jobs would be $100 billion. But the net cost would be much less.

Each Quality of Life worker would pay income taxes—say $1580, which is what the average individual with one dependent now pays and is a reasonable estimate of what an individual with two dependents would pay in 1990. Each worker would contribute 7.7 percent of wages to the social security system, which is $1155. The government would not have to pay for workers' health care through Medicaid; value that savings at the minimum cost of "bare-bones" health insurance plans offered to unemployed workers in 1983, which was $986 per year. The average unemployment compensation of $2065 per person per year would be saved. Finally, each Quality of Life worker would have more money to contribute to the economy than a person receiving unemployment compensation and would generate at least $3750 per year in additional expenditures for clothing, housing, and so forth. Subtracting all these savings and benefits from the $15,000 cost per job gives a net cost of $5465 per job. The total measurable net cost of the entire Quality of Life program for 6.65 million workers would be only $36.3 billion.

And there would be many other savings that cannot be measured by a simple formula, such as savings in food stamps and food kitchens and administrative savings realized by not having to process assistance for the unemployed. There would also be other benefits that are not easily quantified, such as savings in the cost of litigation and cleanup after disasters, if inspection prevented the disasters. If there were more repair and maintenance personnel at work and bridges were not closed for long months for repair, truckers could save millions of dollars in costs incurred by delay; their profits would be higher, and their federal corporate income taxes would be higher, thus offsetting expenditures made for Quality of Life construction jobs. If there were enough prisons staffed with trained rehabilitation personnel, inmates would not be released because there were no beds for them, local and state governments would not have to spend as much for police protection, and taxpayers would not have to fear for their lives or their pocketbooks. In many cases, communities are already seeing the depressing outcome of federal and state expenditure reductions in areas such as education and mental health care. Ill and helpless "shopping-bag" people would not wander city streets if enough Quality of Life jobs were provided.

The list of needed Quality of Life jobs is long indeed. They are part of the system. Because society suffers more for lack of them than it would suffer if it had them, the real net cost per job is probably half the above estimate, or only $18 billion for 6.65 million jobs.

But even at a cost of $5465 per job, $36 billion is a trivial amount, especially when stacked up against the $159 billion annual defense budget. This amount would be only 1.1 percent of gross national product. It is easily affordable. Two or three times as much is affordable, too. So if the more pessimistic future forecast in earlier chapters comes to pass, it will still be well within the nation's power to create work opportunities for everyone. A combination of more Quality of Life jobs and shorter work weeks could easily create fifteen million jobs for a price tag of under $75 billion. (Chapter 10 showed that reducing the work week to 35 hours could create nearly eight million jobs, and as many as twelve million jobs could be provided through Quality of Life opportunities.)

These estimates, admittedly, are just rough "what-ifs." They are not meant to indicate that $15,000 is the best average wage to assume and certainly not to indicate that $15,000 is the ceiling that any Quality of Life worker would expect to earn. There could be and would be many variations in opportunities provided. Some jobs could be part-time work at high wages; others could be full-time work at the minimum wage. Upward mobility would be encouraged, as would lateral movement from publicly assisted work to the private sector and vice versa. The main point indeed is that publicly assisted work should not be so stigmatized as "different" in quality, compensation, or career expectations that only the job have-nots would seek it. Quality of Life jobs are more in the tradition of honored necessities, like police work and firefighting, than of the discredited, make-work countercyclical government programs.

The argument in favor of Quality of Life jobs is so logical that one must conclude that opposition to it is not rational but emotional. As a nation, Americans have been hypnotized by the shibboleth that publicly supported jobs are less worthy than so-called self-sufficient private jobs. But those private jobs are really not so independent of public support. The devotees of Adam Smith have come to the untenable position that it's all right to subsidize farmers, but it's socialistic to use tax dollars to provide health care services or open-air operas. Every dollar of tax credit for privately owned equipment is a subsidy to workers as well as to owners. Every cent of oil depletion allowance is a subsidy to the men on the rig as well as to investors. The only difference is that collectively we have declared that we want oil; we have not yet said that we want the other public services.

Just how many jobs should be created in different categories must be worked out bit by bit. A few numbers suggest the size of the unmet need. There are only 5900 private inspectors in the country. Representing the interests of the public are only 112,000 health and safety inspectors—and since these figures are for 1981 and government funding for inspection has been reduced, there are probably fewer now. These few individuals cannot begin to cover all the sites and buildings that need checking. We could increase their number tenfold and still have too few inspectors.

Look at the health field. There are only 522,000 licensed practical nurses. To care for all the sick and old, the nation could use three to five times as many, plus nurse's aides and orderlies, dietitians, and therapists. Poor people can't create the demand for such services without public assistance, even though they need them desperately.

As far as physical facilities go, conservative estimates by the Urban Institute set the need for additional investment in infrastructure maintenance and repair at $1 trillion; others, such as the Association of General Contractors, estimate the need at as much as $3.3 trillion. For every $1 billion worth of expenditure on construction, the Bureau of Labor Statistics estimates that 24,000 jobs are created. So an accelerated, permanent public works program could provide at least 100,000 jobs a year at prevailing union wages, and many more if the publicly subsidized jobs were compensated at the minimum wage.

Publicly Assisted Jobs Can Be Done Well

The argument advanced against public-sector jobs that they are done less efficiently than work motivated by the possibility of profits does not hold much water either. The National Park Service is a fine example of good work done efficiently and conscientiously. There is no evidence that teachers whose work is financed by federal education grants are less efficient than teachers in private schools. Where government workers are doing a cost-effective job, it is generally for the same reason that private-sector workers are performing well—the workers like their work and have a certain amount of autonomy and responsibility in doing it.

Still, all Quality of Life jobs would not be provided directly by a government agency, and certainly not by a federal government agency. Some would be created by subsidizing additional privately run, nonprofit facilities, such as nursing homes and mental health institutions. Some would be provided by subsidizing existing local institutions, such as schools, so that they could raise teachers' salaries and provide more teacher's aides or computer specialists or math teachers—all sorely needed, as the 1983 National Commission on Education pointed out. Under certain circumstances new Quality of Life jobs might be provided by contracting needed services to private, for-profit organizations, including construction companies, health and safety inspection experts, and waste disposal firms. The form of the subsidy is important, of course, but not as important as making the ultimate leap and deciding that everyone who wants to work and is able to work should have a job.

Given the fears that large budget deficits drive up inflation or keep interest rates higher than they would otherwise be, publicly assisted jobs should not be financed by borrowing. If funds were raised through taxation, an average surcharge of about $400 per tax return would be necessary to pay for the jobs each year. This is about half of what the Reagan administration gave upper-income taxpayers in tax cuts in 1981.

The real question will be whether we can afford not to go the route of publicly supported jobs. In one world are productive citizens who contribute and feel good about the world. In the other is a nation polarized between job haves and job have-nots.

HOW TO PAY

While earlier we calculated that $400, on average, would have to be added to personal income tax liabilities to cover the net cost of a $40 billion Quality of Life program, raising personal income taxes is not the only way to generate this revenue, nor is it necessarily the politically preferred way. No one likes to pay higher taxes, certainly not the middle-class worker stretching to make ends meet. (According to the Joint Committee on Taxation, families and individuals earning between $20,000 and $50,000 account for 50 percent of all individual income taxes paid, even though they make up only 37 percent of all taxable returns.) Another way of paying for Quality of Life jobs would be simply to eliminate waste in current expenditures.

Nearly all presidential candidates promise to eliminate waste, and yet waste remains a permanent problem. Still, it has been well documented that the Pentagon's system of purchasing weapons and parts is out of control. Contractors offer outrageously low bids for building weapons and then, once the contract is locked up, double and triple the price tag. This raises prices of all weapons. The practice of paying defense contractors their costs plus a profit encourages them to put unnecessary equipment on weapons or to design and redesign them unnecessarily. The Pentagon, as protector not only of the nation but of defense contractors, rarely cancels a weapons program, even when it obviously has failed the research tests.

But supporters of a permanent jobs program will have to show Congress a way to pay for it in case savings in military and other programs are not available. This is especially so, given that our estimates of the number of jobs that would have to be provided by the Quality of Life program might be too low. If the pessimistic scenario occurs, over nine million jobs would be needed.

Corporations will enjoy great efficiency and productivity in the work revolution, thanks largely to the introduction of new technology. What created this efficiency is not solely the genius of corporations, but the sum total of the nation's educational and research system. Billions of dollars of tax money are invested in publicly supported schools, laboratories, and even development of specific products.

The robot or the flexible machining centers, both threats to jobs, were made possible because taxes of working people using less sophisticated technology helped finance the accumulated knowledge that gave them birth. Working people indirectly financed the new capital investment that will speed up elimination of their jobs. They permitted and in some instances supported the Accelerated Cost Recovery Act of 1981, after business persuaded Congress that its investments were being inhibited by discriminatory taxes that gave foreign competitors an unfair advantage.

In supporting education, research and development, or tax breaks for business, workers obviously were not overtly planning their own job destruction. But this will be the practical result in many cases.

The heart of the matter is that business efficiency and productivity are no accidents, but the result of many sacrifices by individuals. Thus business and industry have a major moral and ethical responsibility to return a share of the benefits of increased productivity back to the system that made their success possible. One way to go about this would be to enact a sort of excess productivity tax, so that if a firm's output per unit of labor input were greatly increased as a direct result of automation and/or overseas production, the increased earnings would not be retained in the firm or distributed to the stockholders. They would be taxed away to pay for Quality of Life jobs and thus reinvigorate the system that helped make that productivity possible.

But although this might have some intuitive appeal, it could prove very unwieldy in the execution. It would be hard to distinguish between "normal" productivity increases and "excess" productivity increase, or if it was possible, it could inspire a morass of regulation and red tape. Such a tax would certainly be viewed as a disincentive to investment in the United States, since no similar tax is applied elsewhere. And it would be very difficult to police, so avoidance would be encouraged.

Is there another way to accomplish the same objective of capturing the benefits of productivity increases made possible by the whole array of individual and institutional contributions? Yes, because the benefits of increased productivity accrue and spread through the economy as income. Some income goes to workers' wages and benefits; some goes to managers' salaries and benefits. Other income is unearned, through dividends and appreciation of assets. Some of the income earned by business is retained in the business, and some is distributed to shareholders as dividends or to bondholders as interest.

Whether retained inside business or distributed, the incremental income that is the direct product of increased efficiency can be taxed by changing the tax system as a whole.

The Case for Taxes

Let's start with the question of business taxation. Businesses have seen their tax burden eased substantially through congressional action, especially with passage of the Accelerated Cost Recovery Act of 1981. The investment tax credit and accelerated depreciation are tax preferences to encourage greater productivity, particularly in certain industries. Bolstered by a mountain of confusing tax regulations that have developed in *ad hoc* fashion over years of tinkering with the complex tax code, legitimate and desired corporate tax preferences make it difficult to capture the benefits of increased economic efficiency for the public at large. While many business tax reformers urge abolition of the corporate income tax entirely, they do not offer a guarantee that an equivalent amount of money would be disbursed to shareholders to be taxed as individual income.

The complexities involved in changing tax law are much beyond the scope of this book, but the point to be made is that to capture the benefits of increased economic efficiency and to finance publicly supported jobs, income—both earned and unearned—must be the target of taxation. Whether this is accomplished through stiffer dividend taxes, higher capital gains taxes, higher corporate income taxes, or simply changes in the basic income tax rates, it is crucial that the income derived from productivity increases be taxed and distributed back to the people who helped pay for the productivity, and who, as a result of it, don't have jobs.

Budget Balancing Acts

As of 1983 at least, Americans were not psychologically ready to pay higher taxes, because the revenue and expenditure pictures were so out of synchronization. It was that obvious unprecedented federal budget deficits exceeding $100 billion annually would extend far into the future. Expenditures are moving toward 25 percent of gross national product, while anticipated revenues are only about 18.5 percent of gross national product. Revenues are down because the economy has been sluggish, but even as production picks up, tax avoidance is draining billions of dollars from the federal coffers. The federal income tax system is so riddled with exceptions, exclusions, and exemptions that legal tax avoidance is becoming a national pastime. The Congressional Budget Office reported in 1983 that income from investment is either taxed unduly lightly or, to all intents and purposes, not taxed at all. Illegal tax avoidance, in the form of unreported cash transactions of the "underground" economy, is not quantifiable, but it has been estimated at millions of dollars daily. The many ideas advanced to reform the tax system range from a flat tax on all earned and unearned income, to value-added taxes on each phase of the production process, to a tax on consumption. Since presently it is quite possible for a salaried individual earning $20,000 to pay twice as great a percentage of his income—with the same number of dependents—as an individual earning $75,000 in salary and unearned income, Americans have a legitimate reason to seek greater fairness from their tax system. Since tax reform is not the subject of this book, we will merely point out that overall broadening of the tax base, combined with modification in the number of tax brackets and elimination of some preferences, could stop the hemorrhaging of the tax collection system and add billions of new dollars to help close the budget gap and pay for Quality of Life jobs.

Finding the way out of the budget trap is essential in preparing for the work revolution, because unless this is done, the federal deficit will be so high that it will raise interest rates, promote reinflation, and choke off the productivity advances needed to increase gross national product. Fortunately, there is widespread agreement on this point, and a massive bipartisan effort after the 1984 election that focuses on both the budget and on tax reform is reasonably to be hoped for. Existing entitlement programs, such as welfare, food stamps, unemployment compensation, Medicare, Medicaid, and social security will have to be reexamined. They should be reexamined in the light of the work revolution, which will greatly change the nature of the entitlement programs America needs. Many of the existing programs actually create a disincentive to work; those disincentives should be wiped out. But many also stigmatize publicly supported work. Those stigmas can only be removed by redefining public work once and for all as worthwhile work. A Quality of Life jobs program would fit perfectly into this long-overdue budget and tax reform effort.

THE WILL OF THE PEOPLE

During the 1970s it became fashionable among liberal as well as conservative economic analysts to promote the economics of austerity. Inflation and the energy crisis scared them and scared policy makers, too. Such a heavy psychological toll was exacted from Americans that we lost faith in our future. A mood of despair crept over the land as it was reiterated, over and over again, that the economy had stalled and the American people were doomed to a nasty win-or-lose game of beggaring one another in a fight over shares of an economic pie that would never grow again.

That is not the thesis of this book. Rather, our message is that economic growth is likely. The fifth technological revolution around the world is the consequence of man's continuing ingenuity. This ingenuity will, in the future as it has in the past, ultimately result in greater economic opportunity for more people around the globe. But, like all previous technological revolutions, it will also cause hardships and dislocations that will bring suffering to many workers. The biggest difference between the next work revolution and all those that have gone before is that we now know enough about the force and impact of these dislocations to head them off.

The secret that needs to be unlocked is a political secret, not an economic one. It is a sure bet that American production will be more efficient in the future. It is a sure bet that, while ups and downs of business cycles cannot be avoided, the longer-term trend will be toward more output per unit of labor input. Capturing the benefits of this increased productivity is the political issue of the work revolution. It is no different from the issues that have always faced self-governing citizens, except in the pace at which people will be affected.

If we are in for another long wave of capital investment in technology as the Russian economist Kondratieff predicted, we are facing at least fifteen years and as much as fifty years of dislocation as refinements and diffusion of technology take place. But we don't have fifty years to figure out what to do about distributing its benefits. The poverty rate in the United States has jumped 5 percentage points in five years, to 15 percent. Already we have a smoldering urban underclass, confined in our decaying cities without opportunity, without skills, and without hope. They live off their wits in a marginal economy, kept afloat by government support and buoyed by illegal activities. This underclass will multiply itself and fester and seethe into a dangerous political element that will invite control by force.

At the same time, the great middle class is in trouble, threatened by technology and the export of work to other countries. For the first time since the Great Depression, the middle class faces downward economic mobility, as its old well-paying jobs are wiped out by technology and the export of work overseas, with new jobs offering less rewards. Middle-class citizens will not be able to buy the services they are accustomed to from wholly private sources, because they will not have the resources to purchase those services in the open marketplace. They will get less private health insurance, less private day care for their children, etc., as the basic necessities of living eat up more of their household budgets. The workers who built a prosperous America face a dismal future of relative impoverishment.

The tax system we have now cannot prevent the unequal distribution that will result from the work revolution. And the system will not be changed much unless antiquated ideas about who should pay for what kind of work are thrown out. These notions are depriving the nation of a standard of living it could well afford. Paradoxically, we now face an era in which the economic pie will grow, while the will to seize that growth and provide greater fairness in sharing its fruits is dead.

Unless, of course, we realize the promise of the work revolution. Its promise is more interesting work, less drudgery, more leisure. More than that, it promises that a richer nation can afford the luxuries of clean air, clean water, healthy individuals, up-to-snuff public facilities, and whatever else it may want.

The work revolution can be managed, but if we don't get started soon enough, the jobless problem will overwhelm us. It will exacerbate tensions between races, age groups, and the sexes. It will add the burden of patchwork solutions that only worsen the long-term problems to an already overencumbered federal budget. If we get started soon enough, there is time to change skills, get a different education, and prepare as individuals for the upheavals of the future even while, as a society, we adjust our institutions to deal with the problems. The work revolution need not leave a flood of victims in its wake.

SELECTED
BIBLIOGRAPHY

A complete bibliography covering all the subjects that were touched upon in the preparation of this book would challenge the manuscript itself in length. The following lists sources of information on technology, job training, education, career preparation, financing, and structural economic change, without beginning to exhaust the sources. It also lists a few of the many books on political economy in America which carry notable messages—only some of which tend to support our views.

Albus, James S. *Industrial Robot Technology and Productivity Improvement.* Washington, D.C.: Office of Technology Assessment Exploratory Workshop, July 1981.

American Association of Community and Junior Colleges. *Community, Technical and Journal Colleges Fact File.* Vol. 53, No. 2. Washington, D.C., October 1982.

American Iron and Steel Institute. *Steel at the Crossroads: The American Steel Industry in the 1980s.* Washington, D.C., January 1980.

———. *Steel and America: An Annual Report.* Washington, D.C., May 1982.

Applebaum, Eileen. *The Economics of Technical Progress: Labor Issues Arising from the Spread of Programmable Automation Technologies.* Washington, D.C.: Office of Technology Assessment, March 1983.

Ayres, Robert U., and Miller, Steven M. *Robotics, Applications & Social Implications.* Cambridge, Mass.: Ballinger Publishing Co., 1983.

Barnet, Richard J. *The Lean Years.* New York: Simon and Schuster, 1980.

Bluestone, Barry, and Harrison, Bennett. *Capital and Communities: The Causes and Consequences of Private Disinvestment.* Washington, D.C.: The Progressive Alliance, 1980.

Bouvier, Leon F. *Immigration and its Impact on U.S. Society.* Washington, D.C.: Population Reference Bureau, September 1981.

———. *U.S. Population: Where We Are; Where We're Going.* Washington, D.C.: Population Reference Bureau, June 1982.

Bressand, Albert. *The State of the World Economy, Annual Report by the French Institute for International Relations.* Cambridge, Mass.: Ballinger Publishing Co., 1982.

Center for Public Resources. *Basic Skills in the U.S. Work Force.* New York, 1982.

Chiswick, Barry, ed. *The Gateway: U.S. Immigration Issues and Policies, Conference Proceedings*. Washington, D.C. and London: American Enterprise Institute for Public Policy Research, 1982.

Choate, Pat. *Retooling the American Work Force Toward a National Training Strategy*. Washington, D.C.: Northeast-Midwest Institute, July 1982.

Congressional Budget Office. *Dislocated Workers*. Washington, D.C., 1982.

———. *Revising the Individual Income Tax*. Washington, D.C., July 1983.

Cornish, Edward, ed. *Careers Tomorrow: The Outlook for Work in a Changing World*. Washington, D.C.: World Future Society, 1983.

Department of Engineering and Public Policy, School of Urban and Public Affairs, and Department of Social Science. *The Impact of Robotics on the Workforce and Workplace*. Pittsburgh, Pa.: Carnegie-Mellon University, June 1981.

Dunn, Wynonia L. *Status of Statewide Career Information Delivery Systems*. Washington, D.C.: The National Occupational Information Coordinating Committee, August 1982.

Engelberg, Joseph F. *Robotics in Practice*. New York: Amacom, 1980.

Ferman, Louis A., and Gordus, Jeanne P. *Mental Health and the Economy*. Kalamazoo, Mich.: W. E. Upjohn Institute for Employment Research, 1979.

Galbraith, John Kenneth. *The Affluent Society*. New York: New American Library, 1958.

Golladay, Mary A., and Wulfsberg, Rolf M. *The Condition of Vocational Education*. Washington, D.C.: National Center for Educational Statistics, July 1981.

Heilbroner, Robert L. *The Economic Transformation of America*. New York: Harcourt Brace Jovanovich, 1977.

Joint Economic Committee, Congress of the United States. *The Cost of Government Regulation*. Washington, D.C.: U.S. Government Printing Office, April 1978.

———. *East-West Trade: The Prospects to 1985*. Washington, D.C.: U.S. Government Printing Office, August 1982.

———. *Employment and Unemployment*. Washington, D.C.: U.S. Government Printing Office, January 1982.

———. *Impacts of Robotics on Employment*. Washington, D.C.: U.S. Government Printing Office, March 18, 1983.

———. *Japanese Industrial and Labor Policy*. Washington, D.C.: U.S. Government Printing Office, June 23, 1982.

———. *Public Works as a Countercyclical Tool*. Washington, D.C.: U.S. Government Printing Office, June 17, 1980.

———. *The Underground Economy*. Washington, D.C.: U.S. Government Printing Office, November 15, 1979.

———. *U.S. Economic Growth from 1976 to 1986: Prospects, Problems, and Patterns*. Washington, D.C.: U.S. Government Printing Office, December 17, 1976.

Kendrick, John W., and Grossman, Elliot S. *Productivity in the United States*. Baltimore, Md.: The Johns Hopkins University Press, 1980.

Lawrence Livermore National Laboratory. *Technology of Machine Tools*. Vol. 1, Executive Summary. Livermore, Calif.: University of California, October 1980.

Levin, Henry M., and Rumberger, Russell W. *The Educational Implications of High Technology*. Stanford, Calif.: Institute for Research on Educational Finance and Governance, Stanford University, February 1983.

Levitan, Sar, and Johnson, Clifford M. *Second Thoughts on Work*. Kalmazoo, Mich.: W. E. Upjohn Institute for Employment Research, 1982.

Levitan, Sar A., Mangum, Garth L., and Marshall, Ray. *Human Resources and Labor Markets*. New York: Harper & Row, 1972.

Lindquist, Victor R., and Endicott, Frank S. *Northwestern Endicott Report*. Evanston, Ill.: Placement Center, Northwestern University, 1982.

Longworth, R.C., and Neikirk, William. "The Changing American Worker." *Chicago Tribune*, September 1979.

Madigan, Charles, and Neikirk, William. "The New Worker." *Chicago Tribune*, November 1982.

Martin, Gail M. "Industrial Robots Join the Work Force," *Occupational Outlook Quarterly*. Washington, D.C.: U.S. Department of Labor, Fall 1982.

Mier, Robert; Strobeck, Art; and Ranney, David. *Technological Change and Chicago Industry: A Preliminary Study*. Chicago: University of Illinois at Chicago Circle Center for Urban Economic Development, January 1983.

National Center for Educational Statistics. *The Condition of Education*. Washington, D.C., 1982.

National Commission for Employment Policy. *Seventh Annual Report: The Federal Interest in Employment and Training*. Washington, D.C., October 1981.

National Occupational Information Coordinating Committee. *A Framework for Developing an Occupational Information System*. Washington, D.C., October 1979.

———. *Summary of Existing Computer-Based Occupational Information Systems for Program Planning*. Attachment 2 for Administrative Memorandum 83-1. Washington, D.C., March 1983.

———. *The Status of the NOICC/SOICC Network*. Washington, D.C., September 30, 1981.

Office of Technology Assessment, Congress of the United States. *U.S. Industrial Competitiveness: A Comparison of Steel, Electronics, and Automobiles*. Washington, D.C.: U.S. Government Printing Office, July 1981.

Organisation for Economic Co-operation and Development. *OECD Economic Outlook*. Paris: OECD, July 1983.

Panati, Charles. *Breakthroughs: Astonishing Advances in Your Lifetime in Medicine, Science and Technology.* New York: Houghton Mifflin, 1980.

Paul, Krishan K.; Carlos, Ellen A.; and Bushnell, David S. *Vocational Education and Economic Development Case Studies.* Arlington, Va.: American Vocational Association, January 1982.

Robison, David. *Training and Jobs Programs in Action.* Washington, D.C., Committee for Economic Development in cooperation with Work in America Institute, Scarsdale, New York, May 1978.

Saffady, William. *The Automated Office.* Silver Spring, Md.: National Micrographics Assoc., 1981.

Schieber, Sylvester J. *Social Security: Perspectives on Saving the System.* Washington, D.C.: Employee Benefit Research Institute, 1982.

Schwartz, Gail Garfield. "The New Realities of Economic Development," *Southern Review of Public Administration.* Vol. 6, No. 4. Winter 1983.

———. *Building Milwaukee's Labor Force.* Washington, D.C.: Garfield Schwartz Associates, June 1982.

———. *Challenges to Pennsylvania: An Overview of Economic Prospects.* Washington, D.C.: Garfield Schwartz Associates for the Majority Leader of the House of Representatives of the Commonwealth of Pennsylvania, April 1983.

———. *Growth Potential in Maryland.* Baltimore, Md.: Center for Metropolitan Planning & Research, The Johns Hopkins University, June 1981.

———. "High-Tech: Making the Right Connections," *New York Affairs.* Vol. 7, No. 4, New York: New York University, Urban Research Center, 1983.

Schwartz, Lester J., and Irv Brechner. *The Career Finder.* New York: Ballantine Books, 1983.

Science Advisory Panel Task Force Reports. *A National Public Works Investment Policy.* Report prepared for the committee on Public Works, U.S. House of Representatives. Washington, D.C.: U.S. Government Printing Office, December 1974.

Sheppard, C. Stewart, and Carroll, Donald C. *Working in the Twenty-First Century.* New York: John Wiley & Sons, 1980.

Soldo, Beth J. *America's Elderly in the 1980s.* Washington, D.C.: Population Reference Bureau, Inc., November 1980.

Stanback Jr., Thomas M., *Understanding the Service Economy.* Baltimore and London: The Johns Hopkins University Press, 1979.

Subcommittee on Telecommunications, Consumer Protection and Finance of the Committee on Energy and Commerce, House of Representatives. *Telecommunications and Information Products and Services in International Trade.* Washington, D.C.: U.S. Government Printing Office, 1981.

Subcommittee on Trade of the Committee on Ways and Means, House of Representatives. *Quality of Production and Improvement in the*

Workplace. Washington, D.C.: U.S. Government Printing Office, October 14, 1980.

Thurow, Lester C. *The Zero Sum Society.* New York: Basic Books, 1980.

Toffler, Alvin. *The Third Wave.* New York: Bantam Books, April 1981.

U.S. Department of Commerce, Bureau of the Census. *Statistical Abstract of the United States.* 103d Edition. Washington, D.C.: U.S. Government Printing Office, 1982–83.

U.S. Department of Commerce, Bureau of Industrial Economics. *1983 U.S. Industrial Outlook.* Washington, D.C.: U.S. Government Printing Office, 1983.

U.S. Department of Labor, Bureau of Statistics. *Economic Projections to 1990.* Washington, D.C.: U.S. Government Printing Office, March 1982.

———. *The Impact of Technology on Labor in Five Industries.* Washington, D.C.: U.S. Government Printing Office, December 1982.

———. *Occupational Outlook Handbook.* Washington, D.C.: U.S. Government Printing Office, April 1982.

———. *Occupational Outlook Quarterly.* Washington, D.C.: U.S. Government Printing Office, Spring 1982.

———. *Occupational Projections and Training Data.* Washington, D.C.: U.S. Government Printing Office, October 1982.

———. *Occupational Projections and Training Data: A Statistical and Research Supplement.* Appendix C. Washington, D.C.: U.S. Government Printing Office, 1983.

———. *Productivity and the Economy: A Chartbook.* Washington, D.C.: U.S. Government Printing Office, October 1981.

———. *Technological Change and its Labor Impact in Five Energy Industries.* Washington, D.C.: U.S. Government Printing Office, 1979.

———. *Technological Change and its Labor Impact in Five Industries.* Washington, D.C.: U.S. Government Printing Office, 1977.

———. *Technological Change and Manpower Trends in Five Industries.* Washington, D.C.: U.S. Government Printing Office, 1975.

———. *Technology and Labor in Five Industries.* Washington, D.C.: U.S. Government Printing Office, 1979.

———. *Technology and Labor in Four Industries.* Washington, D.C.: U.S. Government Printing Office, January 1982.

———. *Women at Work.* Washington, D.C.: U.S. Government Printing Office, April 1983.

U.S. Trade Representative to the President. *26th Annual Report.* Washington, D.C.: Office of U.S. Trade Representative, November 1982.

Widner, Ralph R.; Schwartz, Gail Garfield; Rainey, Kenneth D.; and Choate, Pat. *Economic Development and Employment: A Survey of Economic Development, Employment, and Training Programs Since 1960.* Washington, D.C.: Manpower Commission on Employment, 1980.

Work in America Institute, Inc. *The Future of Older Workers in America.* Scarsdale, New York, 1980.

INDEX